DANIEL BLUM'S

THEATRE

WORLD

edited by JOHN WILLIS

SEASON 1964-1965

Volume 21

CROWN PUBLISHERS, INC.

New York

Copyright © 1965 by John Willis. Manufactured in the U.S.A.

Library of Congress Catalog Card No. 50-3023

IN MEMORIAM

DANIEL BLUM
1899-1965

Founder and Editor
of
THEATRE WORLD

Bert Andrews Photo

Irene Dailey, Martin Sheen, Jack Albertson
in
"THE SUBJECT WAS ROSES"
Winner of Pulitzer Prize, Drama Critics Circle, and Antoinette Perry Awards

4

TABLE OF CONTENTS

Editorial Assistants: Harold Stephens, Carl Raymund

Staff Photographers: Louis Mélançon, Friedman-Abeles,
Bert Andrews, Alix Jeffry, Van Williams

THE NEW YORK SEASON

The 1964-65 season, from our press seats, had a plethora of incredibly poor straight and musical productions. After the encouraging record of the 1963-64 season, this one was disappointing, not only in quantity, but also in quality. Approximately half the entries were complete failures. However, financially, this season was the biggest grosser on record. This can be justified in part by the price of tickets that rose to a record $9.90.

The best offerings this season were comedies, and exceptionally good ones: "Luv," "The Owl and the Pussycat," and "The Odd Couple." Fewer serious plays were produced, but those that were, failed to attract an audience. Such plays, which deserved longer runs, were "The Physicists," "Hughie," "Poor Bitos," "A Severed Head," and "All In Good Time." Could this indicate that the audience for serious plays is vanishing? Imports were generally unsuccessful, which should be encouraging to our own promising young playwrights. As in almost every season, this one being no exception, a controversial play is presented. "Tiny Alice" by Edward Albee was this season's enigma. Everyone had a different interpretation for it, but all agreed that memorable performances were given in it by John Gielgud and Irene Worth. Among other outstanding performances during the season were those given by Walter Matthau, Zero Mostel, Anne Jackson, Eli Wallach, Sammy Davis, Jr., Julie Harris, Alan Alda, Diana Sands, Alice Ghostley, Geraldine Page, Kim Stanley, Jessica Tandy, Hume Cronyn, Liza Minnelli, Jason Robards, Bea Richards, Maureen Stapleton, and Cyril Ritchard.

It was also a bad season for musicals, the trend being toward serious musical plays rather than musical comedies. The biggest musical hit was "Fiddler On The Roof." Others that were moderately successful were "Golden Boy," "Do I Hear A Waltz?," "Ben Franklin In Paris," and "Bajour." "Half A Sixpence" and its star Tommy Steele, both English imports, proved pleasant additions to Broadway. Although a late entry, but obviously headed for the hit class was "The Roar Of The Greasepaint—The Smell Of The Crowd" by and with Anthony Newley, who is also an English import.

Plays that opened in past seasons and that remained in the hit category during this year were "Hello, Dolly!," "Funny Girl," "Barefoot In The Park," and "Any Wednesday." "The Subject Was Roses" that opened too late in the 1963-64 season to be considered for citations, was amply rewarded this season with the Pulitzer Prize, the Drama Critics Circle Award, and the Antoinette Perry Award. "The Three Sisters," and "The Glass Menagerie" were Broadway's only revivals.

The Repertory Theatre of Lincoln Center in its second season of offerings, failed again to achieve its anticipated success. Differences of opinion, resignations, and changes in management and artistic direction were not helpful in producing a successful season. Arthur Miller's controversial "After The Fall" was retained in the repertoire. His new play "Incident At Vichy" was added, as were "The Changeling" which was a fiasco, and "Tartuffe" which was more agreeably received.

The New York State Theater at Lincoln Center, in its first full year of operation, added prestige to the metropolitan theatre scene with excellent revivals of "The King and I," and "The Merry Widow," with the Schiller Theater of West Berlin in German-language productions of "Don Carlos" and "The Captain of Koepenick," the New York City Ballet, San Francisco Ballet, and American Ballet Theatre.

Jean Dalrymple again made the season at the New York City Center a memorable one. Her exceptionally good revivals, at bargain prices, were "Brigadoon," "Guys and Dolls," "Kiss Me, Kate," and the Gilbert and Sullivan classics. Also at City Center were the Greek Tragedy Theatre, Antonio's Ballets de Madrid, the D'Oyly Carte Company, the brilliant Polish Mime Theatre, Ballet Folklorico de Mexico, and the Moscow Art Theatre in "The Cherry Orchard," "Dead Souls," "The Three Sisters," and "Kremlin Chimes." The opportunity of seeing two productions during the same season of "The Three Sisters" was a rare privilege.

Off-Broadway had a very depressing year. There were 25 less productions than last year, and the obvious lack of quality and good taste in many was discouraging. The best were holdovers from other seasons: "The Fantasticks," "The Knack," and "The Trojan Women." Others worth viewing were "Othello," "Baal," "A View From The Bridge," "The Old Glory," Pinter's "The Room" and "A Slight Ache," "Kiss Mama," "A Sound of Silence," "Dr. Faustus," "Billy Liar," and the delightful "The Decline and Fall of The Entire World As Seen Through The Eyes of Cole Porter Revisited." The entire cast of the last named was excellent. Other notable Off-Broadway performances were given by Michael O'Sullivan, Carolyn Coates, Jaime Sanchez, James Earl Jones, Mitchell Ryan, Susan Towers, Robert Hooks, Scott Hylands, Linda Lavin, Robert Walker, Nicolas Surovy, Julius LaRosa, Cynthia Belgrave, and Lorraine Serabian.

The Association of Producing Artists at the Phoenix, displayed for the third season its high standards that make many Broadway presentations appear amateur. It is hoped that they will be able to realize their ambition for a subsidized Broadway theatre, which they deserve. Their productions of "Man and Superman," "War and Peace," and "Judith" were outstanding and rank with the best of any season. Rosemary Harris was brilliant in all three productions, and is undoubtedly one of our best and most versatile young actresses. The entire company, including directors and production staff, deserves great credit for making the 1964-65 theatre season more enjoyable and worthwhile than it otherwise would have been.

BROADWAY CALENDAR

June 1, 1964 through May 31, 1965

BROADWAY THEATRE

Opened Tuesday, June 2, 1964°
Stephen W. Sharmat presents the Arthur
Lesser Production of Paul Derval's original:

FOLIES BERGÈRE

Music, Henri Betti; Additional Music, Philippe Gerard; Sets and Costumes, Michel Gyarmathy; Choreography, George Reich; Musical
Director, Jo Basile; Conceived and Directed by
Michel Gyarmathy; Associate Producers, Nicholas Strater, Alvin Bojar; In arrangement with
J. Robert Purdom.

CAST

Patachou

Georges Ulmer	Marion Conrad
Nicole Croisille	Les Hoganas
Liliane Montevecchi	Francoise Grés
Vassili Sulic	The Trotter Brothers

Paul Sydell and the Company of
Les Folies Bergère

PROGRAM

ACT I: "Bonjour de Paris," "Can-Can,"
Georges Ulmer, "Souper Fin," "Chopin," Paul
Sydell, "Variété de Danses," Georges Ulmer,
"Cleopatra," Les Hoganas, "A Toute a L'-
Heure."

ACT II: "Texas de France," Georges Ulmer,
"Mariage," The Trotter Brothers, "Gondole á
Venise," Georges Ulmer, "Neige," Patachou,
Finale.

General Managers: Joseph Harris,
Arthur Rubin
Company Manager: Bill Levine
Press: Arthur Cantor, Tony Geiss, Artie
Solomon. Angela Nardelli
Stage Managers: Terence Little, Peter Stern
° Closed November 14, 1964. (191 perform-
ances)

Friedman-Abeles Photos

Left: Patachou

Liliane Montevecchi (right) with Vassili Sulic

Kim Stanley, Shirley Knight, Geraldine Page

MOROSCO THEATRE

Opened Monday, June 22, 1964.°
The Actors Studio, Inc. presents The
Actors Studio Theatre production of:

THE THREE SISTERS

By Anton Chekov; New English version by
Randall Jarrell; Directed by Lee Strasberg;
Scenery, Will Steven Armstrong; Costumes,
Theoni V. Aldredge and Ray Diffen; Lighting,
Feder; Hair Styles, Ronald De Mann; Produc-
tion Coordinator, Richard Blofson; Executive
Assistant, Richard Chandler.

CAST

Masha	Kim Stanley †1
Olga	Geraldine Page †2
Irina	Shirley Knight
Chebutykin	Luther Adler
Solyony	Robert Loggia
Tuzenbach	James Olson
Anfisa	Tamara Daykarhanova
Ferapont	Salem Ludwig
Adjutant	Brooks Morton
Maid	Janice Mars
Vershinin	Kevin McCarthy
Andrei	Gerald Hiken
Kulygin	Albert Paulsen
Natalya	Barbara Baxley
Fedotik	John Harkins
Rode	David Paulsen
Musicians	Janice Mars, Brooks Morton

CARNIVAL PEOPLE: Delos V. Smith, Jr.,
Brooks Morton, Marcia Haufrecht, Sandra Kauf-
man, James Tolkan, Nadine Turney, William
Burns.

A Drama in three acts and four scenes. The
action takes place in the house of the Prozorov's in a provincial town of Russia from May
1897 to Autumn of 1901.

General Manager: Arthur Waxman
Press: Samuel Lurie, Stanley Kaminsky,
Warren Pincus
Stage Managers: Martin Fried, John Strasberg,
Delos V. Smith, Jr.

° Closed October 3, 1964 (119 performances)
† Succeeded by: 1. Geraldine Page, 2. Peggy
Feury
Last production opened at the Ethel Barrymore
Theatre, Dec. 21, 1942, and ran for 123 per-
formances. In the cast were Judith Anderson,
Katharine Cornell, Ruth Gordon, Dennis King,
Kirk Douglas, Tom Powers, McKay Morris,
Edmund Gwenn, Gertrude Musgrove, and
Alexander Knox.

Photos by Martha Holmes, Friedman-Abeles, Henry Grossman

Kim Stanley, Shirley Knight, Kevin McCarthy, Geraldine Page, Luther Adler
Above: Gerald Hiken, Barbara Baxley

LUNT-FONTANNE THEATRE

Opened Friday, September 11, 1964.°
Greek Theatre Association—James A. Doolittle and Felix G. Gerstman present:

WIENER BLUT
(Vienna Life)

Music, Johann Strauss; Libretto, Victor Leon, Leo Stein; New Adaptation, Tony Niessner; Music Arranged by Hans Hagen; Staged by Tony Niessner; Choreography, Fred Meister; Musical Director, Oswald Unterhauser; Designed by Ferry Windberger; Costumes, Hill Rheis-Gromes; Lighting, Thomas Skelton; Produced by Harald A. Hoeller; Hair Styling, Christl Wusto; American Production Superviser, Thomas Skelton.

CAST

Mistress of Ceremonies	Gita Rena
Policeman	Andreij Halasz
Count Balduin Zedlau	Erwin Von Gross
Countess Zedlau	Maria Kowa
Franziska Cagliari	Clementine Mayer
Pepi Pleininger	Dagmar Koller
Josef	Helmut Wallner
Prince Ypsheim-Gindelbach	Wilhelm Popp
Kagler	Hugo Lindinger
Anna	Friederike Mann
Coachman	Werner Karman
Count Bitowski	Emmerich Godin
Countess Bitowski	Else Petry
French Ambassador	Erich Herg
Italian Ambassador	Martino Stamos
English Ambassador	Wolfgang Hackenberg
Prussian Ambassador	Gerhard Kurz
Russian Ambassador	Werner Karman
Lisi	Friederike Mann
Lori	Silvia Holzmayer
Grenadier	Erich Herg
Watchman	Wolfgang Hackenberg
Boy Waiter	Eveline Kollhammer
Proprietor of Heitzing Casino	Werner Karman

SINGING ENSEMBLE: Maria Koloubeck, Silvia Holzmayer, Elfriede Knapp, Angelike Lignu, Friederike Mann, Katherine Stellaki, Wolfgang Hackenberg, Erich Herg, Werner Karman, Gerhard Kurz, Martino Stamos, Achilles Talos.

DANCING ENSEMBLE: Iwa Slatewa, Flora Lojekova, Andrej Halasz, Kurt Schenker, Hulda Fuchs, Katja Dooren, Eveline Kohlhammer, Edda Kreen, Katja Pogacnik, Nora Zechner, Ingrid Nedbal.

MUSICAL NUMBERS: Introduction, "I Am Looking Here Now," "Pepi, He?," "Go On, Write," "Polka," "Good Morning, Mr. Van Pepi," "Polonaise," "Pas de Deux," "Vienna Life," "Viennese Women Love To Sing," "Take It, My Sweet Darling," "Mazurka," "Bohemian Polka," "Czardas," "Lagoon Waltz," "The Blue Danube Waltz," "Go On and Sell My Suit," "A Waltz By Strauss," "Acceleration Waltz," Finale.

UNDERSTUDIES: Zedlau, Gerhard Kurz; Countess Zedlau, Elfriede Knapp; Franziska, Silvia Holzmayer; Pepi, Friederike Mann; Joseph, Wolfgang Hackenberg; Kagler, Werner Karman.

An Operetta in three acts and twelve scenes. The action takes place in Vienna in 1815 at the time of the Congress.

Company Manager: Alfred Fischer
Press: Max Eisen, Bob Feinberg, Jeannie Gibson Merrick, Maurice Turet
Stage Managers: Pat Chandler, Sally Cook

° Closed October 3, 1964 (27 performances)

Dagmar Koller, Helmut Wallner, Erwin Von Gross, Gita Rena. Above: Wilhelm Popp, Helmut Wallner, Hugo Lindinger

HENRY MILLER'S THEATRE

Opened Wednesday, September 16, 1964.°
Arthur Cantor presents:

THE COMMITTEE

Written and Created by The Company; Directed by Alan Myerson; Setting and Lighting, Ralph Alswang; Produced in association with Committee Productions; Production Assistant, Benjamin Siegler.

CAST

Scott Beach	Kathryn Ish
Hamilton Camp	Garry Goodrow
Larry Hankin	Ellsworth Milburn
Irene Riordan	Dick Stahl

ACT I: Overture, The Party, Introduction, Sex On The Campus, The Spies, Oral Exam, Pregnant, The Mechanical Man, Interview, Bar Scene, Folk Song

ACT II: Blue Valley (Calif) PTA, The Store, Summer Vacation, The Virtuoso, Prison Scene, Public Opinion, Liebowitz, The Hour, Street Scene, The Orchestra

A Revue in two acts with material subject to change.

Press: Tony Geiss, Artie Solomon, Angela Nardelli
Stage Managers: Kip Cohen, Irene Riordan

° Closed November 7, 1964. (61 performances)

Pete Peters Photos

Kathryn Ish, Larry Hankin.
Top: entire company

Hamilton Camp   **Irene Riordan**   **Hamilton Camp, Larry Hankin**

Boris Tumarin, Margaret Braidwood, Mildred Dunnock
Top: Ben Gazzara, Mildred Dunnock

Margaret Braidwood, Ben Gazzara

ANTA THEATRE

Opened Thursday, September 17, 1964*
Carroll and Harris Masterson and Norman
Twain in association with ANTA present:

TRAVELLER WITHOUT LUGGAGE

By Jean Anouilh, Translated by Lucienne Hill;
Settings and Costumes, Oliver Messel; Lighting,
Gerald Feil; Directed by Robert Lewis.

CAST

The Butler	William Cottrell
The Duchess	Margaret Braidwood
M. Huspar	Boris Tumarin
Gaston	Ben Gazzara
Mme. Renaud	Mildred Dunnock
Georges Renaud	Stephen Elliott
Valentine Renaud	Nancy Wickwire
Juliette	Rae Allen
The Valet	Anthony Palmer
A Small Boy	Jeffrey Neal
Mr. Truggle	Ronald Dawson

UNDERSTUDIES: Gaston, Georges, Ralph
Waite; Mme., Duchess, Elaine Eldridge; Valentine, Juliette, Alice Thorsell Hirson; Huspar,
William Cottrell; Valet, Truggle, Peter Gumeny; Butler, Ronald Dawson; Boy, Billy King.

A Drama in three scenes. The action takes
place in the Renaud house in a provincial
town in France in 1936.

General Manager: Sherman Gross
Press: Seymour Krawitz, Merle Debuskey
Stage Managers: Del Hughes, Peter Gumeny

* Closed October 24, 1964. (44 performances)

Friedman-Abeles Photos

Mildred Dunnock, Ben Gazzara
Top: Rae Allen, Ben Gazzara

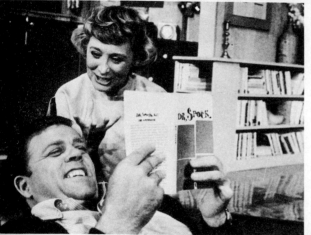

CORT THEATRE

Opened Sunday, September 20, 1964.°
Gerard Oestreicher and Laurence Feldman present:

A GIRL COULD GET LUCKY

By Don Appell; Directed by Mr. Appell; Settings, Robert T. Williams; Costumes, Will Steven Armstrong; Lighting, Jules Fisher; Produced in association with Idar Productions.

CAST
Penny Moore...................................Betty Garrett
Andy Willard .... Pat Hingle
Standby for Miss Garrett, Virginia Vincent

A Comedy in two acts and three scenes. The action takes place in Penny's apartment in New York City.

General Manager: Walter Fried
Press: Bill Doll, Midori Tsuji,
Shirley Herz, Robert Ganshaw
Stage Managers: James Gelb, Susan Savage

° Closed September 26, 1964. (8 performances)

Steve Schapiro Photos

Betty Garrett, Pat Hingle (top and center)

Ruth White, Fred Clark
in
"ABSENCE OF A CELLO"

17

AMBASSADOR THEATRE

Opened Monday, September 21, 1964.°
Michael Ellis and Jeff Britton present:

ABSENCE OF A CELLO

By Ira Wallach; Directed by James Hammerstein; Scenery and Lighting, William Ritman; Costumes, Fred Voelpel; Associate Producer, M. J. Boyer.

CAST

Celia Pilgrim	Ruth White
Andrew Pilgrim	Fred Clark
Marian Jellicoe	Mala Powers
Joanna Pilgrim	Lee Kurty
Emma Littlewood	Ruth McDevitt
Perry Littlewood	Charles Grodin
Otis Clifton	Murry Hamilton

UNDERSTUDIES: Celia, Marian, Eileen Letchworth; Emma, Mabel Cochran; Perry, Bruce Hyde.

A Comedy in three acts. The action takes place in the living room of Andrew Pilgrim's New York City apartment during September of the present year.

Press: Merle Debuskey, Seymour Krawitz
Stage Managers: Charles Maryan, Bruce Hyde

° Closed January 2, 1965. (120 performances)

Friedman-Abeles Photos

Lee Kurty, Fred Clark. Top: Charles Grodin, Ruth White, Fred Clark, Ruth McDevitt, Murray Hamilton. Center: Ruth White, Charles Grodin, Ruth McDevitt, Fred Clark; Mala Powers, Murray Hamilton, Fred Clark

Zero Mostel
in
"FIDDLER ON THE ROOF"

Zero Mostel, Maria Karnilova
Above: Zero Mostel, Michael Granger

IMPERIAL THEATRE
Opened Tuesday, September 22, 1964.°
Harold Prince presents:

FIDDLER ON THE ROOF

Book by Joseph Stein; Based on Sholom Aleichem's Stories; Music, Jerry Bock; Lyrics, Sheldon Harnick; Directed and Choreographed by Jerome Robbins; Settings, Boris Aronson; Costumes, Patricia Zipprodt; Lighting, Jean Rosenthal; Orchestrations, Don Walker; Musical Direction and Vocal Arrangements, Milton Greene; Dance Music Arranged by Betty Walberg; Hair Stylist, D. Rusty Bonaccorso.

CAST

Tevye	Zero Mostel †1
Golde	Maria Karnilova
Tzeitel	Joanna Merlin †6
Hodel	Julia Migenes
Chava	Tanya Everett
Shprintze	Marilyn Rogers
Bielke	Linda Ross †2
Yente	Beatrice Arthur
Motel	Austin Pendleton
Perchik	Bert Convy †3
Lazar Wolf	Michael Granger
Mordcha	Zvee Scooler
Rabbi	Gluck Sandor
Mendel	Leonard Frey †4
Avram	Paul Lipson
Nachum	Maurice Edwards
Grandma Tzeitel	Sue Babel
Fruma-Sarah	Carol Sawyer
Constable	Joseph Sullivan
Fyedka	Joe Ponazecki
Shandel	Helen Verbit
The Fiddler	Gino Conforti †5

VILLAGERS: Tom Abbott, John C. Attle, Sue Babel, Sammy Bayes, Robert Berdeen, Lorenzo Bianco, Duane Bodin, Robert Currie, Sarah Felcher, Tony Gardell, Louis Genevrino, Ross Gifford, Dan Jasin, Sandra Kazan, Thom Koutsoukos, Sharon Lerit, Sylvia Mann, Peff Modelski, Irene Paris, Charles Rule, Carol Sawyer, Roberta Senn, Mitch Thomas, Helen Vervit

UNDERSTUDIES: Tevye, Paul Lipson; Tzeitel, Irene Paris; Hodel, Sandy Kazan; Chava, Sharon Lerit; Perchik, Motel, Leonard Frey; Fyedka, Robert Berdeen; Shprintze, Bielke, Sue Babel; Rabbi, Maurice Edwards; Mendel, Danny Kasin; Avram, Maurice Edwards; Nachum, John C. Attle; Lazar, Paul Lipson; Constable, Ross Gifford; Fiddler, Sammy Bayes; Mordcha, Thom Koutsoukos; Fruma, Irene Paris; Grandma, Sylvia Mann.

MUSICAL NUMBERS: "Tradition," "Matchmaker, Matchmaker," "If I Were A Rich Man," "Sabbath Prayer," "To Life," "Miracle of Miracles," "The Tailor, Motel Kamzoil," "Sunrise, Sunset," "Wedding Dance," "Now I Have Everything," "Do You Love Me?," "I Just Heard," "Far From The Home I Love," "Anatevka," Epilogue.

A Musical Comedy in two acts. The action takes place in Anatevka, a village in Russia, in 1905 on the eve of the revolutionary period.

General Manager: Carl Fisher
Press: Sol Jacobson, Lewis Harmon, Earl Butler
Stage Managers: Ruth Mitchell, James Bronson, Robert Currie

° Still playing May 31, 1965.
† Succeeded by: 1. Luther Adler during vacation, 2. Pia Zadora, 3. Leonard Frey, 4. Dan Jasin, 5. Ken LeRoy, 6. Ann Marisse.

Photos by Friedman-Abeles and Eileen Darby-Graphic Hous

Top Left: Maria Karnilova, Zero Mostel, Beatrice Arthur. Below: Austin Pendleton, Zero Mostel, Joanna Merlin

Austin Pendleton, Bert Convy, Zero Mostel, Maria Karnilova, Joanna Merlin,
Julia Migenes, Tanya Everett, Marilyn Rodgers, Linda Ross
Above: (in bed) Maria Karnilova, Zero Mostel. Top: "The Bottle Dance"

Frank Coda, Victor Spinetti, Murray Melvin, Jack Eddleman

BROADHURST THEATRE

Opened Wednesday, September 30, 1964.°
David Merrick and Gerry Raffles present:

OH WHAT A LOVELY WAR

By Theatre Workshop, Charles Chilton, and the members of the cast; After a treatment by Ted Allan; A Theatre Workship Group Production; Directed by Joan Littlewood; Military Adviser, Raymond Fletcher; Setting and Lighting, John Bury; Costumes, Una Collins, Choreography, Bob Stevenson; Musical Direction, Shepard Coleman; Musical Arrangement, Alfred Ralston; Design Supervision, Klaus Holm; Production Supervisor, Samuel Liff; Technical Advisers, Richard and Ann Bowdler.

CAST

Victor Spinetti	Barbara Windsor
Murray Melvin	Brian Murphy
Fanny Carby	Colin Kemball
Frank Coda	Linda Loftis
Richard Curnock	Ian Paterson
Peter Dalton	George Sewell
Larry Dann	Reid Shelton
Jack Eddleman	Bob Stevenson
Myvanwy Jenn	Valerie Walsh

ACT I: "Row Row Row," "We Don't Want To Lose You," "Belgium Put The Kibosh On The Kaiser," "Are We Downhearted," "It's A Long Way To Tipperary," "Hold Your Hand Out Naughty Boy," "I'll Make A Man Of You," "Pack Up Your Troubles," "Hitchykoo," "Heilige Nacht," "Christmas Day In The Cookhouse," "Goodbye . . . ee."

ACT II: "OH What A Lovely War," "Gassed Last Night," "Roses Of Picardy," "Hush Here Comes A Whizzbang," "There's A Long Long Trail," "I Don't Want To Be A Soldier," "Kaiser Bill," "They Were Only Playing Leapfrog," "Old Soldiers Never Die," "If You Want The Old Battalion," "Far Far From Wipers," "If The Sergeant Steals Your Rum," "I Wore A Tunic," "Forward Joe Soap's Army," "Fred Karno's Army," "When This Lousy War Is Over," "Wash Me In The Water," "I Want To Go Home," "The Bells Of Hell," "Keep The Home Fires Burning," "Sister Susie's Sewing Shirts," Finale.

A Musical Entertainment in two acts.

General Manger: Jack Schlissel
Company Manager: Richard Highley
Press: Max Eisen, Maurice Turet
Stage Director: Kevin Palmer
Stage Manager: Jerry Adler

° Closed January 16, 1965. (125 performances)

Brian Murphy (with umbrella). Top: Valerie Walsh, Myvanwy Jenn, Victor Spinetti, Fanny Carby, Barbara Windsor

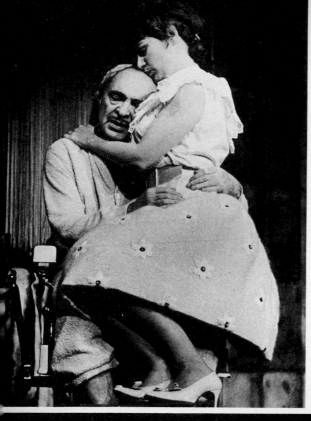

BELASCO THEATRE

Opened Thursday, October 1, 1964.°
Stevens Productions Inc., Bonfils-Seawell
Enterprises, and David Oppenheim present:

THE LAST ANALYSIS

By Saul Bellow; Directed by Joseph Anthony;
Setting and Lighting, David Hays; Costumes,
Ann Roth; Associate Producers, Lyn Austin,
Victor Samrock.

CAST

Philip Bummidge	Sam Levene
Sheldon	Charles Boaz
Louis Mott	Sully Michaels
Imogen	Alix Elias
Winkleman	Leon Janney
First Technician	Walter Williams
Second Technician	Ed Bordo
Third Technician	Phillip Pruneau
Madge	Lucille Patton
Max	Anthony Roberts
Pamela	Ann Wedgeworth
Antique Dealer	Ted Schwartz
Aufschnitt	Will Lee
Bella	Tresa Hughes
Stickles	Bert Conway
Messenger	Ted Schwartz
Tante Frumkah	Minerva Pious
Fiddleman	Michael Vale
Kalbfuss	James Dukas

UNDERSTUDIES: Imogen, Pamela, Sandy
Walsh; Bella, Madge, Tante, Maurine Marlowe.

A Farce in two acts. The action takes
place in Philip Bummidge's apartment in a
loft on New York's West Side at the present
time.

Company Manager: Ben Rosenberg
Press: Samuel Lurie, Warren Pincus,
Stanley F. Kaminsky
Stage Managers: Bill Ross, Perry Bruskin,
Phillip Pruneau

° Closed October 24, 1964. (28 performances)

Friedman-Abeles Photos

Lucille Patton, Minerva Pious, Sam Levene, Tresa Hughes. Top: Sam Levene, Alix Elias

PLYMOUTH THEATRE

Opened Tuesday, October 6, 1964.°
S. Hurok and David Black in association with Jay Julien and Andre Goulston present:

CAMBRIDGE CIRCUS

Written by the Company; Directed by Humphrey Barclay; Music, Bill Oddie, Hugh MacDonald, David Palmer; Designed by Stephen Mullin; Costumes, Judy Birdwood; Lighting, Robert Darling; Musical Arrangement, David Palmer.

CAST

Tim Brooke-Taylor	Jo Kendall
Graham Chapman	Jonathan Lynn
John Cleese	Bill Oddie
David Hatch	

Program

PART I: "Bring Out The Beast," "Cloak and Dagger," "London Bus," "Stage Coach," "Final Episode," "Traffic Island," "Patients, For the Use Of," "Scatty," "How Black Was My Valley," "Boring Straight Song," "BBCBC," "Sing, Sing," "Humour Without Tears."

PART II: "I Wanna Hold Your Handel," "Prophet," "West End Saga," "Music-Hall 1600," "Those Were The Days," "Pride And Joy," "To Bury Caesar," "On Her Majesty's Service," 'Banana," "Bigger Than Both Of Us," "Judge Not," "Foot Note."

A Revue in two parts.

General Manager: Eugene V. Wolsk
Press: Martin Feinstein, Michael Sweeley
Stage Manager: Robert Linden

° Closed October 24, 1964. (23 performances) Reopened Off Broadway Wednesday, October 28, 1964 at Square East, and closed there Sunday, March 21, 1965. (78 performances)

Jo Kendall, John Cleese. Top: Bill Oddie,
Tim Brooke-Taylor, Jonathan Lynn, David Hatch   **25**

MOROSCO THEATRE

Opened Wednesday, October 7, 1964.°
Stevens Productions Inc., Samuel Taylor,
and Bonfils-Seawell Enterprises present:

BEEKMAN PLACE

By Samuel Taylor; Directed by Mr. Taylor;
Setting, Oliver Smith; Lighting, Jack Brown;
Associate Producers, Lyn Austin, Victor Sam-
rock; Assistant to the Director, Fred Hebert;
Production Assistant, Martha Wadsworth;
Clothes Consultant, Suzanne Taylor; Hair Styles,
Michel Kazan.

CAST

Emily Bach-Nielsen	Leora Dana
Christian Bach-Nielsen	Fernand Gravet
Mildred Kelsey	Mary Grace Canfield
Pamela Piper	Arlene Francis
Augusta Piper	Carol Booth
Simon Holt	Laurence Luckinbill
Samuel Holt	George Coulouris

UNDERSTUDIES: Emily, Pamela, Joan Wetmore; Christian, Samuel, Rene Paul; Augusta,
Mildred, Kelly Jean Peters.

A Comedy in three acts. The action takes
place in a house on Beekman Place in the
City of New York during early autumn of
1962.

Company Manager: John Corkill
Press: Frank Goodman, Ben Kornzweig
Stage Manager: Charles Forsythe

° Closed October 31, 1964. (29 performances)

Friedman-Abeles Photos

Arlene Francis, Carol Booth, Laurence Luckinbill
26 Top: Arlene Francis, Fernand Gravet; Fernand Gravet,
Leora Dana, Carol Booth

MARTIN BECK THEATRE

Opened Tuesday, October 13, 1964.°
Allen-Hodgdon Inc. and Stevens Productions Inc. present:

THE PHYSICISTS

By Friedrich Duerrenmatt; Adapted by James Kirkup; Staged by Peter Brook; Scenery, Costumes and Lighting by John Bury; Supervision by Lloyd Burlingame; Production by arrangement with Robert Whitehead.

CAST

Police Inspector Richard Voss	Roberts Blossom
Matron Marta Boll	Doris Rich
Police Photographer Blocher	Jack Woods
Police Stenographer Guhl	Frank Daly
Policemen	John Dutra, Drew Eliot
Police Doctor	Alex Reed
Herbert Georg Beutler (Newton)	Hume Cronyn
Fraulein Doktor Mathilde von Zahnd	Jessica Tandy
Ernst Heinrich Ernesti (Einstein)	George Voskovec
Frau Lina Rose	Frances Heflin
Oskar Rose	David Ford
Adolf-Friedrich	Terry Culkin
Wilfried-Kaspar	Leland Mayforth
Jorg-Lukas	Doug Chapin
Johann Wilhelm Mobius	Robert Shaw
Monika Stettler	Elizabeth Hubbard
Uwe Sievers	Rod Colbin
McArthur	John Perkins
Murillo	Leonard Parker

UNDERSTUDIES: Mathilde, Doris Rich; Mobius, David Ford; Newton, Rod Colbin; Einstein, Roberts Blossom; Inspector, Frank Daly; Oskar, Alex Reed; Marta, Lina, Patricia Ripley; Monika, Susan Carr; Sons, Mark Belsky; Guhl, Blocher, Sievers, John Dutra; Doctor, Jack Woods.

A Drama in two acts. The action passes in the drawing room of a villa belonging to the private sanitarium known as "Les Cerisiers" at the present time.

Press: Harvey B. Sabinson, Lee Solters
Stage Managers: Paul A. Foley, Jack Woods

° Closed November 28, 1964. (55 performances)

Friedman-Abeles Photos

Jessica Tandy, Hume Cronyn, Robert Shaw, George Voskovec
Top: Jessica Tandy, George Voskovec

Jessica Tandy, Frances Heflin. Top: Hume Cronyn

Frances Heflin, Roberts Blossom, Robert Shaw
Top: Jessica Tandy

in "The Physicists"

28

LONGACRE THEATRE

Opened Thursday, October 15, 1964.°
(Moved December 29, 1964 to Henry
Miller's Theatre)
Burt C. D'Lugoff, Robert Nemiroff and
J. I. Jahre present:

THE SIGN IN SIDNEY BRUSTEIN'S WINDOW

By Lorraine Hansberry; Directed by Peter
Kass; Scenery, Jack Blackman; Costumes, Fred
Voelpel; Lighting, Jules Fisher; Campaign Song
by Ernie Sheldon; Recorded by The Moon-
shiners; Production Associate, Alan Heyman;
Associate to the Producers, Beverly Landau;
Assistant to the Producers, George Petrarca;
Production Associate, Murray Levy; Production
Assistants, Jean Lindgren, Joel Dein.

CAST

Sidney Brustein	Gabriel Dell
Iris Parodus Brustein	Rita Moreno
Alton Scales	Ben Aliza
Wally O'Hara	Frank Schofield
Max	Dolph Sweet
Mavis Parodus Bryson	Alice Ghostley
David Ragin	John Alderman
Gloria Parodus	Cynthia O'Neal†
Policeman	Josip Elic

UNDERSTUDIES: Sidney, Alton, Alan Mixon;
Iris, Joyce Flynn; Mavis, Gloria, Dorothy Sef-
ton; David, Kenneth Geist; Max, Josip Elic.

A Drama in three acts and six scenes. The
action takes place at the present time in the
Brustein apartment in Greenwich Village, New
York City.

General Manager: Norman Maibaum
Company Manager: Michael Goldreyer
Press: Merle DeBuskey, Seymour Krawitz,
Ted Goldsmith
Stage Managers: Stephen Gardner,
Kenneth Geist

° Closed Sunday, January 10, 1965. (99 performances)
† Succeeded by Louise Sorel

Friedman-Abeles Photos

**Gabriel Dell, Rita Moreno also top left, and right
with Alice Ghostley**

29

Rita Moreno, Gabriel Dell, and top with
Frank Schofield

Rita Moreno, Alice Ghostley

in "The Sign In Sidney Brustein's Window"

Friedman-Abeles Photo

Sammy Davis, Jr.
in
"GOLDEN BOY"

MAJESTIC THEATRE
Opened Tuesday, October 20, 1964.°
Hillard Elkins presents:

GOLDEN BOY

Book by Clifford Odets and William Gibson;
Based on Mr. Odets' Play of the same name;
Music, Charles Strouse; Lyrics, Lee Adams; Directed by Arthur Penn; Sets, Costumes, and
Projections, Tony Walton; Choreography, Donald McKayle; Lighting, Tharon Musser; Projections Devised by Richard Pilbrow; Musical
Direction, Elliot Lawrence; Orchestrations,
Ralph Burns; Associate Producer, George Platt;
Musical Coordinator, George Rhodes; Assistant
Choreographer, Jaime Rogers; Production Manager, Michael Thoma; Assistant Musical Director, Joyce Brown.

CAST

Tom Moody	Kenneth Tobey
Roxy Gottlieb	Ted Beniades
Tokio	Charles Welch
Joe Wellington	Sammy Davis, Jr.
Lorna Moon	Paula Wayne †1
Mr. Wellington	Roy Glenn
Anna	Jeannette DuBois
Ronnie	Johnny Brown
Frank	Louis Gossett †2
Terry	Terrin Miles
Stevie	Stephen Taylor
Hoodlum	Buck Heller
Eddie Satin	Billy Daniels †3
Benny	Benny Payne
Al	Albert Popwell
Lola	Lola Falana
Lopez	Jaime Rogers
Mabel	Mabel Robinson
Les	Lester Wilson
Drake	Don Crabtree
Theresa	Theresa Merritt
Fight Announcer	Maxwell Glanville
Reporter	Bob Daley
Driscoll	Ralph Vucci

ENSEMBLE: Marguerite Delaine, Baayork
Lee, Robbin Miller, Sally Neal, Louise Quick,
Amy Rouselle, Buck Heller, Harold Pierson,
Kenneth Scott, Lamont Washington.

UNDERSTUDIES: Joe, Lamont Washington;
Lorna, Sheila Sullivan; Eddie, Louis Gossett;
Ronnie, Frank, Albert Popwell; Tom, Don
Crabtree; Roxy, Tokio, Ralph Vucci; Mr. Wellington, Maxwell Glanville; Anna, Amy Rouselle; Drake, Driscoll, Bob Daley; Terry, Stephen Taylor; Lopez, Harold Pierson.

MUSICAL NUMBERS: "Workout," "Night
Song," "Everything's Great," "Gimme Some,"
"Stick Around," "Don't Forget 127th Street,"
"Lorna's Here," "The Road Tour," "This Is
The Life," "Golden Boy," "While The City
Sleeps," "Colorful," "I Want To Be With
You," "Can't You See It?," "No More," "The
Fight."

A Musical in two acts.

General Manager: Joseph Harris
Press: Lee Solters, Harvey B. Sabinson,
Harry Nigro
Stage Managers: Ralph Linn, Vincent Lynne,
Bruce W. Stark, Ralph Vucci

° Still playing May 31, 1965.
† Succeeded by: 1. Sheila Sullivan during vacation, 2. Albert Popwell, 3. Louis Gossett

**Top Left: Charles Welch, Ted Beniades,
Sammy Davis, Jr., Billy Daniels
Below: Sammy Davis, Jr. and chorus**

**Sammy Davis, Jr., Johnny Brown
Above: Sammy Davis, Jr., Paula Wayne**

Sammy Davis, Jr., Paula Wayne
Top: Kenneth Tobey, Sammy Davis, Jr.

Sammy Davis, Jr., Billy Daniels
Top: Sammy Davis, Jr., Jaime Rogers

Robert Preston

34

Jack Fletcher, Robert Preston. Above: Franklin Kiser
Jacqueline Mayro. Top: Robert Preston and chorus

LUNT-FONTANNE THEATRE

Opened Tuesday, October 27, 1964.°
George W. George and Frank Granat present:

BEN FRANKLIN IN PARIS

Play and Lyrics, Sidney Michaels; Music, Mark Sandrich, Jr.; Direction and Choreography by Michael Kidd; Costumes, Motley; Designed by Oliver Smith; Musical Direction and Vocal Arrangements, Donald Pippin; Orchestrations, Philip J. Lang; Dance Music, Roger Adams; Lighting, Jack Brown; Assistant to Producers, Gloria Banta; Technical Supervisor, Ralph O. Willis; Production Assistant, Nelle Nugent.

CAST

Captain Wickes	Sam Greene
Benjamin Franklin	Robert Preston
Temple Franklin	Franklin Kiser
Benjamin Franklin Bache	Jerry Schaefer
Footman	Anthony Falco
Louis XVI	Oliver Clark
Vergennes	Art Bartow
Turgot	Clifford Fearl
Madame La Comtesse Diane de Vobrillac	Ulla Sallert
British Grenadier	Roger LePage
David Lord Stormont	Byron Webster
French Soldier	Ron Schwinn
Pierre Caron de Beaumarchais	Bob Kaliban
Jacques Finque	John Taliaferro
The Artist	John Keatts
Little Boy	Stuart Getz
Pedro Count de Aranda	Jack Fletcher
Bookseller	Herb Mazzini
Janine Nicolet	Susan Watson†
Abbe de Morellet	Herb Mazzini
Spanish Aide-de-Camp	Kip Andrews
Spanish Soldier	Art Matthews
Spanish Ambassador's Daughter	Suzanne France
Yvonne	Lauren Jones

SINGERS AND DANCERS: Barbara Bossert, Mona Crawford, Hilda Harris, Anita Maye, Caroline Parks, Art Bartow, Anthony Falco, Clifford Fearl, John Keatts, Art Matthews, Herb Mazzini, John Taliaferro, Diane Ball, Marilyn Charles, Jean Eliot, Suzanne France, Ellen Graff, Lauren Jones. Sandy Roveta, Kip Andrews, Roger LePage, George Ramos, Eddie Roll, Rec Russel, Ron Schwinn, Lou Zeldis.

UNDERSTUDIES: Franklin, Sam Greene; Comtesse, Caroline Parks; Janine, Sandy Roveta; Temple, Roger LePage; Pierre, Eddie Roll; For Messrs. Webster, Fletcher, Clark and Greene, John Hallow; B. F. Bache, Stuart Getz

MUSICAL NUMBERS: "We Sail The Seas," "I Invented Myself." "Too Charming," "Whatever Became Of Old Temple," "Half The Battle," "A Balloon Is Ascending," "To Be Alone With You," "You're In Paris," "How Laughable It Is," "Hic Haec Hoc," "God Bless The Human Elbow," "When I Dance With The Person I Love," "Diane Is," "Look For Small Pleasures," "I Love The Ladies."

A Musical in two acts and fourteen scenes. The entire action takes place in France during 1776-77.

General Manager: Edward H. Davis
Company Manager: George Oshrin
Press: Lee Solters, Harvey B. Sabinson, David Powers
Stage Managers: William Dodds, Ben Janney, John Hallow

° Closed May 1, 1965. (215 performances)
† Succeeded by Rita Gardner

Friedman-Abeles Photos

Top Right: Oliver Clark, Ulla Sallert
Below: Ulla Sallert, Robert Preston

Franklin Kiser, Robert Preston, Jerry Schaefer

Robert Preston, Ulla Sallert
in
"BEN FRANKLIN IN PARIS"

ROYALE THEATRE

Opened Wednesday, October 28, 1964.°
David Merrick and Donald Albery present:

A SEVERED HEAD

By Iris Murdoch and J. B. Priestley; Directed by Val May; Decor and Costumes, Stewart Chaney; Lighting, Martin Aronstein; Original Designs, Graham Barlow; Production Supervisor, Samuel Liff.

CAST

Martin Lynch-Gibbon	Robin Bailey
Georgie Hands	Jessica Walter
Antonia Lynch-Gibbon	Heather Chasen
Palmer Anderson	Paul Eddington
Rosemary Lynch-Gibbon	Christine Pickles
Alexander Lynch-Gibbon	Robert Milli
Honor Klein	Sheila Burrell

UNDERSTUDIES: Antonia, Honor, Angela Wood; Martin, Alexander, John D. Irving; Palmer, Robert Milli; Georgie, Rosemary, Barbara Caruso.

A Comedy in two acts. The action takes place at the present time in London between Georgie Hands' bed-sitting room in Covent Garden, the drawing room of Martin Lynch-Gibbon's house at Hereford Square, and the study and bedroom of Palmer Anderson's house in Pelham Crescent.

General Manager: Jack Schlissel
Company Manager: Manny Azenberg
Press: Lee Solters, Harvey B. Sabinson, Jay Russell
Stage Managers: Gene Perlowin, Marnel Sumner, Barbara Caruso

° Closed November 21, 1964. (29 performances)

Graphic House Photos

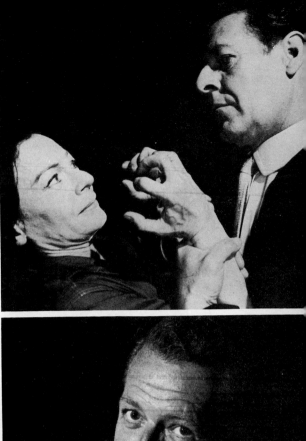

Sheila Burrell, Robin Bailey (also top right)

Jessica Walter, Robin Bailey

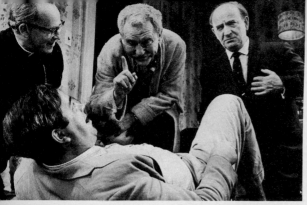

LYCEUM THEATRE

Opened Sunday, November 8, 1964°
David Merrick presents:

I WAS DANCING

By Edwin O'Connor; Directed by Garson Kanin; Designed by Oliver Smith; Costumes, Michael Travis; Lighting, Martin Aronstein; Associate Director, David Pardoll; Associate Producer, Samuel Liff; Production Associate, Alan
DeLynn; Dancing Arranged by Wally Strauss.

CAST

Daniel Considine	Burgess Meredith
Billy Ryan	David Doyle
Delia Bresnahan	Pert Kelton
Father Frank Feeley	Barnard Hughes
Al Gottlieb	Eli Mintz
Tom Considine	Orson Bean

STANDBYS: Delis, Ruth Donnelly; Daniel,
Dan Morgan; Tom, Billy, Dick Van Patten

A Comedy in three acts. The action takes
placed at the present time in Daniel Considine's
bedroom in his son's house.

General Manager: Jack Schlissel
Company Manager: Richard Highley
Press: Harvey B. Sabinson, Lee Solters,
Jay Russell, Lila King
Stage Manager: May Muth

° Closed November 21, 1964. (16 performances)

Eileen Darby-Graphic House

Burgess Meredith. Above: Pert Kelton
Top: Barnard Hughes, David Doyle,
Burgess Meredith, Eli Mintz

38

Top: Barnard Hughes, Eli Mintz, Burgess Meredith
Center: Burgess Meredith, Orson Bean

JHN GOLDEN THEATRE

Opened Monday, November 9, 1964.°
Alexander H. Cohen presents:

COMEDY IN MUSIC

Opus 2

A Nine O'Clock Theatre Production: De-
ned and Lighted by Ralph Alswang; Produc-
n Assistant, Robin Rudd.

CAST

VICTOR BORGE

with

Leonid Hambro

Presented in two parts. The order of the
gram announced by Mr. Borge.

General Manager: Roy A. Somlyo
Company Manager: Seymour Herscher
Press: James D. Proctor
Stage Managers: Jean Barrere, Ross Miller
Closed April 24, 1965. (192 performances)

Victor Borge

Friedman-Abeles Photo

EUGENE O'NEILL THEATRE

Opened Tuesday, November 10, 1964.°
Lester Osterman presents:

SOMETHING MORE!

Book by Nate Monaster; Based on "Portofino P.T.A." by Gerald Green; Music, Sammy Fain; Lyrics, Marilyn and Alan Bergman; Directed by Jule Styne; Scenery and Lighting, Robert Randolph; Costumes, Alvin Colt; Musical Direction, Oscar Kosarin; Orchestrations, Ralph Burns; Vocal Arrangement, Buster Davis; Dance Arrangements and Orchestrations, Robert Prince; Dances and Musical Numbers Staged by Bob Herget; Hair Styles, Ronald DeMann; Production Assistant, Joe Regan.

CAST

Bill Deems	Arthur Hill
Carol Deems	Barbara Cook
Suzy Deems	Neva Small
Freddy Deems	Kenny Kealy
Adam Deems	Eric White
Julie	Katey O'Brady
Dick	Hal Linden
Gladys	Marilyn Murphy
Joe Santini	Rico Froehlich
Tony Santini	Victor R. Helou
Policeman	Rico Froehlich
Mrs. Ferenzi	Peg Murray
Monte Checkovitch	Ronny Graham
Luigi	Victor R. Helou
Lepescu	Michael Kermoyan
Marchesa Valentina Crespi	Joan Copeland
Tony	Christopher Man
Maria	Katey O'Brady
The King	Taylor Reed
The King's Companion	Connie Sanchez
Mr. Veloz	Jo Jo Smith
Mrs. Veloz	Paula Kelly
Commandatorre Vermelli	James Lavery
Clubwoman	Laurie Franks

DANCERS: Joan Bell, Shari Greene, Lynn Kollenberg, Connie Sanchez, Mimi Wallace, Bob Bishop, Steve Jacobs, Richard Lyle, Barry Preston, Bill Starr.

SINGERS: Natalie di Silvio, Laurie Franks, Bobbi Lange, Marilyn Murphy, James Lavery, Taylor Reed, Ed Varrato.

UNDERSTUDIES: Bill, Monte, Hal Linden; Marchesa, Carol, Laurie Franks; Lepescu, Rico Froehlich; Mrs. Ferenzi, Bobbi Lange; Policeman, James Lavery; Luigi, Ed Varrato; Veloz, Bill Starr; Mrs. Veloz, Connie Sanchez; Freddy, Adam, Christopher Man; Suzy, Katy O'Brady.

MUSICAL NUMBERS: "Something More," "Who Fills The Bill," "The Straw That Broke The Camel's Back," "Better All The Time," "Don't Make A Move," "Church Of My Choice," "Jaded, Degraded Am I!," "I've Got Nothin' To Do," "Party Talk," "In No Time At All," "The Master of The Greatest Art Of All," "Grazie Per Niente," "I Feel Like New Year's Eve," "One Long Last Look," "Ode To A Key," "Bravo, Bravo, Novelisto," "Life Is Too Short," "Il Lago de Innamoratti," "Mineola," "Come Sta," Finale.

A Musical Comedy in two acts and seventeen scenes, with prologue. The action takes place at the present time in Mineola, L.I., N.Y., and Portofino, Italy.

General Manager: Richard Horner
Company Manager: Nicholas A. B. Gray
Press: Harvey B. Sabinson, Lee Solters, Leo Stern
Stage Managers: Max Evans, Richard Lyle
° Closed November 21, 1964. (15 performances)

Friedman-Abeles Photos

Top Left: Kenny Kealy, Eric White, Ronny Graham, Neva Small. Below: Barbara Cook, Arthur Hill

Kenny Kealy, Arthur Hill, Barbara Cook, Neva Small, Eric White. Above: Barbara Cook, Peg Murray

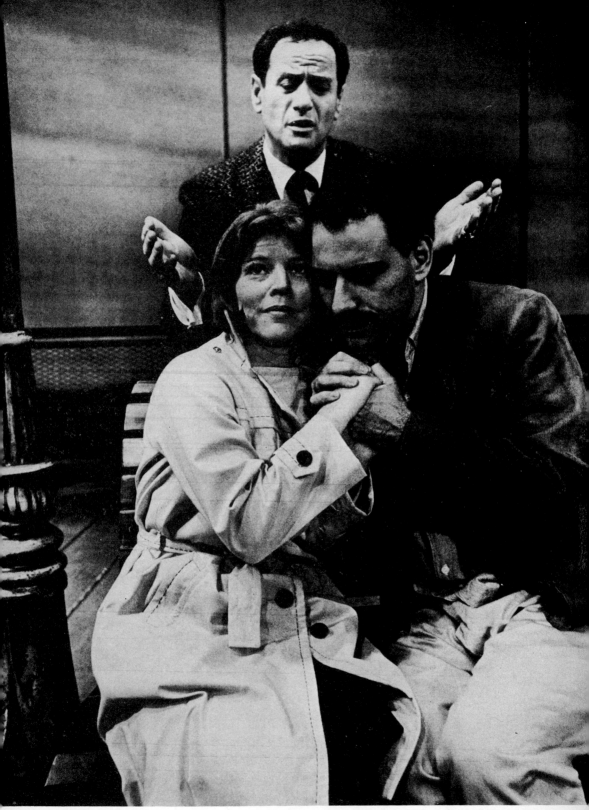

Anne Jackson, Eli Wallach, Alan Arkin
in
"LUV"

BOOTH THEATRE

Opened Wednesday, November 11, 1964.°
Claire Nichtern presents:

LUV

By Murray Schisgal; Directed by Mike Nichols; Designed by Oliver Smith; Lighting, Jean Rosenthal; Costumes, Theoni V. Aldredge; Song, Irving Joseph; Production Assistant, Jacqueline Awad; Acrobatic Stunt Staged by Wayne Storm.

CAST

Harry Berlin..................................Alan Arkin
Milt Manville..................................Eli Wallach
Ellen Manville..................................Anne Jackson

A Comedy in two acts. The action takes place at the present time on a bridge.

General Manager: Robert Kamlot
Press: Frank Goodman, Ben Kornzweig, Robert Ganshaw
Stage Managers: Harvey Medlinsky, Ian Cadenhead

° Still playing May 31, 1965.

Henry Grossman Photos

Eli Wallach, Anne Jackson. Top: Anne Jackson, Alan Arkin

BILLY ROSE THEATRE

Opened Thursday, November 12, 1964.°
Worley Thorne in association with Susan David presents:

CONVERSATION AT MIDNIGHT

By Edna St. Vincent Millay; Staged by Robert Gist; Settings, Charles T. Morrison; Lighting, Barry Garlinger.

CAST

Metcalf	George Murdock
Merton	Larry Gates
John	Al Freeman, Jr.
Lucas	Hal England
Pygmalion	Sandy Kenyon
Carl	James Patterson
Anselmo	John Randolph
Ricardo	Eduard Franz

A Drama in three acts. The action takes place after dinner in the home of a wealthy dilettante in 1938 in New York City.

General Manager: Robert Rapport
Press: Bill Doll & Co., Midori Tsuji, Shirley Herz
Stage Managers: Peter Marko, George Murdock

° Closed November 14, 1964. (4 performances)

Impact Photos

James Patterson   **Hal England**   **Larry Gates**
Top: Al Freeman, Jr., Larry Gates

CORT THEATRE

Opened Saturday, November 14, 1964.°
Harold Prince in association with Michael
Codron and Pledon Ltd. presents:

POOR BITOS

By Jean Anouilh; Translated by Lucienne
Hill; Directed by Shirley Butler; Foreign Production Designed by Timothy O'Brien; American Production supervised by Jean Rosenthal;
Costumes, Donald Brooks; Lighting, Jean Rosenthal; Hair Styles, D. Rusty Bonaccorso.

CAST

Maxime, who plays Saint-Just	Charles D. Gray
Philippe, who plays Jesuit Father	Norman Barrs
Charles	Bernie West
Julien, who plays Danton	Roy Poole
Lila, who plays Marie Antoinette	Jane Lowry
Amanda, who plays Madame Tallien	Nancy Reardon
Vulturne, who plays Mirabeau	C. K. Alexander
Brassac, who plays Tallien	John Devlin
Deschamps, who plays Camille Desmoulins	Michael Lombard
Victoire, who plays Lucille Desmoulins	Diana Muldaur
Bitos, who plays Robespierre	Donald Pleasence
Joseph	Gino Conforti
Delanoue, who plays Merda	Marco St. John
Robespierre as a child	Bryant Fraser

UNDERSTUDIES: Victoire, Amanda, Lila,
Dixie Marquis; Julien, Vulturne, Charles, Bras-
sac, Philippe, Charles Durning; Maxime, Des-
champs, Delanoue, Joseph, James Antonio.

A Comedy in three acts. The action takes
place in a French provincial town, ten years
after the last war.

General Manager: Carl Fisher
Press: Mary Bryant, Louise Weiner
Stage Managers: Ruth Mitchell, Stephen Rich

° Closed November 28, 1964. (17 performances)

Friedman-Abeles Photos

Left: C. K. Alexander, Diana Muldaur, Norman
Barrs, Charles D. Gray, Roy Poole, John Devlin
Top: Charles D. Gray, Donald Pleasence, Norma
Barrs, Gino Conforti, Nancy Reardon, Bernie We
Michael Lombard, John Devlin, C. K. Alexander
Below: Bernie West, Diana Muldaur,
Donald Pleasence

Michael Lombard, Roy Poole, John Devlin, Nancy Reardon, Bernie West, Donald Pleasence,
Charles D. Gray, C. K. Alexander, Diana Muldaur, Jane Lowry

Diana Sands, Alan Alda
in
"THE OWL AND THE PUSSYCAT"

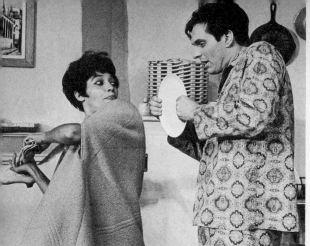

Alan Alda, Diana Sands (also above, top, and right)

ANTA THEATRE

Opened Wednesday, November 18, 1964.°
Philip Rose, Pat Fowler and Seven Arts
Productions present:

THE OWL AND THE PUSSYCAT

By Bill Manhoff; Directed by Arthur Storch;
Scenery and Lighting, Jo Mielziner; Costumes,
Florence Klotz; Projections Created by Anatole
Kovarsky; Music, Mark Lawrence; Arranged by
Norman Paris.

CAST

F. Sherman	Alan Alda
Doris W.	Diana Sands

UNDERSTUDIES: Sherman, Robert Moore;
Doris, Rose Gregorio.

A Comedy in three acts and eight scenes.
The action takes place at the present time in an
apartment in San Francisco.

General Manager: Walter Fried
Press: Merle Debuskey, Seymour Krawitz,
Ted Goldsmith
Stage Manager: Leonard Auerbach
° Still playing May 31, 1965.

Friedman-Abeles Photos

HENRY MILLER'S THEATRE

Opened Thursday, November 19, 1964.°
Morton Gottlieb and Helen Bonfils present:

P. S. I LOVE YOU

By Lawrence Roman; Directed by Henry Kaplan; Scenery and Costumes, Raoul Pene Du Bois; Lighting, Jules Fisher; Miss Page's clothes, Theoni V. Aldredge; Fashion Consultant, Arnold Scaasi; Hair Creations, John Bernard; Furs, Reiss and Frabrizio; Production Assistant, Maggie Abbott.

CAST

Strolling Player	Robert Creash
Julie Cunningham	Geraldine Page
Claude Noyelle	Gilles Pelletier
Vendor	Warren Lyons
Tom Cunningham	Lee Patterson
Germaine Noyelle	Dominique Minot
Blanche	Liliane Simonet
Raymonde	Lynn Carlysle

STANDBYS: Julie, Lynn Carlysle; Tom, Claude, Peter Walker; Germaine, Liliane Simonet.

A Comedy in two acts with a prologue. The action takes place at the present time at Divonne-Les-Bains in France, and in the Paris residences of the Cunninghams and the Noyelles.

General Manager: Richard Seader
Press: Dorothy Ross, Richard O'Brien
Stage Managers: Warren Crane, Warren Lyons

° Closed November 28, 1964. (12 performances)

Werner J. Kuhn Photos

Right and Top: Geraldine Page, Lee Patterson

Lee Patterson, Geraldine Page, Gilles Pelletier, Dominique Minot

Zizi Jeanmaire

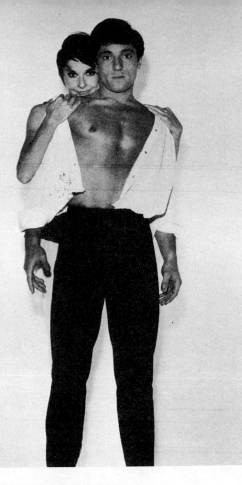

BROADWAY THEATRE

Opened Saturday, November 21, 1964.°
Columbia Theatrical Enterprises, Inc., and
Claude Giraud Productions present under
the auspices of the Association Francaise
d'Action Artistique:

ZIZI

Entire Production Conceived and Staged by
Roland Petit; Costumes, Yves Saint-Laurent;
Musical Director and Conductor, Michel Men-
tion; Associate Conductor, Don Plumby.

CAST

Zizi Jeanmaire
Felix Blaszka
and
The Roland Petit Corps De Ballet

Programme

PART I: Prologue, Zizi, La Cervelle, Les Bras
D'Antoine, Pastiches, La Chambre, Zizi Jeanmaire and Felix Blaszka, Bacorope, La Chalou-
pee, Quail On Toast With Pink Champagne.

PART II: Zizi Sings: Les Yeux Brillants, Les
Tatouages, Charleston, Drole De Musique,
Frankie Et Johnny, Mon Truc En Plumes, Mon
Bonhomme, Je Te Tuerai D'Amour, Eh L'-
Amour.

A Musical Extravaganza in two parts.

General Manager: C. Edwin Knill
Company Manager: Edward C. Fisher
Press: Bill Doll & Co., Midori Tsuji, Shirley
Herz, Richard T. Spittel
Stage Manager: Jean Fananas

° Closed January 2, 1965. (49 performances)

Zizi Jeanmaire (also above, and top left with Felix Blaszka)

49

Gus Trikonis, Herschel Bernardi, Chita Rivera,
Herbert Edelman (also at top)

Chita Rivera

50

SAM S. SHUBERT THEATRE

Opened Monday, November 23, 1964.°
(Moved May 10, 1965 to Lunt-Fontanne
Theatre)
Edward Padula, Carroll and Harris Masterson, Norman Twain present:

BAJOUR

Book, Ernest Kinoy; Based on The New
Yorker Stories by Joseph Mitchell; Music and
Lyrics, Walter Marks; Directed by Lawrence
Kasha; Musical Numbers Staged by Peter Gennaro; Scenery, Oliver Smith; Costumes, Freddy
Wittop; Lighting, Peggy Clark; Vocal Arrangements and Musical Direction, Lehman Engel;
Orchestrations, Mort Lindsey; Dance Music Arranged by Richard De Benedictis; Assistant
Choreographer, Wally Seibert; Associate Producers, Dorian Granowski, Stephen Harmon;
Assistant Conductor, John Lesko; Production
Manager, Duane Camp; Hair Styles, Monsieur
Marc, Joseph Tubens.

CAST

Renting Agent	Dick Ensslen
Cockeye Johnny Dembo	Herschel Bernardi
Vanno	Sal Lombardo
Loopa	Antonia Rey
Patrolmen	Harry Danner, Paul Sorvino, Robert Kristen
Plainclothesman	Harry Goz
Lou MacNiall	Robert Burr
Emily Kirsten	Nancy Dussault[1]
Mrs. Helene Kirsten	Mae Questel
Rosa	Asya
Mitya	Vito Durante
Frankie	Terry Violino
Steve	Gus Trikonis
The King of Newark	Herbert Edelman[2]
Anyanka	Chita Rivera
Marfa	Jeanne Tanzy
Olga	Carmen Morales
Chairlady	Lucie Lancaster
Waiter	Harry Danner
J. Arnold Foster	Ralph Farnworth

DANCERS: Asya, Eileen Barbaris, Michael
Bennett, Connie Burnett, John Cashman, Betsy
Dickerson, Vito Durante, Gene Foote, Bick
Goss, Fernando Grahal, Kazimir Kokich, Marc
Maskin, Stan Mazin, Carmen Morales, Carolyn
Morris, Leland Palmer, Don Rehg, Geri Seignious, Terry Violino, Billi Vitali.

SINGERS: Anita Alpert, Harry Danner, Mariana Doro, Dick Ensslen, Peter Falzone, Ralph
Farnworth, Harry Goz, Liza Howell, Robert
Kristen, Urylee Leonardos, Evy Love, Madeline
Miller, Eugene Morgan, Jeanne Repp, Jessica
Quinn, Paul Sorvino.

UNDERSTUDIES: Anyanka, Carolyn Morris;
Emily, Madeline Miller; Johnny, Herbert Edelman; Lou, Paul Sorvino; Mrs. Kirsten, Lucie
Lancaster; Steve, Stan Mazin; King, Ralph
Farnworth; Loopa, Jeanne Repp; Chairlady,
Mariana Doro; Vanno, Peter Falzone; Marfa,
Evy Love.

MUSICAL NUMBERS: "Move Over, New
York," "Where Is The Tribe For Me?," "The
Haggle," "Love-Line," "Words, Words,
Words," "Mean," "Must It Be Love?," "Bajour," "Soon," "I Can," "Living Simply,"
"Honest Man," "Guarantees," "Love Is A
Chance," "The Sew-Up," "Move Over, America."

A Musical Comedy in two acts and twenty-two scenes. The action takes place at the present time in New Jersey and New York City.

General Managers: Frank Hopkins,
Sherman Gross
Company Manager: Frank Hopkins
Press: Seymour Krawitz, Merle Debuskey,
Ted Goldsmith
Stage Managers: Tony Manzi, Ralph Farnworth

° Still playing May 31, 1965. (216 performances)
† Succeeded by: 1. Virginia Martin during Miss
Dussault's four-weeks illness, 2. Pierre Epstein

Friedman-Abeles Photos

Top Right: Chita Rivera, Mae Questel
Below: Herschel Bernardi, Nancy Dussault

Nancy Dussault, Chita Rivera, Robert Burr
Above: Chita Rivera and gypsies

51

Clarence Williams III, Carolan Daniels, George Rose

PLYMOUTH THEATRE

Opened Monday, November 30, 1964.°
Hume Cronyn-Allen-Hodgdon Inc., Stevens Productions Inc., and Bonfils-Seawell Enterprises present:

SLOW DANCE ON THE KILLING GROUND

By William Hanley; Directed by Joseph Anthony; Designed by Oliver Smith; Costumes, Ann Roth; Lighting, Jack Brown; Production Assistant, Ann McIntosh; Hair Style, Richard of Helena Rubinstein.

CAST

Glas	George Rose
Randall	Clarence Williams III
Rosie	Carolan Daniels

UNDERSTUDIES: Glas, Heinz Hohenwald; Rosie, Roberta Bennett; Randall, Andre Womble.

A Drama in three acts. The action takes place in a small shop in a warehouse-and-factory district of Brooklyn on the night of June 1, 1962. The action is continuous.

Company Manager: Richard Osorio
Press: Harvey B. Sabinson, Lee Solters, Bob Ullman
Stage Managers: William Ross, Heinz Hohenwald

° Closed February 13, 1965. (88 performances)

Friedman-Abeles Photos

Clarence Williams III, Carolan Daniels, and top with George Rose

53

BELASCO THEATRE

Opened Tuesday, December 1, 1964.°
Dore Schary and Walter A. Hyman present:

ONE BY ONE

By Dore Schary; Directed by Mr. Schary; Setting and Lighting, Donald Oenslager; Costumes, Florence Klotz; Women's Clothes, Hannah Troy; Production Assistant, Phyllis Dukore.

CAST

Charles Lacey	Donald Woods
Justy Lacey	Michaele Myers
Kathy Lacey	Sharon Laughlin
Jason Sample	Donald Madden
Frank Sample	Richard McMurray
Grace Sample	Margot Stevenson
Paul Keyes	Jack Heller

UNDERSTUDIES: Grace, Nancy Sheridan; Kathy, Justy, Sandra Smith; Charles, Frank, Harry Young; Jason, Paul, Richard Rust.

A Drama in two acts and five scenes. The action takes place at the present time in the Lacey home on Long Island, New York.

General Manager: Jesse Long
Press: Nat and Irvin Dorfman
Stage Managers: Jeb Schary, Harry Young

° Closed December 5, 1964. (7 performances)

Friedman-Abeles Photos

Donald Madden, Sharon Laughlin (also at top)

Alan Bates
in
"POOR RICHARD"

Joan Alexander, Alan Bates

Joanna Pettct, Alan Bates and
top with Gene Hackman

HELEN HAYES THEATRE

Opened Wednesday, December 2 ,1964.°
Stevens Productions, Inc. presents:

POOR RICHARD

By Jean Kerr; Directed by Peter Wood; Designed by Oliver Smith; Costumes, Theoni V. Aldredge; Lighting, Peggy Clark; Associate Producers, Lyn Austin, Victor Samrock; Production Assistant, Martha Wadsworth.

CAST

Sydney Carroll	Gene Hackman
Catherine Shaw	Joanna Pettet
Richard Ford	Alan Bates
John McFarland	Colgate Salsbury
Virginia Baker	Joan Alexander

UNDERSTUDIES: Catherine, Julie Mannix; Richard, Richard Clarke.

A Comedy in three acts. The action takes place in an apartment in Greenwich Village at the present time.

Company Manager: Ben Rosenberg
Press: Samuel Lurie, Warren Pincus,
Stanley F. Kaminsky
Stage Managers: John Drew Devereaux,
Wayne Carson

° Closed March 13, 1965. (117 performances)

Friedman-Abeles Photos

Alan Bates, Joanna Pettet, Gene Hackman
Top: Alan Bates, Joanna Pettet

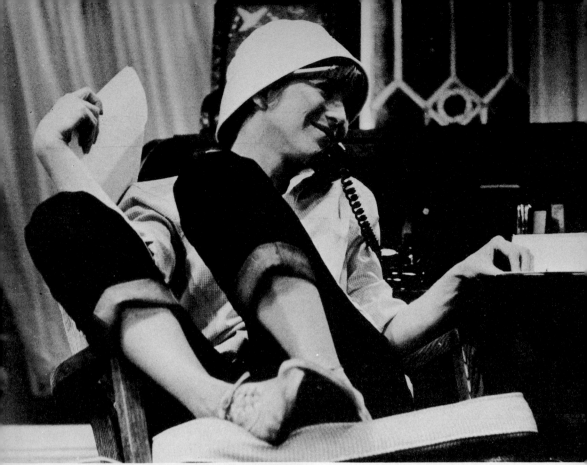

BROOKS ATKINTON THEATRE

Open Monday, December 7, 1964.°
David Black presents:

READY WHEN YOU ARE, C. B.!

By Susan Slade; Directed by Joshua Logan;
Setting and Lighting, Will Steven Armstrong;
Costumes, Theoni V. Aldredge; Production
Manager, Ross Bowman.

CAST

Annie	Julie Harris
Fran	Arlene Golonka
Felicia	Estelle Parsons
Jonas	Lou Antonio
Sadie	Betty Walker

STANDBYS: Annie, Fran, Lynn Bernay, Jo-
nas, Bob Monroe; Felicia, Sadie, Ann Mitchell

A Comedy in two acts and seven scenes.
The action takes place at the present time in
Annie's apartment on Riverside Drive in New
York.

General Manager: Eugene V. Wolsk
Press: Frank Goodman, Ben Kornzweig,
Robert Ganshaw, Paul Solomon
Stage Managers: Doreen Richards, Bob Monroe
° Closed February 13, 1965. (80 performances)

Martha Swope and Bob Golby Photos

Lou Antonio, Julie Harris. Top: Julie Harris

Betty Walker, Lou Antonio, Julie Harris, Estelle Parsons
Top Left: Arlene Golonka, Julie Harris
Below: Julie Harris, Lou Antonio. Right: Julie Harris

Luba Lisa with chorus. Above: (left) Buddy Hackett, Richard Kiley (right) Morocco,
Steve Roland, Karen Morrow, Richard Kiley, Luba Lisa, in window:
Buddy Hackett, Ted Thurston

MARTIN BECK THEATRE

Opened Tuesday, December 15, 1964.°
Joseph Kipness presents:

I HAD A BALL

Book, Jerome Chodorov; Music and Lyrics, Jack Lawrence, Stan Freeman; Directed by Lloyd Richards; Settings and Lighting, Will Steven Armstrong; Costumes, Ann Roth; Musical Direction and Vocal Arrangements, Pembroke Davenport; Dances and Musical Numbers Staged by Onna White; Orchestrations, Philip J. Lang; Dance Music Arranged by Luther Henderson; Hair Styles, Ronald DeMann; Production Assistant, Pat Johnston; Assistant Choreographer, Tom Panko; Assistant Musical Director, Rene Wiegert; Technical Consultant, Jules Fischer.

CAST

Garside	Buddy Hackett
Stan the Shpieler	Richard Kiley
Jeannie	Karen Morrow
Gimlet	Al Nesor
Joe the Muzzler	Jack Wakefield†
Ma Maloney	Rosetta LeNoire
George Osaka	Conrad Yama
Morocco	Morocco
Lifeguard	Marty Allen
Jimmy	Nathaniel Jones
Officer Millhauser	Ted Thurston
Brooks	Steve Roland
Addie	Luba Lisa
Children	Sheldon Golomb, Gina Kaye

SINGERS: Miriamne Burton, Jacqueline Carol, Jacque Dean, Marilyn Feder, Shirley Leinwand, Lispet Nelson, Eugene Edwards, Herbert Fields, Murray Goldkind, Marvin Goodis, Herb Surface, John Wheeler.
DANCERS: Mary Ehara, Sandra Lein, Nancy Lynch, Patti Mariano, Alice Shanahan, June Eve Story, Patti Ann Watson, Marty Allen, Doria Avila, Bob Bernard, Ray Gilbert, Edward J. Heim, Gary Hubler, Scott Hunter, John Sharpe
MUSICAL NUMBERS: "Coney Island, U.S.A.," "The Other Half Me," "Red-Blooded American Boy," "I Got Everything I Want," "Freud," "Think Beautiful," "Addie's At It Again," "Faith," "Can It Be Possible?," "The Neighborhood Song," "The Affluent Society," "Boys, Boys, Boys," "Fickle Finger Of Fate," "I Had A Ball," "Almost," "You Deserve Me," "Tunnel Of Love Chase"

A Musical Comedy in two acts. The action takes place at the present time in and around Coney Island.

General Manager: Philip Adler
Company Manager: S. M. Handelsman
Press: Frank Goodman, Ben Kornzweig, Martin Shwartz, Robert Ganshaw, Paul Solomon
Stage Managers: Mortimer Halpern, Nathan Caldwell, Jr., Bob Bernard

° Still playing May 31, 1965. (183 performances)
† Succeeded by Danny Dayton

Friedman-Abeles Photos

Buddy Hackett, Karen Morrow. Above: Richard Kiley, Buddy Hackett, Steve Roland, Jack Wakefield, Rosetta LeNoire, Al Nesor

Buddy Hackett
in
"I HAD A BALL"

ETHEL BARRYMORE THEATRE

Opened Tuesday, December 15, 1964.*

By arrangement with William Donaldson and Donald Albery, Alexander H. Cohen presents:

BEYOND THE FRINGE '65

Staged by Alexander H. Cohen; Original London Production Directed by Eleanor Fazan; Setting, John Wyckman; Lighting, Ralph Alswang; Production Associates, Andre Goulston, Gabriel Katzka; Production Assistant, Robin Rudd; Staff Assistant, Jane Deckoff.

CAST

Robert Cessna   Donald Cullen
Joe Fabiani   James Valentine

UNDERSTUDIES: Howell Price, Ian Wilder

PROGRAMME

PART I: "Hoe Thoughts From Abroad," "Royal Box," "The Following Paid Political Broadcast," "Bollard," "Blue Trousers," "Weill Song," "The Philosophers," "The Great Train Robbery," "Coloney Bogey," "The Aftermyth Of War."

PART II: "Civil War," "Real Class," "Die Flabbergast," "Portraits From Memory," "One Leg Too Few," "The Death of Nelson," "The Scientist," "The Doctor," "The Duke," "The Miner," "The Restaurant," "The Sermon," "So That's The Way You Like It," "The End Of The World."

A Revue in two acts.

General Manager: Roy A. Somlyo
Company Manager: G. Warren McClane
Press: Max Gendel, Donald Grant, Lea Gendel
Stage Managers: Alan Hall, Howell Price, Ian Wilder

* Closed January 9, 1965. (30 performances) Resumed road tour and closed April 3. 1965. For original production, see THEATRE WORLD, Vol. 19.

Friedman-Abeles Photo

Right: Don Cullen, James Valentine, Joel Fabiani, Robert Cessna

James Valentine, Don Cullen,
Joel Fabiani, Robert Cessna

Robert Cessna, Joel Fabiani,
James Valentine, Don Cullen

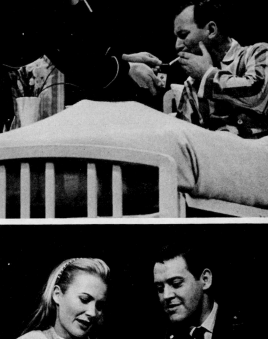

MOROSCO THEATRE

Opened Thursday, December 17, 1964.°
Frederick Brisson by arrangement with
Peter Saunders, Ltd. and Mermaid Theatre
Trust Ltd. presents:

ALFIE!

By Bill Naughton; Director, Gilchrist Calder;
Assistant to the Director, Fred Hebert; De-
signed by Lloyd Burlingame; Lighting Design,
Tharon Musser.

CAST

Alfie	Terence Stamp
Siddie	Joanna Morris
Gilda	Juliet Mills
Humphrey	Jeremy Geidt
Woman Doctor	Vanya Franck
Harry Clamacraft	Donald Ewer
Joe	Jerry Verno
Lily Clamacraft	Marcia Ashton
Carla	Carol Booth
Annie	Mary Hanefey
Lofty	James Luisi
Perc	Peter Fenton
Flo	Sasha Von Scherler
Ruby	Margaret Courtenay
Mr. Smith	George S. Irving

UNDERSTUDIES: Alfie, Hugh Alexander;
Gilda, Joanna Morris; Siddie, Carol Booth;
Humphrey, Lofty, Peter Fenton.

A Comedy in two acts. The action of the
play passes in and around South London at the
present time.

Company Manager: Ralph Roseman
Press: Harvey B. Sabinson, Lee Solters,
Leo Stern
Stage Managers: Charles Forsythe, Hugh
Alexander

° Closed January 2, 1965. (20 performances)

Friedman-Abeles Photos

Top Left: Terence Stamp, Mary Hanefey
Right: Terence Stamp, Donald Ewer

Terence Stamp, Vanya Franck
Above: Juliet Mills, Jeremy Geidt

64

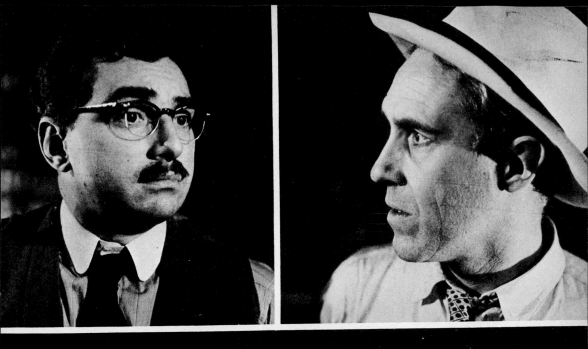

ROYALE THEATRE

Opened Tuesday, December 22, 1964.°
Theodore Mann and Joseph E. Levine in
association with Katzka-Berne present:

HUGHIE

By Eugene O'Neill; Directed by José Quintero; Set and Lighting, David Hays; Costumes, Noel Taylor.

CAST

A Nightclerk..Jack Dodson
"Erie" Smith..Jason Robards

Standby: Dana Elcar

A Drama in one act. The action takes place in the lobby of a small hotel on a West Side street in midtown New York, between three and four in the morning of a summer day in 1928.

General Manager: Paul Libin
Press: Marc Olden, Harold Rand,
Bob Perilla Associates
Stage Manager: Richard Blofson

° Closed January 30, 1965. (51 performances)

Jason Robards, Jack Dodson (also at top)

Friedman-Abeles Photos

65

Irene Worth, William Hutt, and top with John Gielgud

John Gielgud, Irene Worth, and top with
John Heffernan

BILLY ROSE THEATRE

Opened Tuesday, December 29, 1964.*
Theater 1965 (Richard Barr-Clinton Wilder) presents:

TINY ALICE

By Edward Albee; Directed by Alan Schneider; Designer, William Ritman; Gowns, Mainbocher; Lighting, Martin Aronstein.

CAST

Lawyer	William Hutt
Cardinal	Eric Berry
Julian	John Gielgud
Butler	John Heffernan
Miss Alice	Irene Worth

UNDERSTUDIES: Julian, John Heffernan; Miss Alice, Marian Seldes; Lawyer, Butler, Cardinal, Wyman Pendleton.

A Drama in three acts.

General Manager: Michael Goldreyer
Company Manager: Michael Kasdan
Press: Howard Atlee, Michael Alpert, David Roggensack
Stage Managers: Mark Wright, Arthur Pepine, Joseph Cali

* Closed May 22, 1965. (167 performances)

Alix Jeffry Photos

John Gielgud, Irene Worth. Top: Eric Berry, John Gielgud, Irene Worth, William Hutt, John Heffernan

Irene Worth, John Gielgud
in
"TINY ALICE"

Alix Jeffry Photo

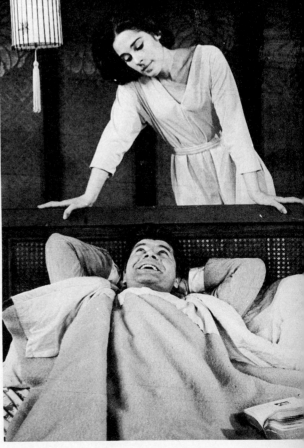

LONGACRE THEATRE

Opened Wednesday, January 6, 1965.°
Norman Twain and Peter S. Katz present:

PETERPAT

By Enid Rudd; Directed by Joe Layton; Settings and Lighting, David Hays; Costumes, Fred Voelpel; Associate Producer, Joseph H. Shoctor; Song "Ben Bullet" by Walter Marks; Music selected and arranged by Walter Marks; Production Assistant, Michael Doro; Organist, Louise Rush.

CAST

Peter _____ Dick Shawn
Pat _____ Joan Hackett

UNDERSTUDIES: Ben Keller, Nancy Pinkerton.

A Comedy in two acts and seven scenes. The action takes place some years ago in a small apartment in New York City, a hotel room, and a summer home.

General Manager: Sherman Gross
Press: Seymour Krawitz, Merle Debuskey
Stage Managers: Del Hughes, Peter Gumeny

° Closed January 23, 1965. (21 performances)

Friedman-Abeles Photos

Dick Shawn, Joan Hackett (also top and left)

LYCEUM THEATRE

Opened Wednesday, January 13, 1965.°
Leonard Sillman, Sandy Farber, Eddie White, in association with Ann Rork, present:

THE FAMILY WAY

By Ben Starr; Directed by Michael Gordon; Setting and Lighting, Ben Edwards; Costumes, Thomas Becher; Miss Wilcox's wardrobe, Baba.

CAST

Bobo Crane	Michael Kearney
Julie Crane	Collin Wilcox
Agnes Graham	Martha Greenhouse
Sylvia Goldman	Fritzi Burr
Richie Goldman	Christopher Man
Phil Brennan	Jack Kelly
Canvasser	Ed Preble
Arthur Smith	Ned Wertimer
Fred Smith	Arlen Dean Snyder
Stan Smith	Edward Crowley

UNDERSTUDIES: Julia, Marya Manning Case; Phil, Arlen Dean Snyder; Sylvia, Agnes, Marilyn Chris; Bobo, Christopher Man; Richie, Steve Chall; Arthur, Ed Preble; Stan, Fred, Salesman, Clark Ranger.

A Comedy in three acts and four scenes. The action takes place at the present time in Julie Crane's Los Angeles apartment.

General Manager: Al Goldin
Company Manager: J. Ross Stewart
Press: Bill Doll, Midori Tsuji, Shirley Herz, Richard Spittel
Stage Managers: Bill O'Brien, Clark Ranger

° Closed January 16, 1965. (5 performances)

Friedman-Abeles Photos

Collin Wilcox, Michael Kearney, Jack Kelly
Top: (L) Martha Greenhouse, Jack Kelly
(R) Ed Crowley, Arlen Dean Snyder, Collin Wilcox

CORT THEATRE

Opened Tuesday, February 2, 1965.°
Martin Lee by arrangement with Hal Wallis Productions and John Gale Productions, Ltd. presents:

BOEING-BOEING

By Marc Camoletti; Adapted by Beverley Cross; Directed by Jack Minster; Designed by Hutchinson Scott; Supervision and Lighting, Lloyd Burlingame; Production Assistant, Joan Davis.

CAST

Janet	Diana Millay
Bernard	Gerald Harper
Bertha	Maureen Pryor
Robert	Ian Carmichael
Jacqueline	Susan Carr
Judith	Joanna Morris

UNDERSTUDIES Nelle Nugent, Hilary Holden, Carleton Carpenter

A Comedy in two acts and three scenes. The action takes place at the present time in Bernard's apartment near Orly Airport in Paris.

General Manager: Victor Samrock
Company Manager: Ralph Roseman
Press: Bill Doll, Midori Tsuji, Richard Spittel, Robert Ganshaw
Stage Managers: Ben Janney, Nelle Nugent, Joan Davis

° Closed February 20, 1965. (23 performances)

Ben Mancuso-Impact Photos

Top: Maureen Pryor, Joanna Morris,
Ian Carmichael, Gerald Harper
Below: Maureen Pryor, Ian Carmichael

Ian Carmichael, Gerald Harper
Above: Diana Millay, Ian Carmichael
Top: Gerald Harper, Susan Carr

71

BROADHURST THEATRE

Opened Saturday, February 6, 1965.°
David Susskind and Daniel Melnick in association with Joseph E. Levine present:

KELLY

Book and Lyrics, Eddie Lawrence; Music, Moose Charlap; Directed and Choreographed by Herbert Ross; Scenic Production, Oliver Smith; Costumes, Freddy Wittop; Lighting, Tharon Musser; Orchestrations, Hershy Kay; Dance Music by Betty Walberg; Associate Producer, Robert L. Livingston; Production Assistants, Janet O'Morrison, Kelly English; Hair Stylist, Ronald DeMann.

CAST

Hop Kelly	Don Francks
Dan Kelly	Wilfrid Brambell
Jack Mulligan	Mickey Shaughnessy
Augie Masters	Leon Janney
Stickpin Sidney Crane	Jesse White
James	Steve Elmore
Carruthers	Brandon Maggart
Fay Cherry	Eileen Rodgers
Charlie	Josip Elic
Sparkenbroke	Bill Richards
Mayor Tully	Hamilton Camp
Englishman	Thomas Rezarf
Angela Crane	Anita Gillette
Tough Kid	Barbara Monte
3 Tough Guys	Louis Kosman, Anthony De Vecchi, Michael Nestor
Sailor	James Moore
The Redhead	Lynn Fields
The Rube	Sterling Clark
Young Girl	Hanne-Marie Reiner
First Young Man	Larry Roquemore
Second Young Man	Paul Charles
The Drunk	Ron Stratton
3 Ladies	Leslie Franzos, Eleanor Treiber, Kathleen Doherty
Lollypop Girl	Bette Jenkins
Beggar	Bill Richards
Bums	James Moore, Larry Roquemore, Bill Richards
Police Chief	J. Vernon Oaks
Policeman	Robert L. Hultman
Chief Dignitary	Stanley Simmonds

DANCING ENSEMBLE: Kathleen Doherty, Lynn Fields, Leslie Franzos, Bette Jenkins, Barbara Monte, Hanne-Marie Reiner, Eleanor Treiber, Sterling Clark, Paul Charles, Anthony De Vecchi, Michael Nestor, Bill Richards, Larry Roquemore, Ron Stratton.

SINGING ENSEMBLE: Georgia Creighton, Ceil Delli, Carol Joplin, Lorene Latine, Donna Monroe, Maggie Task, Walter P. Brown, Steve Elmore, Howard Hartman, Robert L. Hultman, J. Vernon Oaks, William Wendt.

UNDERSTUDIES: Hop, Dan, Hamilton Camp; Angela, Carol Joplin; Fay, Georgia Creighton; Jack, Bill Richards; Mayor, Stanley Simmonds; Charlie, J. Vernon Oaks; Carruthers, Louis Kosman.

MUSICAL NUMBERS: "Ode To The Bridge," "Six Blocks From The Bridge," "That Old Time Crowd," "Simple Ain't Easy," "I'm Gonna Walk Right Up To Her," "A Moment Ago," "This Is A Tough Neighborhood," "Never Go There Anymore," "Life Can Be Beautiful," "Everyone Here Loves Kelly," "Ballad To A Brute," "Heavyweight Champ Of The World," "Me And The Elements."

A Musical Comedy in two acts and thirteen scenes.

General Manager: Philip Adler
Company Manager: Edward Blatt
Press: Nat and Irvin Dorfman, Harold Rand, Marcia Katz
Stage Managers: Randall Brooks, Tom Porter, Kathleen A. Sullivan, Louis Kosman

° Closed February 6, 1965. (1 performance)

Friedman-Abeles Photos

Jesse White, Eileen Rodgers, Mickey Shaughnessy, Leon Janney

Top Left: Eileen Rodgers, Jesse White, Anita Gillette, Mickey Shaughnessy
Below: Anita Gillette, Don Francks

HENRY MILLER'S THEATRE

Opened Wednesday, February 10, 1965.°
Gilbert Miller in association with Stevens
Productions Inc. presents:

DIAMOND ORCHID

By Jerome Lawrence and Robert E. Lee; Directed by José Quintero; Sets and Lighting, David Hays; Costumes, Donald Brooks.

CAST

Maximiliano Orton	Bruce Gordon
Paulita	Jennifer West
Announcer	William Cottrell
Director	Leon B. Stevens
Sound Effects Man	John Garces
Radio Actor	Felice Orlandi
Jorge Salvador Brazo	Mario Alcalde
Studio Executive	Mel Haynes
Garcia	Bruce Kirby
Dona Elena Rivera	Margery Maude
Dr. Domingo Guzmano	Finlay Currie
Newscaster	John Armstrong
First Soldier	Gerald McGonagill
Second Soldier	Borah Silver
Third Soldier	John Garces
Fourth Soldier	James Goodnow
Carlos	William Cottrell
Portero	Louis Guss
Aguila	Leonardo Cimino
Old Man	Rene Enriquez
Waitress	Betty Hellman
Captain	Gerald McGonagill
Lieutenant	Borah Silver
Social Secretary	Patricia Jenkins
Male Secretary	John Garces
Mama	Helen Craig
Old Woman	Mary Bell
Man-With-Cap	Felice Orlandi
Cardinal Frazzini	Leon B. Stevens
Nurse	Betty Hellman
Servants	John Sarno, Felice Orlandi, Rene Enrique, James Goodnow, John Armstrong

STANDBYS: Paulita, Patricia Jenkins; Brazo, Felice Orlandi; Guzmano, Leonardo Cimino.

A Drama in two acts. The action takes place in a Latin-American country in the recent past.

General Manager: George Banyai
Company Manager: Richard Seader
Press: Sol Jacobson, Lewis Harmon, Earl Butler
Stage Managers: Eugene Stuckmann, Bill Story, Warren Crane

° Closed February 13, 1965. (5 performances)

Werner J. Kuhn Photos

Finlay Currie, Mario Alcalde, Margery Maude, Bruce Gordon, Jennifer West
Above: Jennifer West, Bruce Gordon

Top: Leon B. Stevens, Mario Alcalde, Jennifer West, Bruce Gordon, Finlay Currie, Helen Craig

73

Carol Burnett, and above with Dick Shawn

MARK HELLINGER THEATRE

Opened Monday, February 15, 1965.°
Lester Osterman and Jule Styne present:

FADE OUT—FADE IN

Book and Lyrics, Betty Comden and Adolph
Green; Music, Jule Styne; Directed by George
Abbott; Dances and Musical Numbers Staged
by Ernest Flatt; Settings and Lighting, William
and Jean Eckart; Costumes, Donald Brooks;
Musical Direction, John Berkman; Orchestrations, Ralph Burns and Ray Ellis; Vocal Arrangements, Buster Davis; Dance Music Arranged by Richard De Benedictis; Hair Styles,
Ernest Adler; Production Co-ordinator, Dorothy
Dicker; Production Assistant, Joe Regan.

CAST

Pops	Frank Tweddell
Autograph Kids	Roger Allan Raby, Charlene Mehl
Helga Sixtrees	Alice Glenn
Roscoe	Bob Neukum
Billy Vespers	Paul Michael
Byron Prong	Dick Shawn
Lyman	John Dorrin
Hope Springfield	Carol Burnett
Rex	Barney Johnston
Chauffeur	John Richardson
Girl	Trish Dwelley
Cowboy Extra	David Cryer
Gangster Extra	Gene Varrone
Ralph Governor	Mitchell Jason
Rudolf Governor	Dick Patterson
George Governor	Paul Eichel
Frank Governor	John Dorrin
Harold Governor	Gene Varrone
Arnold Governor	David Cryer
Waiters	Richard Frisch, Roger Allan Raby, Steve Elmore
Publicity Men	Dean Doss, Barney Johnston
Convicts	Gene Kelton, John Richardson, Bill Starr, Jerry Gotham
Myra May Melrose	Virginia Payne
Seamstress	Diane Arnold
Custer Corkley	Dan Resin
Max Welch	Richard Frisch
Lou Williams	Tiger Haynes
Dora Dailey	Aileen Poe
Lionel Z. Governor	Lou Jacobi
Dr. Anton Traurig	Reuben Singer
Gloria Currie	Judy Cassmore
Madame Barrymore	Penny Egelston
Lead Dancer	Don Crichton

SINGING ENSEMBLE: Terri Baker, Dell
Brownlee, Trish Dwelley, Carolyn Kemp, Bobbi
Lange, Mari Nettum, David Cryer, John Dor-
rin, Dean Doss, Paul Eichel, Steve Elmore,
Richard Frisch, Barney Johnston, Roger Allan
Raby, Gene Varrone.

DANCING ENSEMBLE: Virginia Allen, Di-
ane Arnold, Lynne Broadbent, Diana Eden,
Alice Glenn, Charlene Mehl, Judy Newman,
Jodi Perselle, Carolsue Shaer, Pat Sigris, Jerry
Gotham, Gene Kelton, John Richardson, Buddy
Spencer, Bill Starr, Ron Tassone, Michael Toles.

UNDERSTUDIES: Byron, Mitchell Gregg; L.
Z., Paul Michael; Hope, Carolyn Kemp; Ru-
dolf, Don Crichton; Traurig, Richard Frisch;
Lou, John Richardson; Myra, Mari Nettum;
Dora, Dell Brownlee; Ralph, Custer, Steve El-
more; Gloria, Terri Baker.

MUSICAL NUMBERS: Overture, "It's Good
To Be Back Home," "Fear," "Call Me Sav-
age," "The Usher From the Mezzanine," "My
Heart Is Like A Violin," "I'm With You,"
"Notice Me," "My Fortune Is My Face," "A
Girl To Remember," "Close Harmony," "You
Mustn't Be Discouraged," "The Dangerous
Age," "L. Z. In Quest Of His Youth," "The
Fiddler and The Fighter Finale," "Fade Out—
Fade In."

A Musical Comedy in two acts and seventeen scenes. The action takes place in Hollywood in the mid-1930's.

General Manager: Richard Horner
Company Manager: Leonard Soloway
Press: Harvey B. Sabinson, Lee Solters,
David Powers
Stage Managers: William Krot, Nicholas A. B.
Gray, Dan Resin

° Closed April 17, 1965. (271 performances)
For original production, see THEATRE
WORLD, Vol. 20. Opened Tuesday, May
26, 1964, at the same theatre and closed
there November 14, 1964 (199 performa-
ances) because of Miss Burnett's illness.

Friedman-Abeles Photos

Carol Burnett (R). Top: Dick Shawn (L)

Dick Shawn, Judy Cassmore
Top: Dick Patterson, Carol Burnett

$$E = mc^2 \, ?$$

$$(a+b)^n = a^n + n \cdots \frac{(n-1)}{!} \, a^{n-2}b$$

$$\frac{n(n-1}{3!} \cdots -3b^3 + \dots +$$

de con―
pro b :
solu

Martin Gabel

Fritz Weaver, and above with Inga Swenson

BROADWAY THEATRE
Opened Tuesday, February 16, 1965.°
Alexander H. Cohen presents:

BAKER STREET

Book by Jerome Coopersmith; Music and
Lyrics, Marian Grudeff and Raymond Jessel;
Adapted from the Stories by Sir Arthur Conan
Doyle; Production Designed by Oliver Smith;
Lighting, Jean Rosenthal; Costumes, Motley;
Directed by Harold Prince; Choreography, Lee
Becker Theodore; Musical Direction, Harold
Hastings; Orchestrations, Don Walker; Dance
Arrangements, John Morris; Production Associ-
ate, Hildy Parks; Special Makeup, Dick Smith;
Hair Styles, D. Rusty Bonaccorso; Produced in
Association with Gabriel Katzka; Diamond Ju-
bilee Parade by Bil Baird's Marionettes; Pro-
duction Assistant, Arthur Whitelaw.

CAST

Captain Gregg	Patrick Horgan
Dr. Watson	Peter Sallis
Mrs. Hudson	Paddy Edwards
Sherlock Holmes	Fritz Weaver
Inspector Lestrade	Daniel Keyes
Irene Adler	Inga Swenson
Daisy	Virginia Vestoff
Baxter	Martin Wolfson
Wiggins	Teddy Green
Duckbellows	Bert Michaels
Nipper	Sal Pernice
Perkins	George Lee
Macipper	Mark Jude Sheil
Murillo	Jay Norman
The Three Killers	Avin Harum, Tommy Tune, Christopher Walken
Tavern Singer	Gwenn Lewis
Professor Moriarty	Martin Gabel

DANCERS: Saral Lee Barber, Barbara Blair,
Lois Castle, John Grigas, Gwenn Lewis, Diana
Saunders

SINGERS: Martin Ambrose, Frank Bouley,
Jack Dabdoub, Gay Edmond, Judie Elkins,
Maria Graziano, Horace Guittard, Peter Johl,
Mara Landi, Hal Norman, Vera Walton.

UNDERSTUDIES: Moriarty, Jack Dabdoub;
Watson, Hal Norman; Mrs. Hudson, Mara Lan-
di; Baxter, Martin Ambrose; Gregg, Horace
Guittard; Irene, Virginia Vestoff.

MUSICAL NUMBERS: "It's So Simple," "I'm
In London Again," "Leave It To Us, Guv,"
"Letters," "Cold Clear World," "Finding
Words For Spring," "What A Night This Is
Going To Be," "London Underworld," "I Shall
Miss You," "Roof Space," "A Married Man,"
"I'd Do It Again," "Pursuit," "Jewelry."

A Musical Adventure of Sherlock Holmes in
two acts and sixteen scenes with a prologue.
The action takes place in and around London
in 1897, the year in which England celebrated
the Diamond Jubilee of the reign of Queen
Victoria.

General Manager: Roy A. Somlyo
Company Manager: Seymour Herscher
Press: James D. Proctor, Louise Weiner,
Don Grant
Stage Managers: Ruth Mitchell, Jake
Hamilton, Nicholas Rinaldi

° Still playing May 31, 1965. (121 performances)

Friedman-Abeles Photos

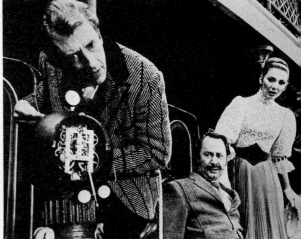

Right Center: Fritz Weaver, Inga Swenson
Top: "The Baker Street Irregulars"

Fritz Weaver, Peter Sallis, Inga Swenson

Martin Gabel, Fritz Weaver, Inga Swenson
in
"BAKER STREET"

ROYALE THEATRE

Opened Thurday, February 18, 1965.°

David Susskind, Daniel Melnick and Joseph E. Levine in association with John and Roy Boulting present:

ALL IN GOOD TIME

By Bill Naughton; Directed by Donald Mc-Whinnie; English Production Designed by Alan Tagg; Lighting Designed and American Production Supervised by Tharon Musser; Costumes, Peter Harvey; Associate Producer, Robert L. Livingston.

CAST

Ezra Fitton	Donald Wolfit
Lucy Fitton	Marjorie Rhodes
Arthur Fitton	Brian Murray
Geoffrey Fitton	John Karlen
Leslie Piper	John Sharp
Liz Piper	Hazel Douglas
Violet Fitton	Alexandra Berlin
Uncle Fred	Richard A. Dysart
Joe Thompson	Eugene Roche
Molly Thompson	Rosalind Ross
Eddie Taylor	Terry Lomax

UNDERSTUDIES: Lucy, Rosalind Ross; Arthur, John Karlen; Leslie, Fred, Joe, Ralph Drischell; Liz, Molly, Diana Webster; Violet, Carol Booth; Geoffrey, Eddie, Don Billett.

A Comedy in three acts and seven scenes. The action takes place in and around the Fitton home in the North of England at the present time.

Company Manager: Alfred Fischer
General Manager: Philip Adler
Press: Nat and Irvin Dorfman, Marcia Katz, Harold Rand
Stage Managers: Marnel Sumner, Don Billett

° Closed March 27, 1965. (44 performances)

Friedman-Abeles Photos

Brian Murray, Alexandra Berlin. Top: Donald Wolfit, Marjorie Rhodes, John Sharp, Hazel Douglas

79

Marjorie Rhodes, Donald Wolfit
in
"ALL IN GOOD TIME"

Patrick McVey, Tom Bosley, Dan Dailey

MOROSCO THEATRE

Opened Tuesday, March 9, 1965.°
Lee Guber, Frank Ford and Shelly Gross present:

CATCH ME IF YOU CAN

By Jack Weinstock and Willie Gilbert; Based on French play by Robert Thomas; Directed by Vincent J. Donehue; Designed and Lighted by George Jenkins; Costumes, Peter Joseph.

CAST

Daniel Corbin .... Dan Dailey
Inspector Levine .... Tom Bosley
Elizabeth Corbin .... Bethel Leslie
Father Kelleher .... George Mathews
Sidney .... Eli Mintz
Mrs. Parker .... Jo Tract
Everett Parker, Jr. .... Patrick McVey

UNDERSTUDIES: Levine, Sidney, Jeremiah Morris; Elizabeth, Mrs. Parker, Rosemary Tory; Kelleher, Patrick McVey; Elizabeth, Jo Tract.

A Comedy Murder Mystery in three acts and four scenes. The action takes place in a summer cottage in the Catskill Mountains on a Labor Day weekend at the present time.

General Manager: Marvin A. Krauss
Company Manager: Richard Osorio
Press: Saul Richman
Stage Manager: Charles Maryan

° Still playing May 31, 1965. (95 performances)

Barry Kramer Photos

Top: Dan Dailey, Tom Bosley, Bethel Leslie

Tom Bosley, Jo Tract. Above: Tom Bosley, Dan Dailey

Dan Dailey, Eli Mintz. Above: Dan Dailey, Bethel Leslie

in "Catch Me If You Can"

82

Art Carney, Walter Matthau
in
"THE ODD COUPLE"

Henry Grossman Photo

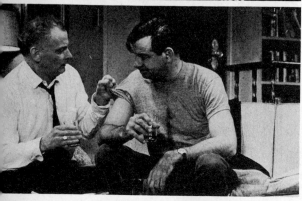

PLYMOUTH THEATRE

Opened Wednesday, March 10, 1965.°
Saint Subber presents:

THE ODD COUPLE

By Neil Simon; Directed by Mike Nichols;
Set Designed by Oliver Smith; Costumes, Ann
Roth; Lighting, Jean Rosenthal; Production
Assistant, James Turner.

CAST

Speed	Paul Dooley
Murray	Nathaniel Frey
Roy	Sidney Armus
Vinnie	John Fiedler
Oscar Madison	Walter Matthau
Felix Ungar	Art Carney
Gwendolyn Pigeon	Carole Shelley
Cecily Pigeon	Monica Evans

UNDERSTUDIES: Oscar, Louis Zorich; Felix,
Paul Dooley; Roy, Vinnie, Bernard Pollock;
Cecily, Gwendolyn, Carol Gustafson.

A Comedy in three acts and four scenes. The
action takes place at the present time on a hot
summer night in Oscar Madison's apartment on
Riverside Drive in New York.

General Manager: C. Edwin Knill
Company Manager: William Craver
Press: Harvey B. Sabinson, Lee Solters,
Harry Nigro, David Powers
Stage Managers: Harvey Medlinsky,
Bernard Pollock

° Still playing May 31, 1965. (93 performances)

Henry Grossman, Friedman-Abeles Photos

Art Carney, Walter Matthau. Above: Paul Dooley,
Art Carney, Sidney Armus

Top: John Fiedler, Sidney Armus, Paul Dooley,
Nathaniel Frey, Walter Matthau, Art Carney

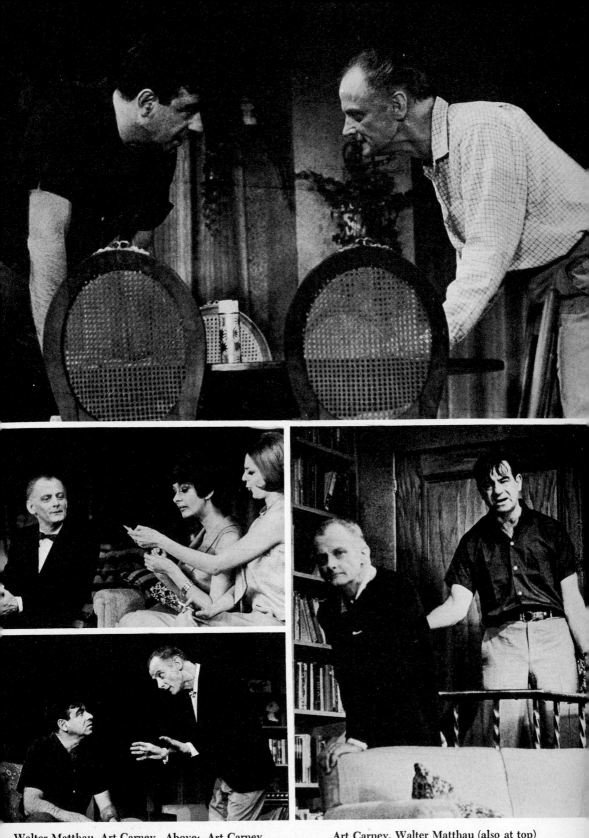

Walter Matthau, Art Carney. Above: Art Carney, Monica Evans, Carole Shelley

Art Carney, Walter Matthau (also at top)

Steve Mills, Ann Corio

HUDSON THEATRE

Opened Tuesday, March 16, 1965.°
Michael P. Iannucci presents:

THIS WAS BURLESQUE

Entire Production Supervised and Directed
by Ann Corio, and based on her recollections;
Musical Conductor, Nick Francis; Choreography,
Paul Morokoff; Costumes, Rex Huntington; Miss
Corio's gowns by Jacks of Hollywood, Martier-
Raymond, and Rex Huntington.

CAST

ANN CORIO

Steve Mills	Harry Conley
Dick Bernie	Paul West
Mac Dennison	Dexter Maitland
Kitty Lynne	Marilyn Marshall

THE BURLEY CUTIES: Nicole Jaffee, Linda
Donovan, Maria Bradley, Barbara Rhodes, Shar-
on Taylor, Jerry Beth Shotwell, Mary Alagia,
Geraldine Barron, Betsy Haug, Rita O'Connor

Program

ACT I: Overture, Prologue, "Hello Everybody," "Flirtation," "Bill Bailey," "Hee Haw,"
"Ecdysiast," "Hotel de France," "Dance L'Ori-
ent," "St. James Infirmary," "Exotic," "School-
room," "Les Poules," Mills and West, Marilyn
Marshall, Finale, Candy Butcher.

ACT II: "Powder My Back," "Sutton Place,"
"White Cargo," Tina Kay, "Evolution of
Dance," "Hall of Fame," "Crazy House," Ann
Corio, Finale.

A Musical Satire in two acts and twenty-
four scenes.

General Manager: Clifford Hayman
Press: Lenny Traube, Eddie Jaffee,
Marion Graham
Stage Manager: Paul Morokoff

° Still playing May 31, 1965.
Opened originally Off-Broadway March 6,
1962 at the Casino East Theatre

Avery Willard Photos

Top: Maria Bradley, Dexter Maitland, Nicole
Jaffe, Dick Bernie, Barbara Rhodes

Sergio Franchi, Elizabeth Allen
in
"DO I HEAR A WALTZ?"

FORTY-SIXTH STREET THEATRE

Opened Thursday, March 18, 1965.°
Richard Rodgers presents:

DO I HEAR A WALTZ?

Music by Richard Rodgers; Lyrics by Stephen Sondheim; Book by Arthur Laurents; Based on his play, "The Time Of The Cuckoo"; Directed by John Dexter; Choreographed by Herbert Ross; Scenery and Costumes, Beni Montresor; Lighting, Jules Fisher; Orchestrations, Ralph Burns; Musical Director, Frederick Dvonch; Dance Music Arranged by Richard de Benedictis; Choreographic Associate, Wakefield Poole; Production Supervisor, Jerome Whyte; Hair Stylists, Phil Leto, Leslie Blanchard, Ara Gallant.

CAST

Leona Samish	Elizabeth Allen
Mauro	Christopher Votos
Signora Fioria	Carol Bruce
Eddie Yaeger	Stuart Damon
Jennifer Yaeger	Julienne Marie
Mrs. McIlhenny	Madeleine Sherwood
Mr. McIlhenny	Jack Manning
Giovanna	Fleury D'Antonakis
Vito	James Dybas
Renato Di Rossi	Sergio Franchi
Man On Bridge	Michael Lamont
Mrs. Victoria Haslam	Helon Blount

SINGERS: Darrell Askey, Syndee Balaber, Bill Berrian, Helon Blount, Rudy Challenger, Pat Kelly, Liz Lamkin, Michael Lamont, James Luisi, Jack Murray, Carl Nicholas, Candida Pilla, Casper Roos, Bernice Saunders, Liza Stuart

DANCERS: Jere Admire, Bob Bishop, Wayne De Rammelaere, Steve Jacobs, Sandy Leeds, Joe Nelson, Janice Peta, Walter Stratton, Nancy Van Rijn, Mary Zahn

UNDERSTUDIES: Leona, Mitzie Welch; Renato, James Luisi; Mrs. McIlhenny, Helon Blount; McIlhenny, Casper Roos; Giovanna, Candida Pilla; Vito, Michael Lamont; Jennifer, Liza Stuart; Eddie, Bill Berrian; Mauro, Mathew Loscalzo.

MUSICAL NUMBERS: "Someone Woke Up," "This Week Americans," "What Do We Do? We Fly!," "Someone Like You," "Bargaining," "Here We Are Again," "Thinking," "No Understand," "Take The Moment," "Moon In My Window," "We're Gonna Be All Right," "Do I Hear A Waltz?," "Stay," "Perfectly Lovely Couple," "Thank You So Much."

A Musical in two acts and eleven scenes. The action takes place in Venice at the present time.

General Manager: Morris Jacobs
Company Manager: Maurice Winters
Press: Frank Goodman, Martin Shwartz, Paul Solomon
Stage Managers: Jean Barrere, Harry Young, Harry Clark

° Still playing May 31, 1965. (84 performances)

Carol Bruce, Christopher Votos, Elizabeth Allen
Above: Elizabeth Allen, Sergio Franchi

88

Larry Fried Photos

Carol Bruce, Julienne Marie, Stuart Damon, Elizabeth Allen, Sergio Franchi, Jack Manning, Madeleine Sherwood, Fleury D'Antonakis. Top Left: Elizabeth Allen, Stuart Damon, Julienne Marie. Center: Sergio Franchi, Elizabeth Allen. Right: Elizabeth Allen

89

Maurice Chevalier

ALVIN THEATRE

Opened Thursday, April 1, 1965.°
Alexander H. Cohen presents:

MAURICE CHEVALIER AT 77

Fred Stamer at the Piano; Lighting by Jean Rosenthal.

PROGRAM

"Thank Heaven For Little Girls," "Stations Of Life," "Place Pigalle," "Cole Porter Medley," "Valentine," "Some People," "Un P'tit Air," "I Remember It Well," "Un Clochard M'a Dit," "You Brought A New Kind Of Love To Me," "When You're Smiling," "Hello, Dolly," "You Must Have Been A Beautiful Baby," "La Lecon de Piano," "Paris Tu Rajeunis," "Louise," "A Las Vegas," "Hello, Beautiful," "Mimi La Blonde," "Accents Melodiques," "I'm Glad I'm Not Young Anymore," "Au Revoir," "Mimi," "Ah Donnez M'en de la Chanson," "George Gershwin Medley," "Spectateurs Spectaculaires," "La Tendresse," "Paris Je T'Aime," "La Miss."

General Manager: Roy A. Somlyo
Company Manager: G. Warren McClane
Press: Bill Doll, Midori Tsuji, Robert Ganshaw, Richard Spittel
Production Manager: Ruth Mitchell

° Closed May 1, 1965, after a limited engagement of 35 performances.

Henry Grossman Photo

Bea Richards
in
"THE AMEN CORNER"

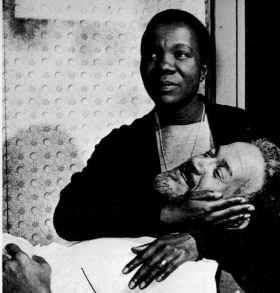

ETHEL BARRYMORE THEATRE

Opened Thursday, April 15, 1965.°
Mrs. Nat Cole presents:

THE AMEN CORNER

By James Baldwin; Directed by Frank Silvera; Designed by Vantile Whitfield; Musical Director, James Carmichael; Choral Director, Alfred Cain; A Frank Silvera-Kell-Cole "Theatre Of Being" Production; Leo Branton, Executive Producer.

CAST

Man	C. P. Walker
First Woman	Amentha Dymally
Second Woman	Yvette Hawkins
Sister Margaret	Bea Richards
Odessa	Gertrude Jeannette
Sister Moore	Isabell Sanford
Sister Boxer	Juanita Moore
Brother Boxer	Whitman Mayo
Sister Jackson	Josie Dotson
David	Art Evans
Luke	Frank Silvera
Sister Sally	Cynthia Belgrave
Sister Rice	Toby Russ
Sister Douglas	Helen Martin

UNDERSTUDIES: Margaret, Cynthia Belgrave; Odessa, Toby Russ; Sisters Moore and Boxer, Brunetta Barnett; Sister Jackson, Yvette Hawkins; Luke, Whitman Mayo; Boxer, C. P. Walker; Sally, Amentha Dymally.

A Drama in three acts. The action takes place at the present time in the church of which Margaret is pastor, and in the apartment above it which is her home in Harlem.

General and Company Manager: Sidney Bernstein
Press: Dorothy Ross, Richard O'Brien
Stage Managers: James Gelb, Ed Cambridge

° Still playing May 31, 1965. (52 performances)

Top: (Left) Bea Richards, (Right) Bea Richards, Frank Silvera. Left Center: Isabell Sanford, Juanita Moore

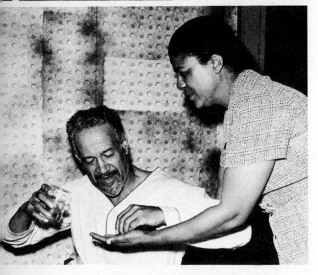

Frank Silvera, Gertrude Jeannette

Friedman-Abeles Photo.

Tommy Steele
in
"HALF A SIXPENCE"

Polly James, Tommy Steele

BROADHURST THEATRE

Opened Sunday, April 25, 1965.°
Allen-Hodgdon, Stevens Productions and Harold Fielding present:

HALF A SIXPENCE

Book by Beverley Cross; Based on H. G. Wells' "Kipps"; Music and Lyrics, David Heneker; Directed by Gene Saks; Dances and Musical Numbers staged by Onna White; Scenery and Costumes, Loudon Sainthill; Musical Direction, Stanley Lebowsky; Lighting, Jules Fisher; Costume Supervision, Jane Greenwood; Original Ballet Music by Robert Prince; Assistant Choreographer, Tom Panko; Vocal Arrangements, Buster Davis; Orchestrations, Jim Tyler; Dance Arrangements and Orchestrations, Robert Prince; Associate Producer, Jane C. Nusbaum; Production Assistant, Joyce Meyerson; Hair Dresser, Bari Braoun.

CAST

Arthur Kipps	Tommy Steele
Sid Pornick	Will Mackenzie
Buggins	Norman Allen
Pearce	Grover Dale
Carshot	William Larsen
Flo	Michele Hardy
Emma	Reby Howells
Kate	Louise Quick
Victoria	Sally Lee
Mr. Shalford	Mercer McLeod
Mrs. Walsingham	Ann Shoemaker
Mrs. Botting	Trescott Ripley
Ann Pornick	Polly James
Young Walsingham	John Cleese
Helen Walsingham	Carrie Nye
Chitterlow	James Grout
Laura	Eleonore Treiber
Girl Student	Rosanna Huffman
Boy Student	Sterling Clark
Photographer	Sean Allan
Photographer's Assistant	Robert Gorman
First Reporter	Reid Klein
Second Reporter	Fred Cline
Gwendolin	Ann Rachel

DANCERS: Diane Blair, Lynn Fields, Sally Ransone, Sterling Clark, Robert Karl, Alan Peterson, Bill Stanton, Ron Schwinn.

SINGERS: Sean Allan, Fred Cline, Robert Gorman, Glenn Kezer, Reid Klein, John Knapp, Max Norman, Carol Richards, Ann Rachel, Constance Moffit, Rosanna Huffman

UNDERSTUDIES: Kipps, Grover Dale; Sid, Ron Schwinn; Buggins, Robert Karl; Pearce, Sterling Clark; Flo, Reby Howells; Victoria, Sally Ransone; Emma, Kate, Diane Blair; Shalford, William Larsen; Carshot, John Knapp; Mrs. Botting, Constance Moffit; Mrs. Walsingham, Trescott Ripley; Ann, Reby Howells, Chitterlow, William Larsen; Laura, Sally Ransone; Helen, Eleonore Treiber; Walsingham, John Knapp; Girl Student, Carol Richards; Boy Student, Robert Gorman.

MUSICAL NUMBERS: "All In The Cause Of Economy," "Half A Sixpence," "Money To Burn," "A Proper Gentleman," "She's Too Far Above Me," "If The Rain's Got To Fall," "The Old Military Canal," "Long Ago," "Flash Bang Wallop," "I Know What I Am," "The Party's On The House," Finale.

General Manager: Victor Samrock
Company Manager: Ben Rosenberg
Press: Bill Doll, Bob Ullman, Robert Ganshaw
Stage Managers: Terence Little, Ernest Austin, William Larsen

° Still playing May 31, 1965. (41 performances)

Friedman-Abeles Photos

Top Left: Grover Dale, Norman Allen, Tommy Steele, Will Mackenzie. **Center:** Ann Shoemaker, John Cleese, Tommy Steele, Carrie Nye

Tommy Steele (C), also at top, and center
with James Grout

Tommy Steele, and above with Polly James

ROYALE THEATRE

Opened Monday, April 26, 1965.°
Theodore Mann and Joseph E. Levine in
association with Katzka-Berne Productions
Inc. present:

AND THINGS THAT GO
BUMP IN THE NIGHT

By Terrence McNally; Directed by Michael
Cacoyannis; Set, Ed Wittstein; Costumes, Noel
Taylor; Lighting, Jules Fisher; Projections, Fred
Eberstadt; Production Assistant, Peter Gold-
farb.

CAST

Fa	Clifton James
Grandfa	Ferdi Hoffman
Sigfrid	Robert Drivas
Lakme	Susan Anspach
Ruby	Eileen Heckart
Clarence	Marco St. John

UNDERSTUDIES: Ruby, Carolyn Coates; Fa,
Grandfa, Bert Conway; Lakme, Lois Unger;
Sigfrid, Clarence, Scott Hylands.

A Drama in three acts. The action takes
place in one night, in one room (the basement
of Ruby's home). The time is now, as it
could be.

General Manager: Paul Libin
Press: Merle Debuskey, Seymour Krawitz,
Larry Belling, Harold Rand
Stage Manager: Ben Janney

° Closed May 8, 1965. (16 performances)

Friedman-Abeles Photos

**Marco St. John, Robert Drivas. Above and left:
Eileen Heckart. Top: Ferdi Hoffman, Robert Dri**

HENRY MILLER'S THEATRE

Opened Thursday, April 29, 1965.°
Elaine Perry and Ben Edwards present:

A RACE OF HAIRY MEN!

By Evan Hunter; Directed by Elaine Perry; Setting and Lighting by Ben Edwards; Costumes, Jane Greenwood; Production Assistant, Arthur Gorton; Hair Styling, Dorman Alison.

CAST

Nick	Martin Huston
Ralph	Brandon de Wilde
Kathy	Joan McCall
Bernstein	April Shawhan

A Comedy in two acts. The action takes place at the present time in a coldwater flat behind First Avenue near Houston Street in Manhattan.

General Manager: George Banyai
Company Manager: Richard Seader
Press: Sol Jacobson, Lewis Harmon
Stage Managers: John Drew Devereaux,
Wayne Carson

° Closed May 1, 1965. (4 performances)

Werner J. Kuhn Photos

Joan McCall, April Shawhan, Martin Huston, Brandon deWilde (also at top) Center: Joan McCall, April Shawhan

Maureen Stapleton, George Grizzard, Piper Laurie
(above with Pat Hingle)

Maureen Stapleton, George Grizzard
(above with Piper Laurie)

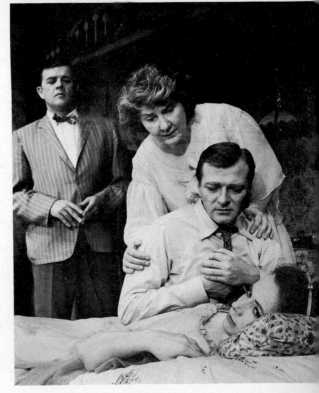

BROOKS ATKINSON THEATRE

Opened Tuesday, May 4, 1965.°
Claude Giroux and Orrin Christy, Jr., present:

THE GLASS MENAGERIE

By Tennessee Williams; Directed by George Keathley; Scenery Supervised and Designed respectively by James A. Taylor and Robert T. Williams; Costumes, Patton Campbell; Lighting, V. C. Fuqua; Music, Paul Bowles; Assistant to the Producers, Angelo Del Rossi.

CAST

The Mother ....Maureen Stapleton
Her Son ....George Grizzard
Her Daughter ....Piper Laurie
The Gentleman Caller.........................Pat Hingle

STANDBYS: Mother, Florence Stanley; Daughter, Maureen McNalley; Son, James Ray; Caller, William Traylor

A Drama in two parts. The action takes place in an alley in St. Louis, now and in the past.

General Manager: George Manyai
Company Manager: Richard Grayson
Press: John Springer Associates,
Walter Alford, Mary Ward
Stage Managers: Wade Miller, Donald
Bumgardner

° Still playing May 31, 1965. The original production opened March 31, 1945 at the Playhouse and ran for 563 performances with Laurette Taylor, Eddie Dowling, Julie Haydon, and Anthony Ross. (See THEATRE WORLD, Vol. 1) Revived at City Center November 21, 1956 for 15 performances with Helen Hayes, James Daly, Lois Smith, and Lonny Chapman. (See THEATRE WORLD, Vol. 13)

Werner J. Kuhn Photos

**Top: (left) Piper Laurie, Maureen Stapleton
(right) George Grizzard**

Pat Hingle, Maureen Stapleton, George Grizzard,
Piper Laurie

Maureen Stapleton
in
"THE GLASS MENAGERIE"

Werner J. Kuhn Phot

OHN GOLDEN THEATRE
Opened Monday, May 10, 1965.°
Alexander H. Cohen presents:

KEN MURRAY'S HOLLYWOOD

Produced in association with Arthur White-
w; Designed and Lighted by Ralph Alswang;
Music arranged and played by Armin Hoffman;
Production Assistant, Davina Crawford.

PROGRAM

PART I: Prelude by Armin Hoffman, Holly-
ood's Number One Movie Fan Ken Murray,
Hollywood Family Album, San Simeon.
PART II: Backstage with "Bill and Coo,"
Hollywood Thirty Years Later.

Movies made and narrated by Ken Murray
during his years in Hollywood.

General Manager: Roy A. Somlyo
Company Manager: G. Warren McClane
Press: Bill Doll & Co., Midori Tsuji,
Robert Ganshaw
Stage Manager: Frank Rowley

Still playing May 31, 1965.

Ken Murray

Liza Minnelli

ALVIN THEATRE

Opened Tuesday, May 11, 1965.°
Harold Prince presents:

FLORA, THE RED MENACE

Book by George Abbott and Robert Russell; Based on Novel "Love Is Just Around The Corner" by Lester Atwell; Directed by George Abbott; Music, John Kander; Lyrics, Fred Ebb; Dance and Musical Numbers Staged by Lee Theodore; Settings, William and Jean Eckart; Costumes, Donald Brooks; Lighting, Tharon Musser; Musical Direction, Harold Hastings; Orchestrations, Don Walker; Dance Arrangements, David Baker; Production Supervisor, Ruth Mitchell; Hair Styles, D. Rusty Bonaccorso.

CAST

F.D.R.'s Voice	Art Carney
Apple Seller	J. Vernon Oaks
Pencil Seller	Clark Morgan
Policeman	Daniel P. Hannafin
Broker	Henry LeClair
Fourth Man	John Taliaferro
Woman	Anne C. Russell
Fifth Man	Anthony Falco
Sixth Man	Les Freed
Seventh Man	Robert Fitch
School Principal	Abbie Todd
Flora	Liza Minnelli
Harry Toukarian	Bob Dishy
Lilly	Anne C. Russell
Artists	Less Freed, John Taliaferro, J. Vernon Oaks, Diane McAfee, Anthony Falco, Marie Santell
Comrade Galka	Louis Guss
Comrade Ada	Mary Louise Wilson
Comrade Jackson	Clark Morgan
Comrade Charlotte	Cathryn Damon
Elsa	Stephanie Hill
The Lady	Dortha Duckworth
Mr. Weiss	Joe E. Marks
Bronco Smallwood	James Cresson
Joe	Danny Carroll
Katie	Marie Santell
Mr. Rearson	Gordon Dilworth
Mr. Stanley	Robert Kaye
Lulu	Jamie Donnelly
Maggie	Elaine Canilla

DANCERS: Elaine Cancilla, Ciya Challis, Barbara Doherty, Judith Doren, Ellen Graff, Mary Ann Niles, Phyllis Wallach, Harry Bell, Robert Fitch, Marcello Gamboa, Charles Kalan, James McArdle, Neil J. Schwartz

SINGERS: Jamie Donnelly, Barbara Christopher, Diane McAfee, Abbie Todd, Anthony Falco, Les Freed, Daniel P. Hannafin, Henry LeClair, J. Vernon Oaks, John Taliaferro

UNDERSTUDIES: Flora, Jamie Donnelly; Harry, Danny Carroll; Ada, Anne C. Russell; Charlotte, Elaine Cancilla; Stanley, J. Vernon Oaks; Lady, Abbie Todd; Elsa, Marie Santell; Galka, Gordon Dilworth; Smallwood, Robert Fitch; Weiss, Henry LeClair; Joe, Charles Kalan.

MUSICAL NUMBERS: "Prologue," "Unafraid," "All I Need Is One Good Break," "Not Every Day Of The Week," "Sign Here," "The Flame," "Palomino Pal," "A Quiet Thing," "Hello, Waves," "Dear Love," "Express Yourself," "Knock, Knock," "The Tree Of Life Ballet," "Sing Happy," "You Are You," Finale.

A Musical Comedy in two acts and fourteen scenes. The action takes place between 1933 and 1935 in New York City.

General Manager: Carl Fisher
Press: Mary Bryant
Stage Managers: John Allen, Frank Gero, Bob Bernard

° Still playing May 31, 1965. (23 performances)

Friedman-Abeles Photos

Top Right: Liza Minnelli (L), Stephanie Hill (C)
Below: Mary Louise Wilson, James Cresson

Bob Dishy, Liza Minnelli. **Above:** Bob Dishy, Cathryn Damon

103

Anthony Newley, Joyce Jillson
Top: Cyril Ritchard, Anthony Newley

Anthony Newley, Murray Tannenbaum, Cyril Ritch:
Top: Cyril Ritchard, Anthony Newley

SAM S. SHUBERT THEATRE

Opened Sunday, May 16, 1965.°
David Merrick in association with Bernard Delfont presents:

THE ROAR OF THE GREASE-PAINT—THE SMELL OF THE CROWD

Book, Music, and Lyrics by Leslie Bricusse and Anthony Newley; Directed by Anthony Newley; Musical Numbers Staged by Gillian Lynne; Designed and Lighted by Sean Kenny; Costumes, Freddy Wittop; Musical Director; Herbert Grossman; Associate Producer, Samuel Liff; Orchestrations, Philip J. Lang; Vocal and Dance Music Arranged by Peter Howard; Staff Associate, Sylvia Schwartz; Assistant Choreographer, Buff Shurr.

CAST

Cocky	Anthony Newley
Sir	Cyril Ritchard
The Kid	Sally Smith
The Girl	Joyce Jillson
The Negro	Gilbert Price
The Bully	Murray Tannenbaum

URCHINS: Rawley Bates, Lori Browne, Lori Cesar, Jill Choder, Gloria Chu, Kay Cole. Marlene Dell, Boni Enten, Mitzi Feinn, Pamela Gruen, Linda Rae Hager, Cyndi Howard, Laura Michaels, Debbie Palmer, Heather Taylor

UNDERSTUDIES: Cocky, Edward Earle; Sir, Rod McLennan; Negro, Bob Broadway; Kid, Jill Choder; Girl, Kay Cole

MUSICAL NUMBERS: "The Beautiful Land," "A Wonderful Day Like Today," "It Isn't Enough," "Things To Remember," "Put It In The Book," "This Dream," "Where Would You Be Without Me?," "Look At That Face," "My First Love Song," "The Joker," "Who Can I Turn To When Nobody Needs Me," "A Funny Funeral," "That's What It Is To Be Young," "What A Man!," "Feeling Good," "Nothing Can Stop Me Now," "My Way," "Sweet Beginning."

A Musical Entertainment in two acts. The action takes place on a rocky place.

General Manager: Jack Schlissel
Company Manager: Vince McKnight
Press: Harvey B. Sabinson, Lee Solters, David Powers
Stage Managers: Gene Perlowin, Bob Broadway, Linda Rae Hager

° Still playing May 31, 1965.

Henry Grossman Photos

Cyril Ritchard, Sally Smith, Anthony Newley
Above: Gilbert Price

105

Cyril Ritchard, Anthony Newley
in
"THE ROAR OF THE GREASEPAINT—THE SMELL OF THE CROWD"

BILTMORE THEATRE

Opened Wednesday, October 23, 1963.°
Saint Subber presents:

BAREFOOT IN THE PARK

By Neil Simon; Directed by Mike Nichols; Setting Designed by Oliver Smith; Costumes, Donald Brooks; Lighting, Jean Rosenthal.

CAST

Corie Bratter	Elizabeth Ashley†1
Telephone Man	Herbert Edelman†2
Delivery Man	Joseph Keating
Paul Bratter	Robert Redford†3
Mrs. Banks	Mildred Natwick†4
Victor Velasco	Kurt Kasznar†5

UNDERSTUDIES: Paul, Gene Rupert†6; Corie, E. J. Peaker†7; Victor, Herbert Edelman†8; Mrs. Banks, Ruth Gregory†9.

A Comedy in three acts and four scenes. The action takes place at the present time in the Bratter apartment on East 48th Street in New York City.

General Manager: C. Edwin Knill
Company Manager: William Craver
Press: Harvey Sabinson, Harry Nigro, David Powers
Stage Managers: Harvey Medlinsky†10, Joseph Keating

° Still playing May 31, 1965.
For original production, see THEATRE WORLD, Vol. 20.
† Succeeded by: 1. Penny Fuller, 2. Stephen Pearlman, 3. Robert Reed, then Anthony Robert, 4. Ruth White during vacation, 5. Sandor Szabo during vacation, 6. Jed Allan, 7. Beverlee McKinsey, 8. Joseph Keating, 9. Ruth Matteson, 10. Robert Marriman

Friedman-Abeles Photos

Mildred Natwick, Penny Fuller, Kurt Kasznar, Anthony Roberts. Top: Penny Fuller, Kurt Kasznar, Anthony Roberts

David Burns, Carol Channing (above and top)

ST. JAMES THEATRE

Opened Thursday, January 16, 1964.°
David Merrick presents:

HELLO, DOLLY!

Book, Michael Stewart; Based on Play "The Matchmaker" by Thornton Wilder; Music and Lyrics, Jerry Herman; Directed and Choreographed by Gower Champion; Settings, Oliver Smith; Costumes, Freddy Wittop; Lighting, Jean Rosenthal; Musical Direction and Vocal Arrangements, Shepard Coleman; Orchestrations, Philip J. Lang; Dance and Incidental Music Arranged by Peter Howard; Assistant to the Director, Lucia Victor; Production Supervisor, Neil Hartley; A David Merrick and Champion-Five Inc. Production.

CAST

Mrs. Dolly Gallagher Levi	Carol Channing
Ernestina	Mary Jo Catlett
Ambrose Kemper	Igors Gavon†
Horse	Jan LaPrade, Bonnie Mathis
Horace Vandergelder	David Burns
Ermengarde	Alice Playten
Cornelius Hackl	Charles Nelson Reilly
Barnaby Tucker	Jerry Dodge
Irene Molloy	Eileen Brennan
Minnie Fay	Sondra Lee
Mrs. Rose	Amelia Haas
Rudolph	David Hartman
Judge	Gordon Connell
Court Clerk	Ken Ayers

TOWNSPEOPLE, WAITERS: Nicole Barth, Monica Carter, Carvel Carter, Amelia Haas, Jan LaPrade, Joan Buttons Leonard, Marilyne Mason, Bonnie Mathis, Else Olufsen, Yolanda Poropat, Bonnie Schon, Barbara Sharma, Mary Ann Snow, Jamie Thomas, Pat Trott, Ken Ayers, Alvin Beam, Joel Craig, Dick Crowley, Gene Gebauer, Joe Helms, Richard Hermany, Neil Jones, Charles Karel, Paul Kastl, Jim Maher, Joe McWherter, John Mineo, Randy Phillips, Lowell Purvis, Michael Quinn, Will Roy, Paul Solen, Ronnie Young.

UNDERSTUDIES: Dolly, Jo Anne Worley; Vandergelder, Gordon Connell; Cornelius, Charles Karel; Irene, Mary Ann Snow; Minnie, Barbara Sharma; Barnaby, John Mineo; Ambrose, Charles Karel; Judge, Michael Quinn; Ernestina, Amelia Haas; Mrs. Rose, Jamie Thomas.

MUSICAL NUMBERS: "I Put My Hand In," "It Takes A Woman," "Put On Your Sunday Clothes," "Ribbons Down My Back," "Motherhood," "Dancing," "Before The Parade Passes By," "Elegance," "The Waiters' Gallop," "Hello, Dolly!," "Come and Be My Butterfly," "It Only Takes A Moment," "So Long, Dearie," Finale.

A Musical Comedy in two acts and fifteen scenes. The action takes place in Yonkers and in Manhattan in the past.

General Manager: Jack Schlissel
Company Manager: Richard Highley
Press: Lee Solters, Harvey Sabinson, Lila King, David Powers
Stage Managers: Frank Dudley, Pat Tolson David Hartman

° Still playing May 31, 1965.
For original production, see THEATRE WORLD, Vol. 20.
† Succeeded by Charles Karel

Eileen Darby-Graphic House Photos

THE MUSIC BOX

Opened Tuesday, February 18, 1964.°
George W. George and Frank Granat and
Howard Erskine, Edward Specter Productions, Peter S. Katz present:

ANY WEDNESDAY

By Muriel Resnik; Directed by Henry Kaplan; Scenery, Robert Randolph; Costumes, Theoni V. Aldredge; Lighting, Tharon Musser; Hair Styles, Mr. Kenneth; Production Assistant, Nelle Nugent.

CAST

John Cleves	Don Porter†1
Ellen Gordon	Sandy Dennis†2
Cass Henderson	Gene Hackman†3
Dorothy Cleves	Rosemary Murphy

UNDERSTUDIES: Ellen, Cynthia Harris; Dorothy, Lucy Prentis; John, John Dutra.

A Comedy in two acts and four scenes. The action takes place at the present time in a garden apartment in the East Sixties in Manhattan.

General Manager: Edward H. Davis
Press: Lee Solters, Harvey Sabinson,
Lila King, David Powers
Stage Manager: Porter Van Zandt

° Still playing May 31, 1965. For original production, see THEATRE WORLD, Vol. 20.
† Succeeded by: 1. George Gaynes, 2. Barbara Cook, 3. Ryan MacDonald, then Kenneth Mars.

Friedman-Abeles Photos

**Barbara Cook, Rosemary Murphy, George Gaynes
(also above with Kenneth Mars)**

FIFTY-FOURTH STREET THEATRE
Opened Thursday, February 27, 1964.°
Joseph Cates presents:

WHAT MAKES SAMMY RUN?

Book, Budd and Stuart Schulberg; Based on Novel by Budd Schulberg; Music and Lyrics, Ervin Drake; Musical Staging, Matt Mattox; Director, Abe Burrows; Settings and Lighting, Herbert Senn and Helen Pond; Costumes, Noel Taylor; Vocal Arrangements and Musical Direction, Lehman Engel; Orchestrations, Don Walker; Dance Arrangements, Arnold Goland; Production Manager, Michael Thoma; Production Supervised by Robert Weiner; A Gates Brothers Production in Association with Beresford Productions Ltd; Production Associate, Rick Mandell, Production Assistant, Jan Gassman; Hair Styles, Frank Reynolds.

CAST

Al Manheim	Robert Alda
Sammy Glick	Steve Lawrence†1
O'Brien	Edward McNally†2
Osborn	John Dorrin†3
Bartender	Ralph Vucci†4
Julian Blumberg	George Coe†5
Rita Rio	Graciela Daniele†6
Tracy Clark	Richard France
Lucky Dugan	Edward McNally
Sheik Orsini	Barry Newman
Technical Advisor	Robert E. Maxwell, Jr.
Sidney Fineman	Arny Freeman
Kit Sargent	Sally Ann Howes†7
H. L. Harrington	Walter Klavun†8
Laurette Harrington	Bernice Massi†9
Seymour Glick	Mace Barrett
Swing Couple	Lynn Gremmler†10, Doug Spingler†11

SINGING ENSEMBLE: Lillian Bozinoff, Natalie Costa, Judith Hastings, Jamie Simmons, Darrell J. Askey, John Dorrin, Richard Terry, Ralph Vucci

DANCING ENSEMBLE: Diann Ainslee, Nancy Carnegie, Barbara Gine, Lavina Hamilton, Bella Shalom, Maralyn Thomas, Jean Blanchard, Marco Gomez, Buck Heller, Nat Horne, Jack Kresy, Natasha Grishin

UNDERSTUDIES: Sammy, Richard France; Kit, Judith Hastings; Al, Mace Barrett; Laurette, Natalie Costa; Tracy, Buck Heller†11; Rita, Diann Ainslee; O'Brien, Lucky, Fineman, Harrington, John Dorrin.

MUSICAL NUMBERS: "A New Pair Of Shoes," "You Help Me," "The Work Song," "A Tender Spot," "Lites-Camera-Platitude," "My Home Town," "Monsoon," "I See Something," "Maybe Some Other Time," "You Can Trust Me," "A Room Without Windows," "Kiss Me No Kisses," "I Feel Humble," "Something To Live For," "Paint A Rainbow," "You're No Good," "The Friendliest Thing," "Wedding Of The Year," "Some Days Everything Goes Wrong."

A Musical Comedy in two acts. The action takes place a generation ago in New York and Hollywood.

General Manager: Marshall Young
Press: Max Eisen, Jean Gibson Merrick, William Greenblatt
Stage Managers: George Thorn, Bob Maxwell, Tom Porter

° Still playing May 31, 1965
For original production, see THEATRE WORLD, Vol 20.
† Succeeded by: 1. Paul Anka during vacation, 2. Leslie Litomy, 3. Warren Galjour, 4. George Blackwell, 5. Stuart Unger, 6. Diann Ainslee, then Barbara Andrews, 7. Bernice Massi, 8. Ralph Stantley, 9. Paula Stewart, 10. Juanita Boyle, 11. Grant Lashley

Top Left: Steve Lawrence, Paula Stewart

Steve Lawrence

WINTER GARDEN
Opened Thursday, March 26, 1964°
Ray Stark presents:

FUNNY GIRL

Book and Story by Isobel Lennart; Music, Jule Styne; Lyrics, Bob Merrill; Directed by Garson Kanin; Musical Numbers Staged by Carol Haney; Scenery and Lighting, Robert Randolph; Costumes, Irene Sharaff; Musical Direction, Milton Rosenstock; Orchestrations, Ralph Burns; Vocal Arrangements, Buster Davis; Dance Orchestrations, Luther Henderson; Associate Producer, Al Goldin; Associate Director, Lawrence Kasha; Presented in association with Seven Arts Productions; Hairstyles, Ronald DeMann.

CAST

Fanny Brice	Barbra Streisand
John	Robert Howard
Emma	Royce Wallace
Mrs. Brice	Kay Medford
Mrs. Strakosh	Jean Stapleton†1
Mrs. Meeker	Lydia S. Fredericks
Mrs. O'Malley	Joyce O'Neil
Tom Keeney	Joseph Macaulay
Eddie Ryan	Danny Meehan†2
Heckie	Victor R. Helou†3
Workmen	Robert Howard, Robert Henson
Snub Taylor	Buzz Miller
Trombone Smitty	Blair Hammond
Five Finger Finney	Alan E. Weeks
Trumpet Soloist	Dick Perry
Bubbles	Shellie Farrell
Polly	Joan Lowe
Maude	Ellen Halpin
Nick Arnstein	Sydney Chaplin
Showgirls	Sharon Vaughn, Diana Lee Nielsen
Stage Director	Marc Jordan
Florenz Ziegfeld, Jr.	Roger DeKoven†4
Mimsey	Sharon Vaughn
Ziegfeld Tenor	John Lankston
Ziegfeld Lead Dancer	George Reeder
Adolph	John Lankston
Mrs. Nadler	Rose Randolf
Paul	Larry Fuller
Cathy	Joan Cory
Vera	Lainie Kazan
Jenny	Diane Coupe
Ben	Buzz Miller
Mr. Renaldi	Marc Jordan
Mike Halsey	Robert Howard

REPORTERS: Blair Hammond, Albert Zimmerman, Alan Peterson, Victor R. Helou, Stephanie Reynolds

SHOWGIRLS: Prudence Adams†5, Joan Cory, Diane Coupe, Lainie Kazan, Diana Lee Nielsen, Sharon Vaughn, Rosemarie Yellen

SINGERS: Lydia S. Fredericks, Mary Louise, Jeanne McLaren, Joyce O'Neil, Rose Randolf, Stephanie Reynolds, Victor R. Helou, Robert Henson, Robert Howard, Marc Jordan, John Lankston, Albert Zimmerman

DANCERS: Edie Cowan, Christine Dalsey, Shellie Farrell, Ellen Halpin, Rosemary Jelincic, Karen Kristen, Joan Lowe, Jose Ahumada, Bud Fleming, Larry Fuller, Blair Hammond, John Nola, Alan Peterson, Alan E. Weeks

UNDERSTUDIES: Fanny, Lainie Kazan; Arnstein, George Reeder.

MUSICAL NUMBERS: "If A Girl Isn't Pretty," "I'm The Greatest Star," "Eddie's Fifth Encore," "Cornet Man," "Who Taught Her Everything," "His Love Makes Me Beautiful," "I Want To Be Seen With You Tonight," "Henry Street," "People," "You Are Woman," "Don't Rain On My Parade," "Sadie, Sadie," "Find Yourself A Man," "Rat-Tat-Tat-Tat," "Who Are You Now?," "The Music That Makes Me Dance."

A Musical in two acts and twenty-four scenes.

General Manager: Al Goldin
Company Manager: John Larson
Press. Frank Goodman, Martin Shwartz, Paul Solomon
Stage Managers: Richard Evans, Tom Stone, Joseph Dooley, Robert Howard

° Still playing May 31, 1965. (476 performances)
For original production, see THEATRE WORLD, Vol. 20.
† Succeeded by: 1. Paula Laurence during vacation, then Fritzi Burr, 2. Lee Allen, 3. Richard Ianni, 4. Alan Manson, 5. Barbara London

Henry Grossman Photos

Sydney Chaplin, Barbra Streisand
Above Center and Top: Barbra Streisand

ROYALE THEATRE
Opened Monday, May 25, 1964.°
(Moved Sept. 7, 1964 to Winthrop Ames Theatre, and on March 23, 1965 to Helen Hayes Theatre)
Edgar Lansbury presents:

THE SUBJECT WAS ROSES

By Frank D. Gilroy; Directed by Ulu Grosbard; Scenery, Edgar Lansbury; Lighting, Jules Fisher; Costumes, Donald Foote; Production Assistants, Linda Gaydos, Al Isaac.

CAST

John Cleary .... Jack Albertson
Nettie Cleary .... Irene Dailey
Timmy Cleary .... Martin Sheen
UNDERSTUDIES: John, Joseph Sullivan; Nettie, Peg Murray; Timmy, Matt Clark

A Drama in two acts and seven scenes. The action takes place in May 1946 in a middle class apartment.

General Manager: Joseph Beruh
Press: Max Eisen, Jeannie Gibson Merrick, Dan Rosen, Paul Solomon
Stage Managers: Paul Leaf, Matt Clark

° Still playing May 31, 1965. Winner of Pulitzer Prize, Antoinette Perry, and Drama Critics Circle Awards. For original production, see THEATRE WORLD, Vol. 20.

Left: Irene Dailey, Jack Albertson, Martin Sheen

Martin Sheen, Jack Albertson

Irene Dailey, Martin Sheen

Martin Sheen

Martin Sheen, Irene Dailey, Jack Albertson

PLAYS FROM OTHER SEASONS THAT CLOSED
DURING THIS SEASON

Play	Opened	Closed	Performances
Mary, Mary	March 8, 1961	Dec. 12, 1964	1572
How To Succeed In Business Without Really Trying	Oct. 14, 1961	March 6, 1965	1415
Never Too Late	Nov. 27, 1962	Apr. 24, 1965	1007
A Funny Thing Happened On The Way To The Forum	May 8, 1962	Aug. 29, 1964	965
Oliver!	Jan. 6, 1963	Nov. 14, 1964	774
High Spirits	Apr. 7, 1964	Feb. 27, 1965	375
Here's Love	Oct. 3, 1963	July 25, 1964	338
110 In The Shade	Oct. 24, 1963	Aug. 8, 1964	330
The Deputy	Feb. 26, 1964	Nov. 28, 1964	316
Dylan	Jan. 18, 1964	Sept. 12, 1964	273
Nobody Loves An Albatross	Dec. 19, 1963	June 20, 1964	212
Blues For Mr. Charlie	Apr. 23, 1964	Aug. 29, 1964	148
Baby Want A Kiss	Apr. 19, 1964	Aug. 22, 1964	145
Hamlet	Apr. 9, 1964	Aug. 8, 1964	137
Marco Millions (in repertory)	Feb. 20, 1964	June 18, 1964	49
But For Whom Charlie (in repertory)	March 12, 1964	July 2, 1964	49
My Fair Lady (City Center)	May 20, 1964	June 28, 1964	47
Royal Shakespeare Company	May 18, 1964	June 6, 1964	24
The White House	May 19, 1964	June 6, 1964	23
Roar Like A Dove	May 21, 1964	June 6, 1964	20

SPECIAL ATTRACTION

Jana Andrsova (C). Above: Frantisek Sifta,
Vlasta Ployharova

CARNEGIE HALL

Opened Monday, August 3, 1964.°
Richard Fleischer in association with Harry Bernsen, Jr., presents:

LATERNA MAGIKA

Director, Ing. Miroslav Vrabec; Deputy Director, Jirina Martinkova; Artistic Director, Oldrich Stodola; Technical Manager, Jan Pokorny; Coordinator, Jeanne Susskind.

"Tales Of Hoffmann"

By Jacques Offenbach; Direction, Orchestration, and Music Conducted by Vaclav Kaslik; Screenplay, Vaclav Kaslik; Boris Michajlov; Josef Svoboda; Choreographer, Jiri Nemecek; Costumes, Jan Skalicky; Set Decorator, Josef Svoboda; Music played by Film Symphonic Orchestra of Prague.

CAST

Hoffmann .... Zdenek Jankovsky, Vladimir Krejcik, Frantisek Sifta, Zdenek Svehla

Role	Sung By	Played By
FILM:		
Spalanzani		
	Antonin Votava	Antonin Votava
Coppelius		
	Jaroslav Horacek	Rudolf Pellar
Cochenille		
	Milan Karpisek	Milan Karpisek
Crespel		
	Karel Kalas	Karel Kalas
Dr. Mirakel		
	Jaroslav Horacek	Rudolph Pellar
Franz		
	Milan Karpisek	Milan Karpisek
Dapertutto		
	Jaroslav Horacek	Rudolph Pellar
Pitichinaccio		
	Milan Karpisek	Milan Karpisek
Courtesan		
	Vera Krilova	Jirina Knizkova

STAGE
Olympia
    Helena
        Tattermuschova ..... Jana Andrsova,
                Helena Pejskova,
                Tatana Hernychova
Antonia
    Anna Penaskova .... Anna Penaskova
    Vlasta Ployharova ..... Vlasta Ployharova
Giulietta
    Libuse Domaninska ... Jana Braunschlagerova

"Variations"

Theme, Screenplay, Text, and Direction by Milos Forman, Jaromil Jires, Boris Michajlov, Alfred Radok, Emil Radok, Jan Rohac, Vladimir Svitacek, K. M. Wallo; Choreographers, Jiri Nemecek, Zora Semberova, Martin Tapak; Music, Zdenek Liska, Jiri Slitr, Jaromir Vomacka; Photography, Jaroslav Kucera, Jan Novak, Vladimir Novotny, Jiri Safar.

CAST

Mistress of Ceremonies .... Gwyda Donhowe
Pianist .... Arthur Kleiner
Violinist .... Ivan Straus
Male Dancer .... Pavel Vesely
Ballet and Ensemble: Members of the National Theater and Laterna Magika

General Manager: Norman Kean
Press: Bill Doll & Co, Robert Ganshaw
Stage Manager; Iris Merlis

° Closed Sunday, August 16, 1964 (27 performances)

THE DANCE

"The Sleeping Beauty"

Vladilen Semenov (C) in "Cinderella"

Vladilen Semenov, Irina Kolpakova in "Raymonda"

ina Kolpakova, Vladilen
enov in "Sleeping Beauty"

Yuri Soloviev, Alla Sizova
in "Le Corsaire"

METROPOLITAN OPERA HOUSE

Opened Tuesday, September 8, 1964.°
S. Hurok presents:

THE LENINGRAD
KIROV BALLET

Director General Pyotr Rachinsky; Artistic
Director, Konstantin Sergeyev; Conductor, Victor Fedotov; Principal Designer, Ivan Sevastian-
ov.

REPERTORY

The Sleeping Beauty, Cinderella, Swan Lake,
Raymonda, Gala Programme.
Company Manager: Edward Perper
Press: Martin Feinstein, Michael Sweeley,
Edward Parkinson, Lillian Libman
Stage Manager: Giovanni Esposito

Kaleria Fedicheva and Right: Inna Zubkovskaya,
Vladilen Semenov in "Swan Lake"

° Closed Saturday, September 26, 1964, after
a limited engagement of 20 performances. 115

METROPOLITAN OPERA HOUSE

Opened Wednesday, April 21, 1965.°
The Royal Opera House, Covent Garden
Ltd., in association with The Arts Council
of Great Britain presents under the management of S. Hurok:

THE ROYAL BALLET

Director, Frederick Ashton; Assistant Di-
rectors, John Field, John Hart, Michael Somes;
Principal Conductor, John Lanchbery; Resident
Choreographer, Kenneth MacMillan; Conductor,
Emanuel Young; Guest Conductor, Joseph Le-
vine.

PRINCIPALS: Margot Fonteyn, Rudolf Nurey-
ev, Svetlana Beriosova, David Blair, Desmond
Doyle, Leslie Edwards, Christopher Gable, Al-
exander Grant, Stanley Holden, Ronald Hynd,
Gerd Larsen, Donald MacLeary, Annette Page,
Merle Park, Georgina Parkinson, Keith Rosson,
Lynn Seymour, Brian Shaw, Antoinette Sibley,
Graham Usher, Franklin White.

REPERTORY: Romeo and Juliet, Swan Lake,
Les Sylphides, Les Biches, Daphnis and Chloe,
The Dream, A Wedding Bouquet, Giselle,
Marguerite and Armand, The Invitation, Laur-
entia, La Bayadere, Les Patineurs.

Company Managers: Les Appleby, Oscar Berlin
Press: Martin Feinstein, Michael Sweeley,
Edward Parkinson
Stage Managers: Leon Arnold,
Arthur Callaghan

° Closed Sunday, May 16, 1965 after a limited
engagement of 31 performances, and em-
barked on a ten weeks tour of The United
States and Canada.

Margot Fonteyn, Rudolf Nureyev in (L) "Swan Lake"
(R) "Romeo and Juliet"

Svetlana Beriosova, Donald Macleary
in "Swan Lake"

Annette Page, Alexander Grant, Merle Park
in "A Wedding Bouquet"

Margot Fonteyn in "Marguerite and Armand"

Svetlana Beriosova in "Les Biches"

METROPOLITAN OPERA HOUSE

Opened Tuesday, May 18, 1965.°

S. Hurok presents:

MOISEYEV DANCE COMPANY

Artistic Director, Igor Moiseyev; Musical Director and Conductor, Nikolai Nekrassov; Choreography by Igor Moiseyev; Guest Conductor, Arthur Lief; Coordinator, Simon Semenoff; Concert Master, Samuel Marder.

REPERTORY

Exercises On A Russian Theme, Exercises On A Ukrainian Theme, Polka, Pontozoo, Lyavonikha, Bulgarian Dances, Trepak, Georgia, Sunday, Partisans, Sanchakou, Zhok, Old City Quadrille, Gypsies, Two Boys In A Fight, Gopak, Dance of The Tartars From Kazan, Yurochka, Suite of Old Russian Dances, Polyanka, A Day On Board Ship, The Three Shepherds, Khorumi

Company Managers: Edward A. Perper,
Maxim Gershunoff
Press: Martin Feinstein, Michael Sweeley,
Lillian Libman
Stage Manager: Jay Kingwill

° Closed Saturday, May 29, 1965 after 13 performances. Re-opened Tuesday, June 15, 1965 at Madison Square Garden for 14 performances, closing Sunday, June 27, 1965.

Stanislas Kulikov, Irina Konyeva, Anatoli Fyodorov, Galina Ivanova in "Sunday". Above: "Partisans" Top: "Polka"

117

Patricia Neway, Barry Robins. Above: Lee Venora,
118 Frank Porretta. Top: Risë Stevens, Darren McGavin

NEW YORK STATE THEATER

Opened Monday, July 6, 1964.°
Music Theater of Lincoln Center presents:

THE KING AND I

Music, Richard Rodgers; Lyrics and Book, Oscar Hammerstein 2nd; Based on Novel "Anna and The King of Siam" by Margaret Landon; Directed by Edward Greenberg; Costumes, Irene Sharaff; Settings, Paul C. McGuire; Original Choreography by Jerome Robbins Reproduced by Yuriko; Musical Director, Franz Allers; Orchestrations, Robert Russell Bennett; Hair Styles, Ronald DeMann; Costume Coordinator, Stephen Blumberg; Technical Director, Robert P. Brannigan.

CAST

Captain Orton	Fred Miller
Louis Leonowens	James Harvey
Anna Leonowens	Risë Stevens
The Interpreter	Rudy Vejar
The Kralahome	Michael Kermoyan
The King	Darren McGavin
Phra Alack	Stuart Mann
The King	Darren McGavin
Phra Alack	Stuart Mann
Ann Leonowens	Risë Stevens
Tuptim	Lee Venora
Lady Thiang	Patricia Neway
Prince Chulalongkorn	Barry Robins
Princess Ying Yaowalak	Gina Kaye
Lun Tha	Frank Porretta
Sir Edward Ramsay	Eric Brotherson

PRINCESSES AND PRINCES: Kathleen Din, Gina Kaye, Lorrie Kochiyama, Debbie Kogan, May Yee Mark, Annette Misa, Robert Ader, David Aguilar, Delfino DeArco, Lawrence Kikuchi, Eddie Kochiyama

THE ROYAL DANCERS: Takako Asakawa, Hadassah Badock, Joan Bates, Lisa Berg, Noemi Chiesa, Paula Chin, Miriam Cole, Bettina Dearborne, Carol Drisin, Jeanne Nichtern, Carol Fried, Phyllis Gutelius, Linda Hodes, Susan Kikuchi, Connie Sanchez, Katherine Wilson

WIVES: Anita Alpert, Theodora Brandon, Dixie Carter, Sharon Dierking, Mona Elson, Carole O'Hara, Hanna Owen, Jean Palmerton

AMAZONS: Leisha Caryle, Beverly Morrison, Joanna Owens, Jeanne Rodriguez

PRIESTS, SLAVES: Walter Adams, Henry Baker, Lazar Dano, Victor Duntiere, William Duvall, Julius Fields, Fred Hamilton, Stuart Mann, Jim McMillan, Ken Richards, Anthony Saverino

UNDERSTUDIES: Anna, Annamary Dickey; King, Michael Kermoyan; Thiang, Anita Alpert; Tuptim, Dixie Carter; Kralahome, Rudy Vejar; Ramsay, Fred Miller; Lun Tha, Ken Richards; Louis, Robert Ader; Prince, James Harvey; Eliza, Bettina Dearborne; Uncle Thomas, Jeanne Nichtern; King Simon, Noemi Chiesa; Angel, Phyllis Gutelius; Topsy, Eva, Carol Fried.

MUSICAL NUMBERS: "I Whistle A Happy Tune," "My Lord and Master," "Hello, Young Lovers," "March of The Siamese Children," "A Puzzlement," "The Royal Bangkok Academy," "Getting To Know You," "We Kiss In A Shadow," "Shall I Tell You What I Think Of You?," "Something Wonderful," "Western People Funny," "I Have Dreamed," "The Small House of Uncle Thomas," "Shall We Dance?"

A Musical in two acts. The action passes in and around the King's Palace in Bangkok, Siam, in the early 1860's.

General Manager: Edward Choate
Press: Richard Maney, Martin Shwartz
Stage Managers: Peter Bronte, Michael Paul Price, Louis Kosman

° Closed August 8, 1964, after a limited engagement of 40 performances.
For original production, see THEATRE WORLD, Vol. 7. Opened March 29, 1951, at the St. James Theatre with Gertrude Lawrence and Yul Brynner and ran for 1246 performances. Last revival at City Center June 13, 1963 with Eileen Brennan and Manolo Fabregas. See THEATRE WORLD, Vol. 20.

Friedman-Abeles Photos

NEW YORK STATE THEATER

Opened Monday, August 17, 1964.°
The Music Theater of Lincoln Center,
Richard Rodgers President and Producing
Director, presents:

THE MERRY WIDOW

By Franz Lehar; Director, Edward Greenberg; Choreography, Zachary Solov; Settings,
Rouben Ter-Arutunian; Costumes, Rene Hubert; Based on version by Edwin Lester; Original Book, Victor Leon, Leo Stein; Book Re-
vision, Milton Lazarus; Musical Director, Franz
Allers; New Lyrics, Forman Brown; Hair
Styles, Ronald De Mann, Jack Mei Ling; Assistant Conductor, Dobbs Franks; Costume Coordinator, Stephen Blumberg.

CAST

Major Domo	George Quick
Nish	Sig Arno
Baron Popoff	Mischa Auer
Natalie, Baroness Popoff	Joan Weldon
Chevalier St. Brioche	Robert Goss
Marquis Cascada	Rudy Vejar
General Novikovich	Joseph Leon
Counselor Khadja	Wood Romoff
Mme. Sylvanie Khadja	Luce Ennis
Mme. Novikovich	Marian Haraldson
Capt. Pierre Jolidon	Frank Porretta
Sonia	Patrice Munsel
Prince Danilo	Bob Wright
Lolo	Carol Flemming
Cloclo	Jean Lee Schoch
Dodo	Annette Bachich
Margot	Kathy Wilson
Joujou	Skiles Ricketts
Froufrou	Birgitta Kiviniemi
Michel	William Duvall
Zozo	Dixie Carter
Principal Dancers	Birgitta Kiviniemi, Dmitry Cheremeteff

SINGING ENSEMBLE: Theodora Brandon,
Dixie Carter, Kenna Christi, Sharon Dierking,
Elaine Johnson, Beverly Morrison, Hanna
Owen, Jean Palmerton, Dixie Stewart, Peggy
Wathen, Bruce Carrithers, Ken Corday, Gene
Davis, William Duvall, Harrison Fisher, Nor-
man Grogan, Vincent Henry, Stuart Mann,
Philip Rash, Ken Richards, Carl Sloat, Stafford
Wing

DANCING ENSEMBLE: Annette Bachich,
Bonnie Gene Card, Carol Flemming, Debra
Lyman, Skiles Ricketts, Jean Lee Schoch, Kathy
Wilson, Ian Bruce, Richard Cousins, Jeremy
Knight-Ives, Richard Maxon Malcolm McCor-
mick, Bob Remick, George Tregre

UNDERSTUDIES: Sonia, Joan Weldon; Dan-
ilo, Robert Gross; Popoff, Joseph Leon; Jolidon,
Ken Corday; Natalie, Luce Ennis; Nish, Wood
Romoff; Novikovich, Bruce Carrithers; Khadja,
Stafford Wing; St. Brioche, Stewart Mann;
Cascada, Philip Rash; Mme. Novikovich, Hanna
Owen; Mme. Khadja, Peggy Wathen; Major
Domo, Norman Grogan; Zozo, Beverly Morri-
son; Michel, Harrison Fisher.

MUSICAL NUMBERS: "When In France," "A
Respectable Wife," "Who Knows The Way To
My Heart?," "Maxim's," "Riding On A Carous-
el," "Marsovian Dance," "Vilia," "Women,"
"Czardas and Waltz," "Romance," "Girl At
Maxim's," "I Love You So (The Merry Widow
Waltz)," Finale.

An Operetta in three acts and four scenes.
The action takes place in Paris about 1905.

General Manager: Edward Choate
Company Manager: Paul Groll
Press: Richard Maney
Stage Managers: Peter Bronte, Michael Paul
Price, George Quick

° Closed Saturday, September 19, 1964. (40
performances), and toured until January 16,
1965 when it closed at the Chicago Opera
House.

Friedman-Abeles Photos

Patrice Munsel (also above center), Bob Wright
Top: Joan Weldon, Mischa Auer, Patrice Munsel,
Frank Porretta

119

Patricia Wilde, Jacques D'Amboise
in "Pas De Dix"

"The Nutcracker"

Allegra Kent, Francisco Moncion
in "The Cage"

Jacques D'Amboise
in "Irish Fantasy"

Mimi Paul, Arthur Mitchell
in "Bugaku"

Patricia Wilde, Nicholas Magallanes
in "Square Dance"

Edward Villella, Patricia Neary
in "Prodigal Son"

Arthur Mitchell
as Puck

Jacques D'Amboise,
Melissa Hayden

NEW YORK STATE THEATRE

Opened Tuesday, September 22, 1964.°
The City Center of Music and Drama,
Inc. presents:

NEW YORK CITY BALLET

General Director, Lincoln Kirstein; Ballet
Masters, George Balanchine, John Taras; Associate Ballet Mistress, Una Kai; Assistant Ballet
Mistress, Francia Russell; Costumes by Karin-
ska; New York City Ballet Orchestra Conduct-
ors, Robert Irving and Hugo Fiorato.

COMPANY

PRINCIPAL DANCERS: Jacques D'Amboise,
Melissa Hayden, Jillana, Allegra Kent, Conrad
Ludlow, Nicholas Magallanes, Patricia Mc-
Bride, Arthur Mitchell, Francisco Moncion, An-
dre Prokovsky, Maria Tallchief, Violette Verdy,
Edward Villella, Patricia Wilde
FEATURED DANCERS: Anthony Blum, Su-
zanne Farrell, Gloria Govrin, Deni Lamont,
Sara Leland, Patricia Neary, Mimi Paul, Rich-
ard Rapp, Robert Rodham, Suki Schorer, Earle
Sieveling, Victoria Simon, Kent Stowell, Carol
Sumner, Roland Vazquez, William Weslow
CORPS DE BALLET: Karin von Aroldingen,
Karen Batizi, Diane Bradshaw, Marjorie Bres-
ler, Elaine Comsudi, Gail Crisa, James DeBolt,
Rosemary Dunleavy, Suzanne Erlon, Truman
Finne, Penelope Gates, Ericca Goodman, Janet
Greschler, Susan Hendl, Gail Kachadurian,
Lise Kenniff, Ruth Ann King, Robert Maiorano,
Kay Mazzo, Teena McConnell, Karen Morell,
Marnee Morris, Larry O'Brien, Shaun O'Brien,
Frank Ohman, Delia Peters, Roger Peterson,
Roger Pietrucha, Susan Pillersdorf, John Prinz,
David Richardson, Leslie Ruchala, Ellen
Shire, Bettijane Sills, Michael Steele, Lynne
Stetson, Virginia Stuart, Margaret Wood.

REPERTOIRE

Raymonda Variations, Four Temperaments, Pas
De Deux, Stars and Stripes, Scotch Symphony,
Episodes, Tarantella, Symphony In C, Swan
Lake, Firebird, Afternoon Of A Faun, Western
Symphony, Bugaku, Movements For Piano and
Orchestra, Gounod Symphony, Interplay, Seren-
ade, Prodigal Son, Allegro Brillante, Fanfare,
Agon, Piege de Lumiere, Concerto Barocco,
Meditation, La Valse, Ebony Concerto, Donize-
etti Variations, Irish Fantasy, Clarinade, The
Cage, Dim Lustre, Ballet Imperial, Ivesiana,
The Nutcracker, Delibes, La Sonnambula, Di-
vertimento No. 15, Con Amore, Monumentum,
Apollo, Greenwood, Harlequinade, Liebeslieder
Walzer, Shadow'd Ground, Don Quixote, A
Midsummer Night's Dream.

General Manager: Betty Cage
Company Manager: Zelda Dorfman
Press: Virginia Donaldson, Doris Luhrs
Stage Managers: Ronald Bates, Kevin Tyler,
Mel Schierman

° Closed Sunday, November 8, 1964. Returned
Friday, December 11, 1964 through February 21, 1965. Final season opened Tuesday,
April 20, 1964, and closed Sunday, June 13,
1965.

Fred Fehl Photos

William Weslow, Patricia Neary, Richard Rapp
in "Scotch Symphony"
Above: "Agon"

121

NEW YORK STATE THEATER

Opened Tuesday, November 24, 1964.°
Gert von Gontard and Felix G. Gerstman
in cooperation with Deutsches Theater,
Inc., N.Y. and under the patronage of the
Federal Republic of Germany and the City
of West Berlin present the SCHILLER
THEATER of West Berlin, Boleslaw Bar-
log Managing Director, in:

DON CARLOS

By Friedrich von Schiller; Directed by Gus-
tav Rudolf Sellner; Sets and Costumes, Franz
Mertz; Lighting, Willi Kohler; Technical Di-
rector, Leo Skodik; Masks, Hermann Rosenthal;
Sound, Ewald Spurfeld; Narrators, Sally Cooke,
Iris Merlis.

CAST

Domingo	Friedrich W. Bauschulte
Don Carlos	Rolf Henniger
Marquis of Posa	Erich Schellow
Elisabeth, Queen of Spain	Eva Katharina Schultz
Princess Eboli	Gisela Stein
Marquise of Mondekar	Uta Hallant
Countess of Fuentes	Claudia Brodzinska
Duchess of Olivarez	Charlotte Joeres
Philip II of Spain	Ernst Deutsch
Duke of Alba	Eduard Wandrey
Count of Lerma	Paul Wagner
Queen's Page Boy	Klaus Herm
Duke of Medina Sidonia	Franz Nicklisch
Alexander Farnese	Joachim Ansorge
Duke of Feria	Walter Tarrach
Clara Eugenia	Robin Sherwood
First Officer	Edgar Ott
Second Officer	Rudolf Brandt
Don Luis Mercado	Rudolf Fernau
Grand Inquisitor	Wolfgang Kuehne

A Drama presented in two acts and eighteen
scenes. The action takes place in sixteenth
century Spain.

Company Manager: Bill Levin
Press: Max Eisen, Jennie Gibson Merrick
Stage Managers: Horst Guldemeister,
Pat Chandler

° Closed Sunday, November 29, 1964 after a
limited engagement of 8 performances.

Ernst Deutsch, Eva-Katharina Schultz
Top: Erich Schellow, Ernst Deutsch

Opened Tuesday, December 1, 1964.°
Gert von Gontard and Felix G. Gerstman in cooperation with Deutsches Theater, Inc., N.Y. under the patronage of the Federal Republic of Germany and the City of West Berlin present the SCHILLER THEATER of West Berlin, Managing Director, Boleslaw Baflog, in:

THE CAPTAIN OF KOEPENICK

By Carl Zuckmayer; Directed by Boleslaw Barlog; Sets and Costumes, Eva Schwarz; Music Arranged by Kurt Heuser; Technical Director, Leo Skodik; Lighting, Willi Kohler; Masks, Herman Rosenthal; Sound, Ewald Spurfeld; Narrators, Sally Cooke, Iris Merlis.

CAST

Captain von Schlettow	Erich Schellow
Wabschke	Klaus Miedel
Adolf Wormser	Herbert Gruenbaum
Willi	Ruediger Tuchel
Wilhelm Voigt	Carl Raddatz
Police Sergeant	Reinhold Bernt
Policeman	Otto Matthies
Paul Kallenberg	Klaus Herm
First Woman	Ilse Page
Second Woman	Claudia Brodzinska
Waiter	Herbert Anders
Dr. Jellinek	Claus Holm
Ploeroesenmieze	Maria Becker
A Royal Grenadier	Edgar Ott
A Civilian	Kurt Weitkamp
Policeman	Max Grothusen
Knell	Walter Tarrach
Office Boy	Werner Schott
Hirschberg	Helge Thoma
First Unemployed	Toni Stohr
Second Unemployed	Rudolf Brandt
Third Unemployed	Horst Heidemann
Deltzeit	Holger Kepich
Hostel Parent	Franz Nicklisch
A Voice	Horst Gueldemeister
Obermueller	Friedrich W. Bauschulte
Prison Chaplain	Rudolf Fernau
Prison Guard	Reinhold Bernt
Warden	Wolfgang Kuehne
First Prisoner	Claus Holm
Second Prisoner	Horst Bollman
Mrs. Hoprecht	Charlotte Joeres
Friedrich Hoprecht	Eduard Wandrey
Mrs. Obermueller	Eva-Katharina Schultz
Fanny	Ilse Page
Sick Girl	Ilse Page
Street Singer	Rudolf Brandt
Girl Street Singer	Kaethe Fuellner
Krakauer	Erhard Siedel
Sally	Horst Gueldemeister
First Railroad Man	Otto Matthies
Second Railroad Man	Wolfgang Kuehne
A Porter	Toni Stohr
Kutzmann	Joachim Ansorge
Kilian	Henning Schlueter
Wendrowitz	Max Grothusen
Rosencrantz	Herbert Gruenbaum
Steckler	Reinhold Bernt
Army Sergeant	Rudolf Brandt
Comenius	Werner Schott
First Grenadier	Horst Bollmann
Second Grenadier	Edgar Ott
Commissioner of Detectives	Walter Tarrach
Stutz	Holger Kepich
Inspector of Detectives	Claus Holm
Police Sergeant	Franz Nicklisch
Passport Official	Rudolf Fernau
Chief of Detectives	Paul Wagner
Patrolman	Toni Stohr
Hurdy-Gurdy Man	Harry Schopp
Singer	Kaethe Fuellner

A German fairy tale presented in two acts and seventeen scenes. The action takes place in Berlin and its environs before World War I. The play is founded on historical fact, but action and characters have been freely handled.

Company Manager: Bill Levin
Press: Max Eisen, Jennie Gibson Merrick
Stage Managers: Horst Guldemeister, Pat Chandler

° Closed Sunday, December 6, 1964 after a limited engagement of 8 performances.

Carl Raddatz, Maria Becker. Top: Carl Raddatz, Eva-Katharina Schultz

NEW YORK STATE THEATER

Opened Tuesday, March 17, 1965.°
Ballet Theatre Foundation, Inc. presents:

AMERICAN BALLET THEATRE

Directors, Lucia Chase, Oliver Smith; Assistant Director, Nora Kaye; General Administrator, Charles Payne; Principal Conductor, Walter Hagen; Assistant Conductor, Jean-Pierre Marty; Guest Conductor, Kenneth Schermerhorn; Regisseur, Dimitri Romanoff; Ballet Master, Fernand Nault; Associate Ballet Master, Enrique Martinez.

CAST

Lupe Serrano	John Kriza
Ruth Ann Koesun	Royes Fernandez
Eleanor D'Antuono	Toni Lander
Bruce Marks	Sallie Wilson
Gayle Young	Scott Douglas

Guests: Sonia Arova, Carmen deLavallade, John Gilpin

ENSEMBLE: Janie Barrow, Susan Borree, Joseph Carow, Mary Gelder, Lawrence Gradus, Gail Israel, Ted Kivitt, Karen Krych, Victoria Leigh, Christine Mayer, Veronika Mlakar, Janet Mitchell, Paul Sutherland, Basil Thompson, Edward Verso, Tom Adair, Diane Anthony, Karena Brock, Camille Rosby, Ellen Everett, Eliot Feld, William Glassman, Virginia Griffee, Judi Griffler, Bob Hall, Reese Haworth, Robert Holloway, Stephania Lee, Judith Lerner, Michaela Mattox, Paul Nickel, Gillian Orpin, Marie Paquet, Marcos Paredes, Barbara Remington, Rosalin Ricci, Christine Sarry, Gretchen Schumacher, Rosanna Seravalli, Burton Taylor, Diana Weber, Richard Zelens.

REPERTOIRE: Les Sylphides, Black Swan Pas de Deux, Etudes, Fancy Free, Theme and Variations, The Wind In The Mountains, Sylvia Pas de Deux, Graduation Ball, Grand Pas Glazounov, Fall River Legend, Esmeralda Pas de Deux, Billy The Kid, Peter and The Wolf, The Four Marys, Jardin Aux Lilas, Sargasso, Dark Elegies, Giselle, Miss Julie, La Fille Mal Gardee, Les Noces, The Combat, Caprichos. Nutcracker Pas de Deux, The Frail Quarry, Don Quixote Pas de Deux, L'Inconnue.

Company Manager: Donald Antonelli
Press: Robert S. Taplinger Associates, Fred Weterick
Stage Managers: Franklin Keysar, Joseph Carow

° Closed Sunday, April 11, 1965, after a limited engagement of 32 performances.

124

Jack Mitchell Photos

Sallie Wilson, Bruce Marks in "Sargasso". Above: "Etudes". Top: "The Wind In The Mountains," "Les Noces". Below: "Billy The Kid," "Les Sylphides"

NEW YORK STATE THEATRE

Opened Tuesday, April 13, 1965.°
New York State Theater presents:

SAN FRANCISCO BALLET

Lew Christensen, General Director; Leon Kalimos, Managing Director; Gerhard Samuel, Conductor; Lawrence Foster, Associate Conductor; Decor and Costumes, Cal Anderson.

COMPANY

Jocelyn Vollmar, Sally Bailey, Virginia Johnson, Cynthia Gregory, Robert Gladstein, Terry Orr, David Anderson, R. Clinton Rothwell, Shari White, Gail Visentin, Lynda Meyer, Christie Sharp, Lee Fuller, Henry Berg, Gerard Leavitt, Henry Kersh, Joan DeVere, Marolyn Gyorfi, Betsy Erickson, Eloise Tjomsland, Barbara Begany, Maureen Wiseman, Ann Marie Longtin, Rex Bickmore, Bill Breedlove, Frank Ordway, William Johnson, Kristine Heinemann, Uta Enders, Salicia Smith, Deanne Rowland, David Coll.

REPERTOIRE

Lucifer, Life, Divertissement d'Auber, Sinfonia, Caprice, Beauty and The Beast, Shadows, Fantasma, The Set.

Press: Virginia Donaldson, Doris Luhrs

° Closed Sunday, April 18, 1965 after a limited engagement of 8 performances.

Henri McDowell Photos

Cynthia Gregory, David Anderson

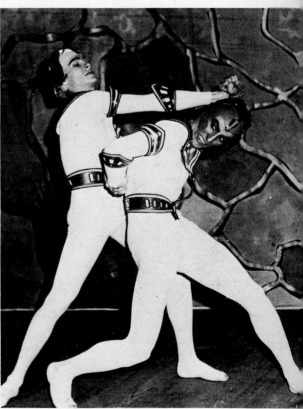

Lynda Meyer, David Anderson, Robert Gladstein, R. Clinton Rothwell, Bill Breedlove, Henry Kersh in "Life" (above: "Life")

R. Clinton Rothwell, David Anderson in "Lucifer"

ANTA WASHINGTON
SQUARE THEATRE

Opened Thursday, January 23, 1964.°
Repertory Theater of Lincoln Center presents:

AFTER THE FALL

By Arthur Miller; Directed by Elia Kazan; Production and Lighting Designed by Jo Mielziner; Music Composed by David Amram; Costumes, Anna Hill Johnstone; Hairstyles, Lee Victor.

CAST

Quentin	Jason Robards, Jr.†1
Felice	Zohra Lampert
Holga	Salome Jens
Mother	Virginia Kaye†2
Dan	Michael Strong
Father	Paul Mann
Nurses	Faye Dunaway†3, Diane Shalet
Doctor	Scott Cunningham
Maggie	Barbara Loden
Elsie	Patricia Roe†4
Louise	Mariclare Costello
Lou	David J. Stewart
Mickey	Ralph Meeker†5
Man in the park	Stanley Beck
Woman with parrot	Diane Shalet
Carrie	Ruth Attaway
Chairman	David Wayne†6
Rev. Harley Barnes	Hal Holbrook†7
Porter	Jack Waltzer
Secretary	Crystal Field†8
Lucas	Harold Scott†9
Clergyman	James Greene

OTHERS: Stanley Beck, Faye Dunaway, Patricia Fay, James Greene, Clinton Kimbrough, John Phillip Law, Barry Primus, Diane Shalet, Jack Waltzer.

A Drama in two acts. The action takes place in the mind, thought, and memory of Quentin, a contemporary man.

General Manager: Stanley Gilkey
Press: Barry Hyams, Susan Bloch
Stage Managers: Frederick deWilde, Robert Downing, Howard Fisher, Frank Hamilton, Don McGovern

° Closed Saturday, May 29, 1965. For original production, see THEATRE WORLD, Vol. 20.
† Succeeded by: 1. Hal Holbrook, 2. Patricia Roe, 3. Lanna Saunders, 4. Faye Dunaway, 5. Joseph Wiseman, 6. Graham Jarvis, 7. James Dukas, 8. Patricia Fay, 9. Don McGovern

Martha Swope Photos

Barbara Loden

Michael Strong, Patricia Roe
Above: Hal Holbrook

Inge Morath Phot

Philip Law, Barbara Loden. Above: Diane Shalet,
chael Strong. Top Right: Stanley Beck, Diane Shalet

ANTA WASHINGTON SQUARE THEATRE

Opened Thursday, October 29, 1964.°
Repertory Theater of Lincoln Center (Directors, Elia Kazan, Robert Whitehead; Executive Consultant, Harold Clurman) presents:

THE CHANGELING

By Thomas Middleton and William Rowley; Directed by Elia Kazan; Settings and Lighting, David Hays; Costumes, Ben Edwards; Music composed by David Amram; Madmen's Choreography, Crystal Field.

CAST

Vermandero	Paul Mann
Beatrice	Barbara Loden
Alonzo	Harold Scott
Tomazo	Scott Cunningham
Alsemero	John Philip Law
Jasperino	James Greene
DeFlores	Barry Primus
Pedro	Clinton Kimbrough
Diaphanta	Lanna Saunders
Maids to Beatrice	Mariclare Costello, Faye Dunaway
Antonio	Stanley Beck
Franciscus	Jack Waltzer
Lollio	David J. Stewart
Alibius	Michael Strong
Isabella	Diane Shalet
Scullery Maid	Crystal Field

MADMEN, SERVANTS, HUNTERS, CLOWNS, PRIESTS AND OTHERS: George Bartenieff, C. Thomas Blackwell, Mark Epstein, Alexander Gam, John Garces, Graham Jarvis, Richard Khan, Stephen Peters, Wendell K. Phillips, Sr., Herbert Ratner, John Sarno, Andreas Voutsinas.

A Drama in three acts. The action takes place in Alicant, a Valencian seaport on the east coast of Spain; near the harbor of the city; in the rooms of Vermandero's castle; and in the madhouse of Alibius.

General Manager: Stanley Gilkey
Press: Barry Hyams, Robert Pasolli, Susan Bloch
Stage Managers: Frederick deWilde, Robert Downing, Howard Fischer, Frank Hamilton

° Closed December 23, 1964, after playing in repertory.

ANTA WASHINGTON
SQUARE THEATRE

Opened Thursday, December 3, 1964.°
Repertory Theater of Lincoln Center (Directors, Elia Kazan, Robert Whitehead; Executive Consultant, Harold Clurman) presents:

INCIDENT AT VICHY

By Arthur Miller; Directed by Harold Clurman; Designed by Boris Aronson; Lighting, Jean Rosenthal; Costumes, Jane Greenwood.

CAST

LeBeau	Michael Strong
Bayard	Stanley Beck
Marchand	Paul Mann
Police Guard	C. Thomas Blackwell
Monceau	David J. Stewart
Gypsy	Harold Scott
Waiter	Jack Waltzer
A Boy	Ira Lewis
A Major	Hal Holbrook
First Detective	Alek Primrose
Old Jew	Will Lee
Second Detective	James Dukas
LeDuc	Joseph Wiseman
Police Captain	James Greene
Von Berg	David Wayne
Professor Hoffman	Clinton Kimbrough
Ferrand	Graham Jarvis
Prisoners	Pierre Epstein, Stephen Peters, Tony Lo Bianco, John Vari

UNDERSTUDIES: Daniel Ades, James Dukas, Pierre Epstein, Tony Lo Bianco, Stephen Peters, Alek Primrose, John Vari.

A Drama presented without intermission. The action takes place late in the morning of a September day in 1942 in a detention room in Vichy, France.

General Manager: Stanley Gilkey
Press: Barry Hyams, Robert Pasolli,
Susan Bloch
Stage Managers: Frederic deWilde, Robert Downing, Howard Fischer, Frank Hamilton, Jay Harnick, Don McGovern

° Closed May 2, 1965 after playing in repertory.

Barry Hyams Photos

Will Lee, David Wayne, David J. Stewart, Michael Strong
Above: Joseph Wiseman, David Wayne
Top: Entire Cast

ANTA WASHINGTON
SQUARE THEATRE

Opened Thursday, January 14, 1965.°
Repertory Theater of Lincoln Center (Harold Clurman, Executive Consultant) presents:

TARTUFFE

By Jean-Baptiste Poquelin (Moliere); Translated into English Verse by Richard Wilbur; Directed by William Ball; Setting, David Hays; Costumes, Jane Greenwood; Lighting, John Gleason; Music Composed by Lee Hoiby.

CAST

Prologue	Hal Holbrook
Tartuffe	Michael O'Sullivan
Children	Deidre Moore, Brad Leigh
Mme. Pernelle	Patricia Roe
Dorine	Sada Thompson
Mariane	Joyce Ebert
Elmire	Salome Jens
Damis	Laurence Luckinbill
Cleante	Claude Woolman
Valere	Paul Shenar
Flipote	Diane Shalet
Midwife	Mariclare Costello
Orgon	Larry Gates
Laurent	Alek Primrose
M. Loyal	Hal Holbrook
Officer to the King	John Philip Law
Servants	James Greene, Jack Waltzer
Loyal's Clerks	Graham Jarvis, Roy R. Scheider
Sergeants	Daniel Ades, Graham Jarvis, Tony Lo Bianco, Roy R. Scheider

UNDERSTUDIES: Daniel Ades, Mariclare Costello, Faye Dunaway, James Greene, Graham Jarvis, John Phillip Law, Alek Primrose, Roy R. Scheider, Diane Shalet, Jack Waltzer.

A Comedy presented in two parts. The action takes place in the middle of winter in 1665 on Orgon's estate in France.

Acting Administrator: Stanley Gilkey
Press: Barry Hyams, Susan Bloch
Stage Managers: Frederic deWilde, Robert Downing, Howard Fischer, Frank Hamilton, Jay Harnick, Don McGovern

° Closed May 22, 1965 after playing in repertory.

Barry Hyams Photos

y Gates, Joyce Ebert, Sada Thompson, Paul Shenar, ome Jens. Above: Michael O'Sullivan, Larry Gates

Top: Michael O'Sullivan, Salome Jens

NEW YORK CITY CENTER

Opened Monday, August 31, 1964.°
The City Center of Music and Drama, Inc.
in association with The Greek Theatre
Association of Los Angeles presents:

THE GREEK TRAGEDY THEATRE
(Piraikon Theatron)

Dimitrios Rondiris, Founder-Producer-Director
in

MEDEA

By Euripides; Translation, D. Sarros; Production, D. Rondiris; Choreography, Loukia; Music, K. Kydoniatis.

CAST

Nurse	E. Zerva, K. Sifaki
Tutor	K. Galanakis, N. Lykomitros
Medea	E. Vergi, A. Papathanassiou, T. Nikiforaki
Creon	E. Messidis, N. Lykomitros
Jason	A. Xenakis
Aegeus	N. Lykomitros
Messenger	N. Chadziskos, N. Lykomitros

Leading Women of Chorus: E. Konstantinou, K. Sifaki, H. Karolou, N. Vorrea, D. Diakatou
Chorus of Women: J. Korobilli, E. Tsoukala, K. Zakka, K. Improhori, M. Igoumenidou, F. Vitali, M. Kazakou, E. Kokoli, G. Boura, D. Kefala

Announcers for simultaneous translation: Anne Lebeck, Margaret Coulter

Opened Monday, September 7, 1964.°

ELECTRA

By Sophocles; Translation, J. Gryparis; Production, D. Rondiris; Choreography, Loukia; Music, K. Kydoniatis.

CAST

Tutor	A. Xenakis, E. Messidis
Orestes	N. Chadziskos, K. Galanakis
Electra	A. Papathanassiou, E. Vergi
Chrysothemis	H. Karolou, E. Konstantinou
Clytemestra	T. Nikiforaki, E. Zerva
Aegisthus	N. Lykomitros, E. Messidis
Pylades	K. Galanakis, N. Lykomitros

Leading Women of the Chorus: E. Konstantinou, K. Sifaki, N. Vorrea, D. Diakatou
Chorus of Women: J. Korobili, E. Tsoukala, K. Zakka, K. Improhori, M. Igoumenidou, F. Vitali, M. Kazakou, E. Kokoli, G. Boura, D. Kefala

Production Coordinator: Alexis Boden
Press: Jean Dalrymple, Tom Trenkle

° Closed Sunday, September 13, 1964. "Medea" was presented for 8 performances the first week, and "Electra" for 8 performances the second week of the limited engagement.

Elsa Vergi (also above with chorus), Antonis Xenakis in "Medea"

Elite Photos

Chorus with D. Nikolaidou, A. Papathanassiou (also top right)
Top left: A. Papathanassiou, Antonis Xenakis in "Electra"

NEW YORK CITY CENTER

Opened Tuesday, September 15, 1964.°
S. Hurok in association with the City Center of Music and Drama presents:

ANTONIO
and
THE BALLETS DE MADRID

Direction, Choreography, and Lighting by Antonio; Assistant Director, Juan Ayala; Conductor, Benito Laret; Guest Conductor, Arthur Lief; Basset Master, Hector Zaraspe.

COMPANY
Antonio

Rosita Segovia	Alicia Diaz
Paco Romero	Hector Zaraspe

Guest Artist: Rosario

SOLOISTS: Pastora Ruiz, Marta Calavia, Angela Del Moral, Mariana, Luis Fuentes, Victor Ullate, Norberto, Pepe Soler, Rosa Garcia

CORPS DE BALLET: Carlos Fernandez, Andres Moreno, Marina, Carmen Roche, Remedios Fernandez, Imperio, Manuela Perez, Luis Flores, Conchita Vidal, Rafael Moreno, Maria Luisa Martin, Jose Vazquez

SINGERS: Clara Maria Alcala, Senita De Jerez, Chano Lobato

GUITARISTS: Manuel Moreno, Juan Moreno, Carlos Sanchez, Paco Sevilla

REPERTORY: Concierto Espanol, El Martinete, Suite of Basque Dances, The Three Cornered Hat, Estampa Flamenca, Suite of Sonatas, El Amor Brujo, La Taberna Del Toro, Triana, Zorongo Gitano, Viva Navarra.

Company Manager: Oscar Berlin
Press: Martin Feinstein, Michael Sweeley, Ed Parkinson
Stage Manager: Guillermo Keys Arenas

° Closed Sunday, September 27, 1964, after a limited engagement of 16 performances.

　　John Blomfield Photos

"La Taberna Del Toro". Above: "Basque Dances"
Top: Antonio and Rosario

NEW YORK CITY CENTER

Opened Tuesday, November 17, 1964.°
The D'Oyly Carte Opera Trust, Ltd., under the management of S. Hurok, presents:

THE D'OYLY CARTE OPERA COMPANY

In repertory in operas written by W. S. Gilbert and composed by Arthur Sullivan; Under the personal supervision of Bridget D'Oyly Carte; Musical Director, Isidore Godfrey, Associate Conductor, James Walker; Director of Productions, Herbert Newby.

IOLANTHE

Conducted by Isidore Godfrey; Settings Designed by Peter Goffin.

CAST

The Lord Chancellor	John Reed
Earl of Mountararat	Donald Adams
Earl Tolloller	David Palmer
Private Willis	Kenneth Sandford
Strephon	Jeffrey Skitch
Queen of The Fairies	Gillian Knight
Iolanthe	Gillian Humphreys
Celia	Margaret Eales
Lelia	Pauline Wales
Fleta	Jennifer Marks
Phyllis	Valerie Masterson

Chorus of Dukes, Marquises, Earls, Viscounts, Barons and Fairies.

Opened Thursday, November 19, 1964.

TRIAL BY JURY

Conducted alternately by James Walker and Isidore Godfrey; Setting Designed by Peter Goffin; Costumes, George Sheringham.

CAST

The Learned Judge	Jeffrey Skitch
Counsel for the Plaintiff	Alan Styler
Defendant	Philip Potter
Foreman of the Jury	Anthony Raffell
Usher	George Cook
Associate	Keith Bonnington
Plaintiff	Jennifer Toye
First Bridesmaid	Joy Mornay

Chorus of Jurymen, Bridesmaids, and Public

Followed by:

H.M.S. PINAFORE

Conducted alternately by Isidore Godfrey and James Walker; Settings and Costumes, Peter Goffin; Back Cloth, Joseph and Phil Harker.

CAST

The Rt. Hon. Sir Joseph Porter	John Reed
Capt. Corcoran	Jeffrey Skitch
Ralph Rackstraw	David Palmer
Dick Deadeye	Donald Adams
Bill Bobstay	George Cook
Bob Becket	Anthony Raffell
Josephine	Ann Hood
Hebe	Pauline Wales
Mrs. Cripps (Little Buttercup)	Gillian Knight

Chorus of First Lord's Sisters, Cousins, Aunts, Sailors, and Marines.

John Blomfield Photos

op Right: Jeffrey Skitch, Gillian Knight in "Iolanthe"
Below: Jeffrey Skitch, Philip Potter, Jennifer Toye, Alan Styler in "Trial By Jury"

Ann Hood, David Palmer. Above: George Cook, Gillian Knight in "H.M.S. Pinafore"

Opened Tuesday, November 24, 1964.

THE PIRATES OF PENZANCE

Conducted alternately by James Walker and Isidore Godfrey; Settings Designed by Peter Goffin.

CAST

Major-General Stanley	John Reed
The Pirate King	Donald Adams
Samuel	Anthony Raffell
Frederic	Philip Potter
Sergeant of Police	George Cook
Mabel	Valerie Masterson
Edith	Gillian Humphreys
Kate	Peggy Ann Jones
Isabel	Pauline Wales
Ruth	Gillian Knight

Chorus of Pirates, Police, and General Stanley's Daughters

Opened Thursday, November 26, 1964.

THE MIKADO

Conducted alternately by Isidore Godfrey and James Walker; Production Directed by Anthony Besch; Costumes Designed by Disley Jones and Charles Ricketts.

CAST

The Mikado of Japan	Donald Adams
Nanki-Poo	Philip Potter
Ko-Ko	John Reed
Pooh-Bah	Kenneth Sandford
Pish-Tush	Alan Styler
Go-To	George Cook
Yum-Yum	Jennifer Toye
Pitti-Sing	Peggy Ann Jones
Peep-Bo	Gillian Humphreys
Katisha	Gillian Knight

Chorus of Schoolgirls, Nobles, Guards, and Coolies

Opened Thursday, December 3, 1964.

RUDDIGORE

Conducted alternately by Isidore Godfrey and James Walker; Settings and Costumes by Peter Goffin.

CAST

Sir Ruthven Murgatroyd	John Reed
Richard Dauntless	David Palmer
Sir Despard Murgatroyd	Kenneth Sandford
Old Adam Goodheart	George Cook
Sir Roderic Murgatroyd	Donald Adams
Rose Maybud	Ann Hood
Mad Margaret	Peggy Ann Jones
Dame Hannah	Gillian Knight
Zorah	Jennifer Toye
Ruth	Jennifer Marks

Chorus of Bucks and Blades, Ancestors and Professional Bridesmaids.

SMALL PARTS, UNDERSTUDIES, AND CHORUS: Glyn Adams, Keith Bonnington, Liam Cummings, Jon Ellison, Eric Greenall, John Hugill, Thomas Lawlor, James Lewington, Gordon Mackenzie, John Maguire, James Marsland, Alfred Oldridge, Derek Peatfield, Vivien Carman, Dawn Davies, Margaret Eales, Gloria Farndell, Abby Hadfield, Susan Maisey, Jennifer Marks, Marian Martin, Joy Mornay, Elizabeth Mynett, Sylvia Vale, Anna Vincent.

Company Manager: Lester Appleby
Press: Martin Feinstein, Michael Sweeley
Stage Managers: Jack Habbick, Geoffrey Lloyd
° Closed Sunday, December 20, 1964. (40 performances)

John Blomfield Photos

Finale of Act I of "Ruddigore"

Top Left: Donald Adams, John Reed in "The Pirates Of Penzance". **Below:** Scene from "The Mikado" with Donald Adams

Opened Wednesday, December 23, 1964.°
The New York City Center Light Opera
Company, Jean Dalrymple, Director, presents:

BRIGADOON

Books and Lyrics, Alan Jay Lerner; Music,
Frederick Loewe; Directed by John Fearnley;
Dances and Musical Numbers Staged by Agnes
de Mille, assisted by James Jamieson; Settings,
Oliver Smith; Lighting, Peggy Clark; Costumes,
Stanley Simmons; Conductor, William Jonson;
Hair Styles, Ernest Adler; Julius Rudel, Musical Director.

CAST

Tommy Albright	Peter Palmer
Jeff Douglas	Scott McKay
Sandy Dean	Will MacKenzie
Meg Brockie	Louise O'Brien
Archie Beaton	Earl MacDonald
Harry Beaton	Edward Villella
Andrew MacLaren	Alexander Clark
Jean MacLaren	Imelda De Martin
Fiona MacLaren	Linda Bennett
Angus McGuffie	Daniel Hannafin
Charlie Dalrymple	Harry David Snow
Maggie Anderson	Gemze De Lappe
Mr. Lundie	Clarence Nordstrom
Bagpiper	Maurice Eisenstadt
Frank	Si Vario
Jane Ashton	Sharon Ritchie

SWORD DANCERS: Ben Gillespie, Paul Olson, Wayne Boyd, Dennis Cole, Charles Mc-Craw, Ron Tassone.

SINGERS: Diana Chase, Maria Hero, Linda Johnson, Virginia Kerr, Bobbi Lange, Leonore Lanzillotti, Joyce Olson, Jeanne Shea, Abbie Todd, Sallie Valante, Lynn Wendell, Brown Bradley, Peter Clark, William J. Coppola, Rex Downey, Glenn Kexer, Henry Lawrence, Jim Lynn, Bob Neukum, Stan Page, Stephen Rydell.

DANCERS: Virginia Allen, Lynne Broadbent, Joanna Crosson, Diana Ede, Lucia Lambert, Loi Leabo, Gracia Littauer, Mavis Ray, Judy Thelen, Mona Tritsch, Esther Villavicencio, Toodie Wittmer, Paul Berne, Wayne Boyd, Allan Byrns, Dennis Cole, Joseph Fioretti, Ben Gillespie, Charles McCraw, Paul Olson, Victor Pierantozzi, Ron Tassone, Michael Toles.

UNDERSTUDIES: Harry, James Jamieson; Tommy, Stan Page; Jeff, Allan Byrns; Fiona, Jeanne Shea; Meg, Bobbi Lange; Archie, Bob Neukum; Angus, Sandy, William J. Coppola; Jean, Loi Leabo; Maggie, Esther Villavicencio; Charlie, Steve Rydell; Lundie, Andrew, Glenn Kezer; Frank, Tom Ellis; Jane, Diana Ede.

MUSICAL NUMBERS: "Once In The Highlands," "Brigadoon," "Down On MacConnachy Square," "Waitin' For My Dearie," "I'll Go Home With Bonnie Jean," "The Heather On The Hill," "The Love Of My Life," "Jeannie's Packin' Up," "Come To Me, Bend To Me," "Almost Like Being In Love," "The Wedding Dance," "Sword Dance," "The Chase," "There But For You Go I," "My Mother's Wedding Day," "Funeral Dance," "From This Day On," Finale.

A Musical in two acts and eleven scenes with a prologue. The action takes place in May of last year in the Scottish Highlands and New York City.

Company Manager: George Zorn
Press: Tom Trenkle
Stage Managers: John Maxtone-Graham,
William H. Batchelder, Tom Ellis

° Closed Sunday, January 3, 1965. (17 performances)
Premiered March 13, 1947 and ran for 581 performances. See THEATRE WORLD, Vol. 3. Last revival January 30, 1963 at New York City Center for 16 performances. See THEATRE WORLD, Vol. 19.

Alix Jeffry Photos

Top Right: Louise O'Brien, Scott McKay, Peter Palmer, Linda Bennett. Below: Peter Palmer, Linda Bennett

Edward Villella, Gemze DeLappe

NEW YORK CITY CENTER
Opened Tuesday, January 5, 1965.*
S. Hurok presents:

THE POLISH MIME THEATRE

Henryk Tomaszewski, Director; Costumes, Krzysztof Pankiewicz, Marcin Wenzel, Kazimierz Wisniak; Music, Augustyn Bloch, Andrzej Markowski, Stanislaw Michalek, Jerzy Pakulski, Jadwiga Szajna-Lewandowska; Scenarios and Production, Henryk Tomaszewski; Assistant Director, Leon Gorecki; Technical Director, Ludwik Kwatersik; Lighting, Ayszard Osmulski.

PROGRAM

Jaselka, The Labyrinth, The Woman, The Nightmare, The Book, Jacob and The Angel, The Kernel and The Shell, The Post Office.

Company Manager: Oscar Berlin
Press: Martin Feinstein, Michael Sweeley
Stage Manager: Simon Semenoff

* Closed Sunday, January 17, 1965, after a limited engagement of 16 performances.

Stanislaw Brzozowski, Elizabeth Jaroszewicz, Andrzej Szczuzewski in "The Detective". Above: Stanislaw Brzozowski, Jerzy Kozlowski, Pawel Rouba, Ludmila Dabrowska in "Jaselka"

"Woyzeck," Above: The Kernel And The Shell" Top: "The Book"

NEW YORK CITY CENTER

Opened Tuesday, January 19, 1965.°
S. Hurok presents:

BALLET FOLKLORICO DE MEXICO

General Director and Choreographer, Amalia Hernandez; Costumes Designed by Dasha; Scenery Designed by Robin Bond, Feliciano Bejar, Agustin Hernandez, A. Lopez Mancera; Assistant to the Director, Nellie Happee; Musical Coordinator, Ramon Noble; Lighting, Thomas Skelton.

PROGRAM

PART I: The Aztec Gods, Dances of Old Michoacan, Wedding In The Huasteca, Los Tarascos, Fiesta in Veracruz.

PART II: Masks Of Guerrero, Wedding In Tehuantepec, The Deer Dance, Fiesta In Jalisco.

General Manager: Estela A. de Mateos
Company Manager: Kurt Newmann
Press: Martin Feinstein, Michael Sweeley,
Tomas Quiroga, Amico Barone
Stage Manager: Louise Guthman

° Closed Sunday, January 31, 1965, after a limited engagement of 16 performances.

Fiesta In Jalisco" (also top). Above: "Aztec Gods"
Top Right: Jorge Tyller in "Deer Dance"
Below: "Los Tarascos"

NEW YORK CITY CENTER

Opened Thursday, February 4, 1965.°
S. Hurok presents in cooperation with the
City Center of Music and Drama:

MOSCOW ART THEATRE

Boris Pokarzhevsky, Director

DEAD SOULS

Adapted by Mikhail Bulgakov from the Novel
by Nikolai Gogol; Initial Artistic Production
Supervisor, Konstantin Stanislavsky; Regisseurs,
V. G. Sakhnovsky, E. S. Teleshava; Designer,
V. A. Simov; Stage Managers, N. N. Gottikh,
A. D. Ponsov; Simultaneous English translation
by Miki Iveria and Edward Greer.

CAST

Chichikov, Pavel Ivanovich	Vladimir Belokurov
Secretary of the Trustee Committee	Mikhail Yanshin
Innkeeper	Nikolai Alexeyev
Waiter	Lev Zolotukhin
The Governor	Victor Stanitsyn
Governor's Servant	Sergei Blinnikov, Vladimir Popov
Antipater Zakharovich	Gregory Konsky
Ivan Grigorevich	Yuri Nedzvetsky
Alexei Ivanovich	Alexei Zhiltsov
Perkhunovsky	Iosef Raevsky
Berebendovsky	Boris Smirnov
Cuckoo	Mikhail Medvedev
The Lieutenant Governor	Mark Prudkin
His Wife	Kira Golovko
Manilov	Mikhail Kedrov, Yuri Leonidov
Lizanka	Galina Kalinovskaya
Sobakevich, Mikhail Semenovich	Alexei Gribov, Sergei Blinnikov
Nozdrev	Boris Livanov
Mizhuev	Nikita Kondratev
Pliushkin	Boris Petker
Proshka	Alexei Pokrovsky
Mavra	Anastasia Georgievskaya
Porfiry	Mikhail Zimin
Korobochka	Anastasia Zueva
Fetinia	Klementina Rostovtseva
The Postmaster	Alexander Komissarov
The Governor's Daughter	Anna Kedrova
Anna Grigorevna	Olga Labzina
Sofia Ivanovna	Tatiana Zabrodina
Parashka	Nina Guliaeva
Macdonald Karlovich	Iosef Raevsky
Sysoy Pafnutevich	Nikolai Alexeyev
Colonel of the Gendarmery	Vassily Markov
Jailer	Nikolai Semernitsky

A Satirical Drama in three acts. The action
takes place in the Russian provincial town of
N. towards the end of the 1830's.

° Closed Sunday, February 28, 1965 after a
limited engagement in repertory totalling 31
performances

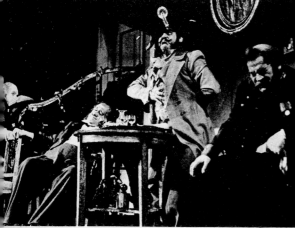

Boris Livanov (Center)

Boris Livanov, Vladimir Belokurov. Top: Boris
Livanov (also center), Nikita Kondratev

NEW YORK CITY CENTER

Opened Tuesday, February 9, 1965.°
S. Hurok in cooperation with the City
Center of Music and Drama presents: the
Moscow Art Theatre production of:

THE CHERRY ORCHARD

By Anton Chekhov; Producer and Director,
Victor Stanitsyn; Designer, L. N. Silich; Sound
Supervisor, Vladimir Popov; Stage Managers,
N. N. Gottikh, A. D. Ponsov.

CAST

Ranevskaya, Liubov
  Andreyevna ....Alla Tarassova
Anya ....Larissa Kachanova
Varya...............................Tatiana Lennikova
Gaev, Leonid Andreyevich........Pavel Massalsky
Lopakhin, Ermolai Alexeyevich ....Mikhail Zimin
Trofimov, Pyotr Sergeyevich....Leonid Gubanov
Semyonov-Pishchik, Boris
  Borisovich ....Mikhail Yanshin
Charlotta Ivanovna.............Angelina Stepanova
Epikhodov, Semyon
  Pantaleyevich.............. Alexander Komissarov
Duniasha .... Klementia Rostovtseva
Firs...............Alexei Gribov, Vladimir Popov
Yasha ....Yuri Leonidov
A Passer-by ....Gregory Konsky
Station Master.................Yuri Nedzvetsky
Post Office Employee.............Alexei Pokrovsky

A Drama in four acts. The action takes
place at the beginning of this century at the
landowner Ranevskaya's estate near a large
metropolis.

° Presented in repertory. Final performance
Saturday, February 27, 1965.

Alla Tarassova, Larissa Kachanova,
Pavel Massalsky

Alla Tarassova, Larissa Kachanova. Above:
Leonid Gubanov, Alla Tarassova

139

NEW YORK CITY CENTER

Opened Thursday, February 11, 1965.°
S. Hurok in cooperation with the City
Center of Music and Drama presents the
Moscow Art Theatre production of:

THE THREE SISTERS

By Anton Chekhov; Staged by Iosef Raev-
sky; Decor, V. V. Dmitriev; Sound Supervision,
Vladimir Popov; Assistant Director, Isola Apin;
Stage Managers, N. N. Gottikh, Alexei Ponsov;
Simultaneous English translations by Miki Iver-
ia and Edward Greer.

CAST

Andrei	Nikolai Alexeyev
Natalia	Klementina Rostovtseva
Olga	Kira Golovko
Masha	Marguarita Yureva
Irina	Raissa Maximova
Kulygin	Vladimir Belokurov
Vershinin	Pavel Massalsky, Mikhail Bolduman
Tuzhenbakh	Leonid Gubanov
Soleny	Yrui Leonidov
Chebutykin	Alexei Pokrovsky
Fedotik	Pyotr Chernov
Rode	Alexei Pokrovsky
Ferapont	Vladimir Popov, Mikhail Medvedev
Anfissa	Anastasia Zueva
Orderly	Victor Petrov
Chambermaid	Galina Kalinovskaya
Street Singer	Tatiana Lennikova
Boy	Nina Guliaeva

A Drama in four acts. The action takes
place at the beginning of this century in a
Russian provincial city, at the home of the
Prozorov sisters.

° Presented in repertory. Final performance
Monday, February 22, 1965.

Top: Raissa Maximova, Kira Golovko, Marguarita
Yureva. Top Left: Marguarita Yureva, Pavel
Massalsky. Below: Klementina Rostovtseva,
Raissa Maximova

Klementina Rostovtseva, Nikolai Alexeyev
Above: Leonid Gubanov, Raissa Maximova

Opened Wednesday, February 24, 1965.°
S. Hurok in cooperation with the City
Center of Music and Drama presents the
Moscow Art Theatre production of:

KREMLIN CHIMES

By Nikolai Pogodin; Directors, Vladimir
Nemirovich-Danchenko, Leonid Leonidov, M.
O. Knebel, Josef Raevsky, Vassily Markov; De-
signer, V. V. Dmitriev; Sound Supervisor, N.
N. Gottikh; Stage Managers, A. D. Ponsov, N.
N. Gottikh; Simultaneous English translation by
Miki Iveria and Edward Greer.

CAST

Lenin	Boris Smirnov
Dzerzhinsky	Vassily Markov
Rybakov	Lev Zolotukhin
Zabelin	Boris Livanov, Mikhail Bolduman
Zabelina	Alla Tarassova
Masha	Marguarita Anastasseva
Chudnov	Gregory Konsky
Roman	Nikolai Alexeyev
Anna	Anastasia Zueva
Liza	Tatiana Zabrodina
Stepka	Nina Guliaeva
Marussia	Larissa Kachanova
Kozanok	Mikhail Medvedev
Senior Worker	Sergei Blinnikov
Bearded Worker	Vladimir Belokurov
Apprentice	Victor Petrov
Beggar Woman	Anastasia Georgievskaya
Old Lady with a child	Olga Labzina
Lady with knitting	Angelina Stepanova
Terrified Lady	Sofia Garrel
A Skeptic	Yuri Nedzevetsky
An Optimist	Yuri Leonidov
A Cook	Tatiana Lennikova
Chairman of Housing Committee	Vladimir Popov
An Officer	Pyotr Chernov
Lenin's Secretary	Nikolai Alexeyev
Glagolev	Pavel Massalsky
Housekeeper	Raissa Maximova
Watchmaker	Boris Petker
Foreign Author	Mark Prudkin
Doll Peddler	Olga Labzina
Red Army Man	Leonid Gubanov
Passing Worshiper	Nikita Kondratiev
Clergyman	Alexei Zhiltsov
Profiteer	Yuri Nedzvetsky
Lard Peddler	Klementina Rostovtseva
Woman with shawl	Tatiana Lennikova
Woman with lace	Marguarita Yureva
Man in boots	Alexander Komissarov

Street Urchins Alexei Pokrovsky, Victor Petrov,
Nina Guliaeva

A Drama in two acts and nine scenes. The
action takes place in Moscow, and the Kremlin.

Company Manager: Edward A. Perper
Press: Martin Feinstein, Michael Sweeley
Stage Manager: Leonard Auerbach

° Presented in repertory that closed on Sunday,
February 28, 1965 after a limited engagement of 31 performances for all productions.

Top Right: Boris Livanov, Vasily Markov, Boris
Smirnov. Below: Boris Livanov, Marguarita
Anastasseva

Boris Smirnov, Boris Livanov
Above: Boris Smirnov, Mark Prudkin   141

NEW YORK CITY CENTER

Opened Wednesday, April 14, 1965.°
The New York City Center Gilbert and
Sullivan Company presents in repertory:

H.M.S. PINAFORE

Book by W. S. Gilbert; Music, Arthur Sullivan; Director, John Bishop; Conductor, Felix Popper; Scenery and Costumes, Patton Campbell.

CAST

The Rt. Hon. Sir Joseph Porter	Norman Kelley
Captain Corcoran	William Chapman, Richard Fredricks
Ralph Rackstraw	John Stamford, William Greene
Dick Deadeye	Paul Ukena
Bill Bobstay	William Ledbetter
Bob Becket	Lee Cass
Josephine	Anne Elgar, Carol Bayard
Cousin Hebe	Marlena Kleinman
Little Buttercup	Muriel Greenspon

PATIENCE

Book, W. S. Gilbert; Music, Arthur Sullivan; Staged by Dorothy Raedler; Conducted by Julius Rudel; Scenery and Costumes, Motley; Choreography, Thomas Andrew.

CAST

Colonel Calverley	William Chapman
Major Murgatroyd	James Wilson
Lt. The Duke of Dunstable	Richard Krause
Reginald Bunthorne	Emile Renan
Archibald Grosvenor	David Smith
Mr. Bunthorne's Solicitor	Thomas Andrew
The Lady Angela	Marlena Kleinman
The Lady Saphir	Helen Guile
The Lady Ella	Virginia Bitar
The Lady Jane	Claramae Turner
Patience	Patricia Welting, Anne Elgar

THE MIKADO

Book, W. S. Gilbert; Music, Arthur Sullivan; Director, Dorothy Raedler; Conductor, Charles Wilson; Scenery and Lighting, Donald Oenslager; Costumes, Patton Campbell.

CAST

The Mikado of Japan	George Gaynes, Paul Ukena
Nanki-Poo	William Diard, Richard Krause
Ko-Ko	Norman Kelley, James Wilson, Herbert Beattie
Pooh-Bah	Herbert Beattie, Lee Cass, Norman Kelley
Pish-Tush	David Smith
Yum-Yum	Mary Jennings, Virginia Bitar, Patricia Welting
Pitti-Sing	Mary Burgess
Peep-Bo	Marlena Kleinman, Helen Guile
Katisha	Claramae Turner, Elaine Bonazzi, Muriel Greenspon

Claramae Turner, Emile Renan in "Patience"

William Diard, Mary Jennings in "The Mikado"

THE PIRATES OF PENZANCE

Book, W. S. Gilbert; Music, Arthur Sullivan; Staged by Dorothy Raedler; Conducted by Dean Ryan; Scenery, H. A. Condell.

CAST

Major-General Stanley	Emile Renan
The Pirate King	Paul Ukena, William Chapman
Samuel	William Ledbetter
Frederic	William Diard, William Greene
Sergeant of Police	Herbert Beattie, Lee Cass
Mabel	Anne Elgar
Edith	Virginia Bitar
Kate	Mary Burgess
Isabel	Helen Guile
Ruth	Muriel Greenspon

THE YEOMAN OF THE GUARD

Book, W. S. Gilbert; Music, Arthur Sullivan; Staged by Allen Fletcher; Conducted by Julius Rudel; Stage Director, Ruth M. Hider; Scenery, Stephen O. Saxe; Costumes, Alvin Colt.

CAST

Sir Richard Cholmondeley	Paul Ukena
Colonel Fairfax	John Stamford
Sergeant Meryll	George Gaynes
Leonard Meryll	Richard Krause
Jack Point	Norman Kelley
Wilfred Shadbolt	Herbert Beattie
The Headsman	Thomas Andrew
First Yeoman	William Greene
Second Yeoman	William Ledbetter
First Citizen	Harris Davis
Second Citizen	Glenn Dowlen
Elsie Maynard	Mary Jennings
Phoebe Meryll	Mary Burgess
Dame Carruthers	Elaine Bonazzi
Kate	Virginia Bitar

ENSEMBLE: Joan August, Barbara Beaman, Paul Corder, Harris Davis, Marcelline Decker, Anthea de Forest, Glenn Dowlen, Joyce Gerber, Margaret Goodman, Helen Guile, Don Henderson, Lila Herbert, David Hicks, Robert Lee Kelly, Jodell Kenting, Hanna Owen, Richard G. Park, Charlotte Povia, Frank Redfield, Anthony Safina, Alexander Savchuck, John Smith, Marie Young, Don Yule. Solo Dancer, Rochelle Zide.

Company Manager: George Zorn
Press: Nat and Irvin Dorfman
Stage Managers: Hans Sondheimer, Bill Field, Dan Butt, Frank Wicks

° Closed Sunday, April 25, 1965 after a limited engagement of 15 performances.

142

Fred Fehl Photos

NEW YORK CITY CENTER

Opened Wednesday, April 28, 1965.°
The New York City Center Light Opera
Company, Jean Dalrymple-Director, pre-
sents:

GUYS AND DOLLS

Music and Lyrics, Frank Loesser; Book, Jo
Swerling and Abe Burrows; Based on Story and
Characters by Damon Runyon; Directed by
Gus Schirmer, Jr.; Choreography, Ralph Beau-
mont; Costumes, Frank Thompson; Adaptation
of Jo Mielziner's original designs by Peter
Wolf; Lighting, Peggy Clark; Hair Styles,
Ernest Adler; Conducted by Irving Actman;
Production Assistant, Ernest Dobbs.

CAST

Nicely-Nicely Johnson	Jack DeLon
Benny Southstreet	Joey Faye
Rusty Charlie	Ed Becker
Sarah Brown	Anita Gillette
Arvide Abernathy	Clarence Nordstrom
Mission Band	Jeanne Schlegel, Clarence

Nordstrom, Maria Hero, Claire Waring,
Arthur Santry, Joy Franz

Harry The Horse	Tom Pedi
Lt. Brannigan	Frank Campanella
Nathan Detroit	Alan King
Angie The Ox	Vern Shinnal
Miss Adelaide	Sheila MacRae
Sky Masterson	Jerry Orbach
Joey Biltmore	Ed Becker
Mimi	Ginna Carr
General Matilda Cartwright	Claire Waring
Big Julie	Jake LaMotta
Drunk	Stuart Mann
Waiter	Philip Lucas

DANCERS: Rita Agnese, Suzanne Channel,
Dorothy D'Honau, Tina Faye, Shelley Frankel,
Leslie Franzos, Ginny Gan, Altouise Gore,
Shari Greene, Maureen Hopkins, Joan Kruger,
Violetta Landek, Maria Strattin, Frank Cop-
pola, Luigi Gasparinetti, Frenando Grahal,
Mark J. Holliday, Daniel Joel, Carlos Macri,
Mitchell Nutick, Paul Owsley, Charles Reeder,
Marc Scott, Ronald Stratton

SINGERS: Joy Franz, Maria Hero, Jeanne
Schlegel, Ken Ayres, Edward Becker, Walter P.
Brown, Victor P. Helou, Henry Lawrence, Phil-
ip Lucas, Jim Lynn, Stuart Mann, John Peck,
Michael Quinn, Darrell Sandeen, Arthur San-
try.

UNDERSTUDIES: Adelaide, Betty Hyatt Lin-
ton; Sky, John Peck; Sarah, Joy Franz; Nicely,
Benny, Victor Helou; Arvide, Arthur Santry;
General, Jeanne Schlegel; Rusty, Michael
Quinn.

MUSICAL NUMBERS: "Opening," "Fugue
For Tin Horns," "Follow The Fold," "The
Oldest Established," "I'll Know," "A Bushel
and A Peck," "Adelaide's Lament," "Guys and
Dolls," "San Juan," "If I Were A Bell," "My
Time Of Day," "I've Never Been In Love
Before," "Take Back Your Mink," "More I
Cannot Wish You," "The Crap Game Dance,"
"Luck Be A Lady," "Sue Me," "Sit Down,
You're Rockin' The Boat," "Marry The Man
Today."

A Musical Comedy in two acts and seventeen scenes. The action takes place in New
York City and in San Juan, Puerto Rico.

General Manager: Homer Poupart
Company Manager: Catherine Parsons
Press: Tom Trenkle
Stage Managers: Herman Shapiro, Paul J.
Phillips, Bert Wood

° Closed Sunday, May 9, 1965, after a limited
engagement of 15 performances. For original production see THEATRE WORLD, Vol-
ume 7. In the original cast were Vivian
Blaine, Isabel Bigley, Robert Alda, and Sam
Levene. It ran for 1200 performances. The
last revival was at N.Y. City Center July 21,
1959, with Lloyd Bridges, Margot Moser, Harvey Stone, and Iva Withers. See THEATRE
WORLD, Vol. 16.

Alix Jeffry Photos

Top: Claire Waring, Jerry Orbach, Anita Gillette
Below: Jack DeLon, Alan King, Joey Faye

Sheila MacRae, and above with Alan King

Opened Wednesday, May 12, 1965.°
The New York City Center Light Opera
Company (Jean Dalrymple, Director) pre-
sents:

KISS ME, KATE

Music and Lyrics by Cole Porter; Book by
Sam and Bella Spewack; Dances and Musical
Numbers Staged by Hanya Holm; Production
Directed by John Fearnley and Billy Matthews;
Musical Director and Orchestra Conducted by
Pembroke Davenport; Associate Conductor, Os-
car Kosarin; Dance Music Arranged by Gene-
vieve Pitot; Scenery, Robert O'Hearn; Costumes,
Stanley Simmons after originals by Lemuel
Ayers; Lighting, Peggy Clark; Hair Styles, Er-
nest Adler; Production Assistant, Ernest Dobbs.

CAST

Fred Graham	Bob Wright
Harry Trevor	Alexander Clark
Lois Lane	Nancy Ames
Ralph (Stage Manager)	William H. Batchelder
Lilli Vanessi	Patricia Morison
Paul	Tiger Haynes
Hattie	Alyce Elizabeth Webb
Stage Doorman	Eugene R. Wood
Bill Calhoun	Kelly Brown
Cab Driver	Bill Kennedy
First Man	Jesse White
Second Man	Victor Helou
Harrison Howell	Royal Beal
Specialty Dancers	Charles Cook, Ernest Brown
Doctor	Don Henderson
Nurses	Patricia Finch, Lynn Wendell
Messengers	Anthony Santiago, Michael Whaley, Loren Hightower
Banker	Richard Lyle
Truck Driver	Ben Gillespie

"Taming Of The Shrew" Players

Bianca	Nancy Ames
Baptista	Alexander Clark
Gremio	William Wendt
Hortensio	Stephen John Rydell
Lucentio	Kelly Brown
Katherine	Patricia Morison
Nathaniel	Ben Gillespie
Gregory	Richard Lyle
Philip	Anthony Santiago
Petruchio	Bob Wright
Haberdasher	Loren Hightower
Innkeeper	Philip Rash
Waiter	Brown Bradley

DANCERS: Myrna Aaron, Joanna Crosson, Ki-
ki Minor, Rande Rayburn, Joy Serio, Lucia
Lambert, Esther Villavicencio, Ben Gillespie,
Loren Hightower, Richard Lyle, Paul Olson,
Don Redlich, Anthony Santiago, Michael Wha-
ley

SINGERS: Patricia Finch, Margaret Goz, Mad-
eline Kahn, Jeanne Shea, Maureen Smith,
Elsie Warner, Lynn Wendell, Maggie Worth,
Brown Bradley, Jack L. Fletcher, Don Hender-
son, Bill Kennedy, Philip Rash, Stephen John
Rydell, William Wendt

UNDERSTUDIES: Lilli, Maggie Worth; Fred,
Jack L. Fletcher; Lois, Jeanne Shea; Harry,
Harrison, Eugene R. Wood; Hattie, Margaret
Goz; Paul, Ernest Brown; Hortensio, Philip
Rash; Gremio, Bill Kennedy; Doorman, Don
Henderson.

MUSICAL NUMBERS: "Another Op'nin',
Another Show," "Why Can't You Behave?,"
"Wunderbar," "So In Love," "We Open In
Venice," "Tom, Dick or Harry," "I've Come
To Wive It Wealthily In Padua," "I Hate
Men," "Were Thine That Special Face," "I
Sing Of Love," "Kiss Me, Kate," "Too Darn
Hot," "Where Is The Life That Late I Led?,"
"Always True To You In My Fashion," "Bian-
ca," "Brush Up Your Shakespeare," "Pav-
anne," "I Am Ashamed That Women Are So
Simple," Finale.

A Musical Comedy in two acts and seventeen
scenes. The action takes place on the stage of
the Ford Theatre in Baltimore.

General Manager: Homer Poupart
Company Manager: Catherine Parsons
Press: Tom Trenkle
State Managers: John Maxtone-Graham,
William H. Batchelder, Alyce Elizabeth Webb

° Closed Sunday, May 30, 1965. (23 per-
formances)
For original production, see THEATRE
WORLD, Vol. 5. In the cast were Patricia
Morison, Alfred Drake, Lisa Kirk, and Harold
Lang. It opened Dec. 30, 1948 and ran for
1077 performances.

Alix Jeffry Photos

Jesse White, Patricia Morison, Bob Wright,
Nancy Ames, Kelly Brown, Alexander Clark
Above: Charles Cook, Tiger Haynes, Ernest Brown

Bob Wright, Patricia Morison

OFF-BROADWAY

SULLIVAN STREET PLAYHOUSE
Opened Tuesday, May 3, 1960.°
Lore Noto presents:

THE FANTASTICKS

Book and Lyrics by Tom Jones; Music, Harvey Schmidt; Suggested by the Play "Les Romantiques" by Edmond Rostand; Directed by Word Baker; Musical Direction and Arrangements, Julian Stein; Designed by Ed Wittstein; Associate Producers, Sheldon Baron, Dorothy Olim, Robert Alan Gold; Assistant to the Producer, Sherman Wayne.

CAST
The Narrator	John Cunningham†1
The Girl	Royce Lenelle†2
The Boy	Jack Blackton†3
The Boy's Father	George Riddle†4
The Girl's Father	Maurice Edwards†5
The Actor	Lowry Miller
The Man Who Dies	Robert A. Worms†6
The Mute	James Cook†7
The Handyman	Richard Drake

MUSICAL NUMBERS: Overture, "Try To Remember," "Much More," "Metaphor," "Never Say No," "It Depends On What You Pay," "Soon It's Gonna Rain," "Rape Ballet," "Happy Ending," "This Plum Is Too Ripe," "I Can See it," "Plant A Radish," "Round and Round," "They Were You," Finale.

A Musical in two acts.

Press: Harvey Sabinson, David Powers
Stage Managers: Geoffry Brown, Edward Garrabrandt, Ronald Link

° Still playing May 31, 1965. (2,112 performances) For original production, see THEATRE WORLD, Vol. 16.

† Succeeded by: 1. John Boni, 2. B. J. Ward, 3. Gary Krawford, Bob Spencer, 4. Donald Babcock, David Sabin, 5. John J. Martin, 6. Curt Williams, 7. Frank Giraci, Richard Barrie.

Bert Andrews

CIRCLE IN THE SQUARE
Opened Monday, December 23, 1963.°
Theodore Mann presents:

THE TROJAN WOMEN

By Euripides; Translated by Edith Hamilton; Staged and Choreographed by Michael Cacoyannis; Music, Jean Prodromides; Costumes, Theoni V. Aldredge; Lighting, Jules Fisher; Chorus Master, Erin Martin.

CAST
Hecuba	Carolyn Coates, Gretchen Kanne
Talthybius	Alan Mixon†1
Cassandra	Carrie Nye†2
Andromache	Joyce Ebert†3
Astynax	Christopher Mann†4, Michael Walker
Helen	Jane White†5
Menelaus	Robert Mandan†6
Voice of Poseidon	Rod Steiger
Greek Soldiers	James O'Hanlon†7, Alan Wendl†8

TROJAN WOMEN: Kay Chevalier, Elaine Kerr, Karen Ludwig, Erin Martin, Dixie Marquis, Dimitra Steris, Maria Tucci, Gretchen Kanne, Marilyn McKenna, Florence Peters, Brita Brown, Tamara Daniel, Lucy Martin, Etaine O'Malley, Lorraine Serabian, Laura Stuart, Joanna Walton, Ann Tarlov.

A Drama presented without intermission. The action takes place outside the walls of Troy following the fall of Troy.

Press: Lawrence Witchell, David Lipsky
Stage Manager: Don Garner, Ron Bruncati

° Closed May 30, 1965. (600 performances) For original production, see THEATRE WORLD, Vol. 20.

† Succeeded by: 1. George Morgan, 2. Elaine Kerr, 3. Shirley Cox, 4. Frank Coleman 4th, 5. Dimitra Steris, 6. Philip Sterling, 7. James McDonald, 8. Donald Hague

Sam Siegel Photos

Left: B. J. Ward, John Boni. Top: John J. Martin, Bob Spencer, B. J. Ward, Donald Babcock

Robert Mandan, Dimitra Steris, Carolyn Coates in "The Trojan Women"

THE NEW THEATRE
Opened Wednesday, May 27, 1964.°
The Establishment Theatre Company Inc.
presents:

THE KNACK

By Ann Jellicoe; Directed by Mike Nichols; Scenery, Ed Wittstein; Clothes, Theoni V. Aldredge; Lighting, Roger Morgan; Executive Producer, Ivor David Balding; Assistant to the Producers, Annie Langdon; Technical Director, David Geary; Production Manager, Eli Ask.

CAST

Tom	Brian Bedford
Colin	Roddy Maude-Roxby†1
Tolen	George Segal†2
Nancy	Alexandra Berlin†3

UNDERSTUDIES: Ronald Roston, Susan Tyrrell

A Comedy in three acts. The action takes place at the present time in Tom's flat in Colin's house in London.

Company Manager: Thomas B. Burrows
Press: Bill Doll & Co., Shirley Herz, Robert Ganshaw
Stage Managers: Eli Ask, Ronald Roston

° Still playing May 31, 1965.
For original production, see THEATRE WORLD, Vol. 20.
† Succeeded by: 1. Sam Waterston, 2. Brian Murray, Paul Savior, 3. Lee Lawson

Martha Swope Photos

Left: Sam Waterston, Brian Bedford, Lee Lawson, Paul Savior. Above: Paul Savior, Lee Lawson

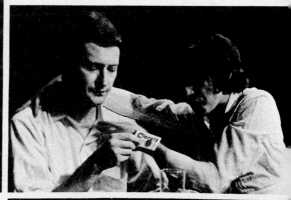

VILLAGE SOUTH THEATRE

Opened Monday, June 1, 1964.°
Ellen Stewart presents:

SO, WHO'S AFRAID OF EDWARD ALBEE?

By David Starkweather; Directed by Robert Dagny; Lighting, John Dodd.

CAST

Colin	Dan DeMott
Mabel	Judy Granite

and

THE RECLUSE

By Paul Foster; Directed by Robert Dagny; Lighting, John Dodd.

CAST

The Recluse	Sala Staw
Jezebel	Bryarly Lee

Press: Walter David
Stage Manager: James Dwyer

° Closed Sunday, June 7, 1964. (8 performances)

Sala Staw. Above: Dan DeMott, Judy Granite

Anna Russell

Opened Monday, June 15, 1964.°
Richard L. Martin presents:

ALL BY MYSELF

Sketches, Lyrics, and Music by Anna Russell; Directed by Kurt Cerf; Setting, Robert E. Darling; Costumes, Stephanya; At the piano, Frank Bartholomew; Technical Assistant, LaRue Watts; Executve Assistant, Sally Steindler.

CAST

Anna Russell

ACT I: A Summer Festival, Festival President, Prima Donna, Madrigal Group, Lieder Singer, Ballad Singer, At The Art Exhibit, Contemporary Music, Les Cigarettes, South American Polite and Rude, Cossack, Community Sing.

ACT II: Backwards With The Popular Song, The Latest, Schizophrenic, Chlorophyl Solly, Santa Claus, Red Hot Mamma, That Man, Hamletto.

A One-Woman Revue presented in two parts.

General Manager: Manheim L. Fox
Press: Karl Bernstein, Ben Kornzweig, Michael Sean O'Shea
Stage Manager: Mitchell Edmonds

° Closed Saturday, July 18, 1964. (40 performances)

MERMAID THEATRE

Opened Thursday, June 18, 1964.°
The Social and Educational Drama Association presents:

ONE IS A LONELY NUMBER

By Burnes Anderson; Directed by Lester Philcox; Associate Director, Ronald Roston; Set, Jennifer Carroll; Lighting, Fred Bohne.

CAST

Susan Westerly	Mary Lynn Layton
Spike	Carmine Stipo
Charlie Gardiner	Henry D. Heffner
Kate Westerly	Ann Noble
Rev. Robert Potter	Ronald Roston
Ruby Miller	Helen Martin
Miss Phillips	Tracey Phelps
Grandmother	Gil Gilliland

A Drama in three acts and four scenes. The action takes place at the present time in a room in a tenement building.

Press: David Lipsky
Stage Manager: Gil Gilliland

° Closed Sunday, June 21, 1964. (6 performances)

Right: Helen Martin, Mary Lynn Layton

ACTORS PLAYHOUSE

Opened Wednesday, June 24, 1964.°
Jay Stanwyck presents:

WORLD OF ILLUSION

Written and Directed by Lionel Shepard; Music, Alan De Mause; Slides, Rosalind Zaman; Lighting, Eric Gertner; Production Coordinator, Alice Knick.

CAST

Lionel Shepard

Hallie Goodman	Daniel Landau
Lily Tomlin	Richard Gilden, Narrator

Alan De Mause, Guitar Lynn Cushman, Flute

PART I: Introduction, Mime and Man, In The Beginning, The Pattern, Rebirth and The Life Cycle, The Pattern Continues, The Cage, William Overcast, The Giant, Rope.

PART II: The Jabberwock, The Brass Ring, The Golden Boat, Improvisations, Pastorale, Rope.

A Mime's view of Man's World in fables with music and narration, presented in two parts.

Company Manager: Jay Stanwyck
Press: Chester Fox, Max Karper
Stage Managers: Eric Gertner, Leroy Taylor

° Closed Sunday, August 23, 1964, after a limited engagement.

Hallie Goodman, Lionel Shepard, Daniel Landau, Lily Tomlin

Severn Darden, Barbara Dana, Alan Arkin
Right: Alan Arkin, Barbara Dana

GATE THEATRE

Opened Monday, September 14, 1964.°
Stuart Duncan and Edgar Lansberry present:

THE ALCHEMIST

By Ben Jonson; Directed by Stephen Porter;
Scenery and Costumes, Lloyd Burlingame;
Lighting, Gilbert Hemsley.

CAST

Face	Roy R. Scheider
Subtle	John Heffernan
Doll Common	Carole Macho
Dapper	Alan Mixon
Abel Drugger	Wayne Tippit
Sir Epicure Mammon	Philip Minor
Pertinax Surly	Robert Stattel
Ananias	James Cahill
Tribulation Wholesome	Mario Siletti
Kastril	Ira Lewis
Dame Pliant	Cynthia Bebout
Lovewit	Edward Grover

Neighbors, Officers Madison P. Mason, James
Nesbit Clark, Louise Stein, Robert Gerlach

A Comedy presented in two parts. The action takes place in Lovewit's house in the Blackfriars District of London in the autumn of 1610.

General Manager: Joseph Beruh
Company Manager: Al Isaac
Press: Karl Bernstein
Stage Managers: Fred Rein, Madison P.
Mason

° Closed Saturday, October 24, 1964. (46 performances)

Friedman-Abeles Photos

A VIEW FROM UNDER THE BRIDGE

Scenes and Dialogue created by the company;
Directed by Sheldon Patinkin; Music, William
Mathieu and Alan Arkin; Lyrics, Paul Sills,
David Shepherd, David Arkin, Leigh Hunt,
Roger Bowen, Alan Arkin; Stage Photograph
Slides, Alan Arkin; Technical Direction and
Lighting Design, Dan Butt; Theatre and Stage
Designed by Ralph Alswang.

CAST

Alan Arkin	Barbara Dana	Severn Darden

A Revue in two parts. Everything is subject to change . . . with or without notice.

General Manager: Felice Rose
Press: Seymour Krawitz, Merle Debuskey

° Closed Sunday, October 25, 1964. (94 performances)

Friedman-Abeles Photo

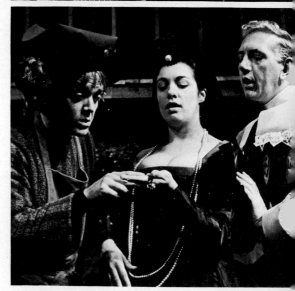

Wayne Tippit, Carole Macho, John Heffernan

THEATRE FOUR

Opened Wednesday, September 23, 1964.°
Bonard Productions in association with
Katherine and Justin Sturm present:

THAT HAT!

Book, Music, and Lyrics by Cy Young; Adapted from "An Italian Straw Hat" by Eugene Labiche and Marc-Michel; Directed and Choreographed by Dania Krupska; Musical Direction and Arrangements, Gerald Alters; Scenery and Costumes, Bill Hargate; Lighting, Patricia Collins; Production Assistants, Judy Rosenthal, John Canemaker; Associate Choreographer, Stuart Hodes.

CAST

Horse	Fabian Stuart, Dallas Edmunds
Ferdinand Goddard	Pierre Olaf
Uncle Virgil	Jerome Collamore
Osbert Norman	Alfred Dennis
Helene Norman	Merle Louise
Photographer	Ted August
Casper Bernard	Joe Ross
Angele Bernard	Carmen Alvarez
Baroness de Champigny	Elmarie Wendel
Clara	Barbara Sharma
Emile Duval	Jose Duval
Flower Girl	Ann Rachel
Gentleman Friend	Bradford Craig
Maybelle	Jeanna Belkin
Virginie	Jean Deeks
Felix	David Bean
Theobald	Lew Horn
Head Shop Girl	Joyce Maret
Jacques	John Canemaker
Viscount	John Toland
Count	Lew Horn
Countess	Jean Deeks
Jean	Louis Johnson
Nisnardi	Bradford Craig

RELATIVES: Ted August, John Canemaker, Dallas Edmunds, Beth-Lynne Low, Joyce Maret, Ann Rachel, Sandy Reed, Fabian Stuart.

MUSICAL NUMBERS: "Exposition," "Italian Straw Hat," "My Husband," "Do A Little Exercise," "Draw Me A Circle," "It's All Off," "Sound Of The Night," "I Love A Man," "Interlude," "Sounds of The Day," "A Tete a Tete," "The Apology," "My, It's Been Grand," "We Have Never Met," "Give Me A Pinch," "A Pot Of Myrtle," "The Mad Ballet," "This World of Confusion," Finale.

A Musical Comedy in two acts and fourteen scenes. The action takes place in 1895 in Paris.

Manager: Ronald S. Lee
Press: Howard Atlee, Anne Woll
Stage Manager: David Bamberger

° Closed Wednesday, September 23, 1964. (1 performance)

Bert Andrews Photo

Kelly Wood, Nancy Carroll in "Cindy"

Pierre Olaf in "That Hat!"

ORPHEUM THEATRE

Opened Thursday, September 24, 1964.°
(Moved Tuesday, January 19, 1965 to the Cricket Theatre)
Chandler Warren and Philip Temple (by arrangement with Stuart Wiener and Jerry Grace) present:

CINDY

Lyrics and Music, Johnny Brandon; Book, Joe Sauter and Mike Sawyer; Directed and Choreographed by Marvin Gordon; Musical Director, Sammy Benskin; Orchestrations, Clark McClellan; Scenery, Robert T. Williams; Costumes, Patricia Quinn Stuart; Lighting, Martin Aronstein; Technical Director, Skip Palmer; Piano, Sammy Benskin; Drums, Herb Lovelle; Musical Numbers Restaged for the Cricket Theatre by Tommy Karaty; Directed for the Cricket Theatre by Ruth Nastasi.

CAST

Storytellers:	
Thelma Olvier	Herself
Rick Landon	Himself
Mark Stone	Himself†1
Cindy Kreller	Kelly Wood†2
Lucky	Jerry Wilkins†3
Della Kreller	Mary Betten†4
Golda Kreller	Amelia Varney
Papa Kreller	Frank Nastasi†5
David Rosenfeld	Mike Sawyer
Mama Kreller	Nancy Carroll†6
Ruth Rosenfeld	Lizabeth Pritchett††7
Chuck Rosenfeld	Joseph Masiell†8

MUSICAL NUMBERS: "Overture," "Once Upon A Time," "Let's Pretend," "Is There Something To What He Said?," "Papa, Let's Do It Again," "A Genuine Feminine Girl," "Cindy," "Think Mink," "Tonight's The Night," "Who Am I?," "Ballroom Squence," "Entr' Acte," "Opening," "If You've Got It, You've Got It," "The Life That I Had Planned For Him," "If It's Love," "Got The World In The Palm Of My Hands," "Call Me Lucky," "Laugh It Up," "What A Wedding," "Finale."

A Musical in two acts and twelve scenes. The action takes place in the Kreller Delicatessen and Home, and the Rosenfeld penthouse.

Company Manager: Anne Sloper, Harold Herman
Press: Bernard and Avivah Simon
Stage Managers: Skip Rognlien, Skip Palmer

° Closed Sunday, May 2, 1965. (318 performances).
° Opened originally at the Gate Theatre on March 19, 1964, and closed June 21, 1964. See THEATRE WORLD, Vol. 20.
† Succeeded by: 1. Michael Loman, Charles Abbate, Robert Becker, 2. Isabelle Farrell, 3. Tommy Karaty, Rick Landon, 4. Alice Beardsley, 5. David Howard, 6. Milly Weitz, 7. Elizabeth Parrish, Evelyn Bell, 8. Joe Bellomo

Bert Andrews Photo

ACTORS PLAYHOUSE

Opened Thursday, October 1, 1964.°
Dorothy G. Fields and John B. Lauria in
association with Patricia Martin present:

KISS MAMA

By George Panetta; Directed by Ruth Rawson;
Setting and Costumes, Jack Cornwell; Lighting, Roger Morgan; Production Assistant, Harry Grier; Production Associates, Jules Bacal,
Jerome Handman, Sid Lerner, Gene Schinto.

CAST

Mama	Augusta Ciolli
Papa	Rudolf Weiss
Betty	Peggy Pope
Frank	Tom Pedi
George	Julius LaRosa†1
Susie	Francine Beers
Peter	Val Bisoglio
Evelyn	Rose Gregorio†2

A Comedy in two acts and five scenes. The
action takes place in our time, in the Spring, in
the living room of the Caparuta house some-
where in New York City.

General Manager: Roy Franklyn
Press: Abner D. Klipstein, Maxine Keith
Stage Manager: Henry Sutton

° Closed Sunday, January 24, 1965. (142 per-
formances)
† Succeeded by: 1. Tony Musante, 2. Linda
Lavin

Julius LaRosa, Rose Gregorio, Augusta Ciolli,
Rudolph Weiss

PHOENIX THEATRE

Opened Monday, October 5, 1964.°
The Phoenix Theatre presents:

THE TRAGICAL HISTORIE OF DOCTOR FAUSTUS

By Christopher Marlow; Directed by Word
Baker; Settings, Ed Wittstein; Costumes, Patri-
cia Zipprodt and Martha Gould; Music, Robert
Prince; Lighting, Jules Fisher; Choreography,
D. Kagan; Technical Directors, Ken Kothe, Ted
Graeber; Production Assistants, Miskit Airth,
Ann Ledley.

CAST

The Scholars:

Faustus	Lou Antonio†
Wagner	Julian Miller
First Scholar	William Larsen
Second Scholar	David Margulies

The Angels:

Good	Nancy Barrett
Evil	Tobi Weinberg

The Devils:

Mephistophilis	James Ray
Lucifer	Gary Maxwell
Belzebub	Richard Branda
Cornelius, Wrath, Martino	Vincent Baggetta
Valdez, Raymond, Emperor Carolus V	Ian Jenkins
Gluttony, Bruno	William Larsen
Pope, Darius	David Margulies
Pride, Cardina, Frederick	Dylan Green
Horse-Courser, Archbishop	William Devane
Covetousness, Empress, Lady-in-Waiting	Lisa Richards
Sloth, German Lady, Duchess of Anholt	Suzanne Osborne
Lechery, German Lady, Helen	Dorothy Tristan
Ugly Wife, German Lady, Inn Hostess	Sue Murdock
Envy, German Lady, Anholt Lady	Jill Michaels
Servant, Flag Boy	George Addis
Cardinal	Dickson Beall
German Lord, Cardinal	James Hall
Cardinal	Hagen Powell
Servant, Flag Boy	David Sigel
Benvolio, Servant, Monk	Stanley Soble
Curtain Boy, Baliol, Page	Janet Spencer
Curtain Boy, Belcher, Page	Carol Dooley

The Clowns:

Robin	Kevin Mitchell
Dick	Jake Dengel
Ralph	Robert Greenwald
Wagner's Boy	Robert Ronan

A Drama presented in two parts. The action
takes place in the Sixteenth Century, in and
around the world.

General Manager: Norman Kean
Production Manager: Marilyn S. Miller
Press: Ben Kornzweig, Robert Ganshaw,
Paul Solomon
Stage Managers: George Daveris, Robert
Greenwald

° Closed Sunday, November 29, 1964. (64
performances)
† Succeeded by Ken Ruta.

Lou Antonio, James Ray. Above: Ken Ruta,
Tobi Weinberg

150

Alix Jeffry Photos

THEATRE DE LYS

Opened Friday, October 9, 1964.°
Fredana Productions present:

GOGO LOVES YOU

Book by Anita Loos; Music by Claude Leveillee; Lyrics by Gladys Shelley; Directed by Fred Weintraub; Musical Numbers Staged by Marvin Gordon; Musical Arrangements and Direction, Everett Gordon; Setting, Kert Lundell; Costumes, Alfred Lehman; Lighting, Jules Fisher; Assistant to Producers, Anna Marie Stramese; Production Assistant, David Whittemore.

CAST

Hortense	Sandy Suter
Bert	Gene Lindsey
Papa Potasse	Walter "Dutch" Miller
Count Stanislaus De La Ferronniere	Arnold Soboloff
Gogo	Judy Henske
Mme. Bernoux	Dorothy Greener
Amelia	Janet Lee Parker
LaBaume	Ted Chapman
Racinet	Roy Hausen
Dancers	JoAnn Lehmann, Nomi Mitty, Rosemarie Ocasio, Donna Smith, Peter Hamparian, Jim Hovis

MUSICAL NUMBERS: "Parnasse," "Prima Donna," "Bazoom," "He Can, I Can," "Gogo," "There Is No Difference," "Keep In Touch," "My Uncle's Mistress," "Happy Love Affair," "Tell Me The Story Of Your Life," "Woman Makes The Man," "Life Is Lovely," "College Of L'Amour," "Savoir Faire," "Quell Heure Est-il?," Finale.

A Musical Comedy in two acts and eleven scenes. The action takes place in France.

General Manager: Joe Beruh
Company Manager: Myron Weinberg
Press: Dorothy Ross, Richard O'Brien
Stage Manager: Heinz Hohenwald

° Closed Saturday, October 10, 1964. (2 performances)

Werner J. Kuhn Photo

Dorothy Greener, Judy Henske, Arnold Soboloff in "Gogo Loves You"

Michael Berkson, George Marcy

MAYFAIR THEATRE

Opened Sunday, October 18, 1964.°
Marion Javits presents, by arrangement with Michael Codron:

HANG DOWN YOUR HEAD AND DIE

Devised by David Wright; Directed and Choreographed by Braham Murray; Designed by Fred Voelpel; Musical Direction, Jonathan Anderson; Supervised by Stevens Productions Inc.; Production Associate, Ronald Bruguiere.

CAST

Michael Berkson	Gerome Ragni
Ben Bryant	Remak Ramsay
Jordan Charney	Virginia Mason
David Garfield	Jenny O'Hara
Charles Gray	Jill O'Hara
Robert Jackson	Teri Phillips
George Marcy	Ria Tawney
Paul Michael	Nancy Tribush
James Rado	

A Revue in two parts.

Company Manager: Moses Baruch
Press: Samuel Lurie, Warren Pincus, Stanley F. Kaminsky
Stage Managers: Iris Merlis, Ria Tawney

° Closed Sunday, October 18, 1964. (1 performance)

Friedman-Abeles Photo

ASTOR PLACE PLAYHOUSE

Opened Monday, October 19, 1964.°
Muriel Morse and Jay Stanwyck present:

THAT 5 A.M. JAZZ

By Will Holt; Directed by Michael Kahn;
Sets, Lloyd Burlingame; Lighting, Milton Duke;
Musical Staging, Sandra Devlin; Associate Producer, Joe Regan; Music and Lyrics for Part
II by Will Holt; Musical Arrangements, Ted
Simons; Production Coordinator, Alice Knick;
Technical Director, David Abel.

CAST

Part I—"The First"
5 A.M.—A World's Fair

The First	James Coco
The Maker	Jerry Jarrett
Little Eva	Ruth Jaroslow

Part II—"5 A.M. Jazz"
5 A.M.—A Hotel Suite in Las Vegas

Frances	Dolly Jonah
Warren	Lester James
Musicians	The Sons Of The West
Piano	Will Holt
Guitar	Vinnie Rogers

MUSICAL NUMBERS: "Some Sunday,"
"Campaign Song," "Gonna Get A Woman,"
"The Happy Daze Saloon," "The All-American
Two-Step," "Sweet Time," "Nuevo Laredo,"
"Those Were The Days."

A Play with music.

General Manager: Muriel Morse
Press: Abner D. Klipstein, Maxine Keith
Stage Manager: Fred Reinglas

° Closed Sunday, January 10, 1965. (94 performances)

James Coco, Jerry Jarrett, Ruth Jaroslow
Above: Lester James, Dolly Jonah

Fred Hodges, Frank O'Connor, A. J. Embie,
Sam Haigler Henry, Rick Wernli, Howard Honig
in "The Comforter"

BLACKFRIARS' THEATRE

Opened Wednesday, October 21, 1964.°
The Blackfriars' Guild presents:

THE COMFORTER

By Rev. Edward A. Molloy; Directed by Walter Cool; Settings and Lighting, Allen Edward
Klein; Costumes, Alice Merrigal.

CAST

Giovanni Stefanori	Jack O'Connor, Frank Melfo
Father Robert Leiber	Fred Hodges, Nicholas Murray
Monsignor Domenico Tardini	Rick Wernli, David Ross Fendrick
Monsignor Giovanni Montini	Howard Honig, Frank Emerson
Luigi Cardinal Maglione	Sam Haigler Henry, Wolf S. Landsman
Pope Pius XII	A. J. Embie, Donald Bishop
Monsignor Orsinego	William McGuire, Tom Kelsey
Monsignor Duca	Cornelius Frizell, Michael Bruen
Monsignor Valeri	Steven Parris, Anthony Osnato
Monsignor Cortesi	Lawrence J. Buckley, Eugene Heller
Monsignor Godfrey	John F. Rush, Dennis P. Barry
Rabbi Anton Zolli	Paul Ernest, Leslie LaMont
Monsignor Baldelli	John F. Rush, Dennis P. Barry
Pietro Nenni	Steven Parris, Anthony Osnato
Alcide De Gasperi	Lawrence J. Buckley, Eugene Heller
Dom Guiseppe Morosini	Richard Christian-Danus, Ray Fisher
Field Marshall Albert Kesselring	William McGuire, Tom Kelsey
Reporter	Richard Christian-Danus, Ray Fisher
Pope Paul VI	Howard Honig, Frank Emerson

(First actors listed perform Wednesday, Thursday, Friday, and Saturday evenings, second
named perform Tuesday evenings, and Saturday and Sunday matinees.)

A Drama in two acts and six scenes with a
prologue and epilogue. The action takes place
in The Pope's summer residence at Castel Gandolfo, and in The Vatican, from 1939 to 1964.

Stage Managers: Robert Charles, Judy Smith

° Closed Sunday, December 13, 1964. (62
performances)

Bert Andrews Photos

PLAYERS THEATRE

Opened Monday, October 26, 1964.°
Joe Manchester in association with J. M.
Fried presents:

THE SECRET LIFE OF WALTER MITTY

Book, Joe Manchester; Based on Story by
James Thurber; Additional Dialogue, Mervyn
Nelson; Music, Leon Carr; Lyrics, Earl Shu-
man; Staged by Mervyn Nelson; Choreography, Bob Arlen; Sets and Lighting, Lloyd Burlingame; Arrangements, Ray Ellis; Costumes,
Joseph Stecko; Costumes, Al Lehman; Production Assistant, Michele Mordana.

CAST

Walter Mitty .... Marc London
Agnes Mitty .... Lorraine Serabian
Maude .... Susan Lehman
Peninnah .... Christopher Norris
Harry .... Rudy Tronto
Willa .... Cathryn Damon
Irving .... Charles Rydell
Ruthie .... Lette Rehnolds
Fred Gorman .... Eugene Roche
Hazel .... Rue McClanahan
Insurance Broker .... Edmund Belson
Real Estate Salesman .... Peter DeMaio
Travel Agent .... Christian Grey
Adelaide .... Caroline Worth Darnell
McMillan .... Nick Athas
Cameo Roles .... Nick Athas, Edmund Belson,
   Caroline Worth Darnell, Peter DeMaio,
   Christian Grey, Susan Lehman, Rue Mc-
   Clanahan, Lette Rehnolds
Orchestra .... Sande Campbell, Bill Stanley,
   Larry Jacobs, Al DeMateo

MUSICAL NUMBERS: "The Secret Life,"
"The Walter Mitty March," "By The Time I'm
Forty," "Walking With Peninnah," "Drip,
Drop Tapoketa," "Aggie," "Don't Forget,"
"Marriage Is For Old Folks," "Hello, I Love
You," "Willa," "Confidence," "Two Little
Pussycats," "Fan The Flame," "She's Talking
Out," "You're Not," "Lonely Ones."

A Musical Comedy in two acts with epilogue
and prologue. The action takes place at the
present time in Waterbury, Conn., in the every-
day and secret life of Walter Mitty.

Press: Frank Goodman, Ben Kornzweig
Stage Managers: Bob Mullen,
Christian Grey

° Closed Sunday, January 3, 1965. (96 performances)

Friedman-Abeles Photos

Lorraine Serabian, Marc London, Rudy Tronto,
Gene Roche, Cathryn Damon. Above: Susan
Lehman, Marc London, Lorraine Serabian,
Christopher Norris

RENATA THEATRE

Opened Wednesday, October 28, 1964.°
Tom Millott in association with Rea Warg
presents:

SHOUT FROM THE ROOFTOPS

By Jess Gregg; Directed by Tom Millott;
Scenery and Costumes, Duane A. Cline; Light-
ing, Mickey J. Burns, Jr.; Incidental Music,
William J. Goldenberg.

CAST

Dena .... Susan Towers
Russ .... Donald Scardino
Aldo Cerelli .... Jerome Guardino
Whitey .... Fran Malis
Claire Dirkee .... Betty Low
Connie Cerelli .... Grayson Hall
Floyd Cobas .... George Coe
Father Wriggins .... William Hughes

A Drama in three acts and seven scenes.
The action takes place at the present time on a
tenement roof.

Press: Sol Jacobson, Lewis Harmon,
Earl Butler
Stage Manager: Blair McFadden

° Closed Sunday, November 8, 1964. (15 performances)

Bert Andrews Photo

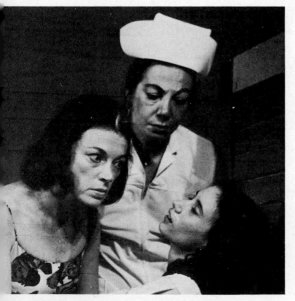

Grayson Hall, Fran Malis, Susan Towers

Jack Ryland, Lester Rawlins, Roscoe Lee Browne

AMERICAN PLACE THEATRE

Opened Sunday, November 1, 1964.°
The American Place Theatre in association
with Jean B. Webster presents:

THE OLD GLORY

By Robert Lowell; Source material: Haw-
thorne's "My Kinsman, Major Molineux," Morton's "New Canaan," Melville's "Benito Cereno"; Directed by Jonathan Miller; Scenery
and Lighting, Will Steven Armstrong; Costumes, Willa Kim; Music, Yehudi Wyner; Choreography, Esther Brooks; Artistic Supervisor,
Wynn Handman; Associate, Michael Tolan;
Production Assistant, Michael Schultz; Technical Director, Don Berry.

Part I

"My Kinsman, Major Molineux"

CAST

Robin	Thomas J. Stubblefield
Boy (his brother)	Blaise Morton
Ferryman	Clayton Corbin
Redcoats	William Jacobson, Robert Tinsley
First Barber	Jay Doyle
Tavern Keeper	George Spelvin
Man with pewter mug	James Zaferes
Clergyman	Thomas Barbour
Prostitute	Scottie MacGregor
Colonel Greenough	Tom McDermott
Man in periwig	Heywood Hale Broun
Watchman	Jack Ryland
Major Molineux	Gaylord C. Mason

CITIZENS OF BOSTON: Howard Martin,
Luke Andreas, Conway Wilson-Young, Richard
Kjelland, Sigrunn Waage, Antonie Becker, M.
Emmet Walsh, Martha Neag, James Zaferes,
Jill Malin, Paul Plummer, Virginia Brown,
George A. Sharpe.

A Political Cartoon. The action takes place
in Boston just before the American Revolution.

Part II

"Benito Cereno"

CAST

Capt. Amasa Delano	Lester Rawlins
John Perkins	Jack Ryland
Don Benito Cereno	Frank Langella
Babu	Roscoe Lee Browne
Atufal	Clayton Corbin
Francesco	Michael Schultz

SPANISH SAILORS: Luke Andreas, William
Jacobson, James Zaferes

AMERICAN SAILORS: Conway Wilson-
Young, Robert Tinsley, Richard Kjelland, M.
Emmet Walsh, Howard Martin

NEGRO SLAVES: Woodie King, Lonnie Ste-
vens, George A. Sharpe, Herman Fitzgerald,
Ernest Baxter, Aston Young, June Brown, Mary
Foreman, Gene Foreman, Judith Byrd, M. S.
Mitchell, Lane Floyd, Paul Plummer, Walter
Jones, Ethan Courtney

A Realistic Tragedy. The action takes place
about 1800 on the decks of the President
Adams, an American sailing vessel, and the San
Domingo, a Spanish slave ship.

General Manager: John Hornberger
Press: Martin Shwartz, Joe Wolhander
Stage Managers: Peter Galambos,
Michael Schultz

° Closed Saturday, December 12, 1964. (36
performances)
"Benito Cereno" re-opened at the Theatre
DeLys, under the sponsorship of Lucille Lor-
tel, Inc., and Jean B. Webster, Thursday,
Jan. 14, 1965. Mark Lenard as Capt. Del-
ano, and James Patterson as Benito were the
only major changes. During the run, Clayton
Corbin was succeeded by Cliff Frazier, then
Lane E. Floyd. This revival closed Sunday,
March 28, 1965, after 86 performances.

Friedman-Abeles Photos

**Top and Left Center: Lester Rawlins,
Roscoe Lee Browne, Jack Ryland, Frank Langella**

THEATRE FOUR

Opened Sunday, November 8, 1964.°
Robert S. Fishko, John A. Prescott, David Rubinson, in association with George Avakian, present:

THE CRADLE WILL ROCK

By Marc Blitzstein; Directed by Howard Da Silva; Musical Director, Gershon Kingsley; Musical Consultant, Leonard Bernstein; Choreography, Rhoda Levine.

CAST

Moll	Lauri Peters
Gent	Ted Scott
Dick	Wayne Tucker
Cop	Ben Bryant
Reverend Salvation	Chris Warfield
Editor Daily	Dean Dittmann
Yasha	Hal Buckley
Dauber	Clifford David
President Prexy	Hal Buckley
Professor Trixie	Clifford David
Professor Mamie	Nichols Grimes
Scott	Chris Warfield
Dr. Specialist	Ben Bryant
Druggist	Peter Meersman
Mrs. Mister	Nancy Andrews
Junior Mister	Joseph Bova
Sister Mister	Rita Gardner†
Mr. Mister	Gordon B. Clarke
Steve	Nichols Grimes
Sadie Polock	Karen Cleary
Gus Polock	Ted Scott
Bugs	Wayne Tucker
Larry Foreman	Jerry Orbach
Ella Hammer	Micki Grant
Clerk	Gershon Kingsley

A Drama with music in two acts and ten scenes. The action takes place in Steeltown, U.S.A. during a union drive.

Company Manager: Arthur Glicksman
General Manager: Robert Cherin
Press: Samuel J. Friedman, Jane Friedman
Stage Manager: Ron Bruncati

° Closed Sunday, January 17, 1965. (82 performances)
† Succeeded by Kay Cole.

Friedman-Abeles Photos

**Left: Joseph Bova, Rita Gardner
Above: Peter Meersman, Nichols Grimes,
Wayne Tucker, Karen Cleary, Ted Scott**

CHERRY LANE THEATER

Opened Monday, November 16, 1964.°
Theater 1965 (Richard Barr-Clinton Wilder) presents:

THE GIANTS' DANCE

By Otis Bigelow; Directed by Jack Sydow; Designed by William Ritman; Costumes, Fred Voelpel.

CAST

Geoffrey	Leonard Drum
Queen Boudicca	Alice Drummond
Prince Yvain	Bill Fletcher
Princess Alissande	Kelly Jean Peters
Merlin	Dillon Evans
King Ambrose of Brittona	Boris Tumarin
Arch-Druid Grigas	Wyman Pendleton
Rufus Septimus	Terence Scammell
General Nud	Herbert Voland
Soldiers	George Sampson, James Scheller

UNDERSTUDIES: Ambrose, Merlin, Grigas, Ted Tiller; Geoffrey, Nud, Murray Gitlin; Yvain, Rufus, George Sampson; Boudicca, Alissande, Vicki Blankenship.

A Comedy in three acts. The action takes place in the Palace of Ambrose I of Brittona, a kingdom in the west of England, in the year 470 A.D.

General Director: Michael Kasdan
Administrative Director: Barry Plaxen
Press: Howard Atlee, Michael Alpert, David Roggensack
Stage Managers: Arthur Pepine, Murray Gitlin

° Closed Saturday, November 21, 1964. (6 performances)

Alix Jeffry Photo

Boris Tumarin, Wyman Pendleton, George Sampson, Terence Scammell, James Scheller, Leonard Drum 155

ONE SHERIDAN SQUARE

Opened Tuesday, November 17, 1964.°
Dionus Ltd. presents:

ROUTE 1

By John Wolfson; Directed by Robert Mac-
Gowan; Designed by Dave Moon; Costumes,
Clifford Capone; Lighting, William B. Warfel;
Production Coordinator, Dean Delk; Technical
Director, William B. Warfel; Production As-
sistant, Maggie Dominic.

CAST

Father Beausargus	David O. Petersen
Raunch Hump	Walter Rhodes
Purity Blackbush	Joyce Jillson
Celery Firch	Victoria Rauch
Coon Hump	John Canemaker
Mother Hump	Avril Gentles
Reverend Flap	Jay Barney
Mother Firch	Betty Bright

A Comedy in one act. The action takes
place on Mother Hump's radish farm outside
Blastoma, Florida, Route 1, south of the Georgia border in spring.

General Manager: Jay Rosenblatt
Press: David Lipsky
Stage Manager: Robert C. Buzzell

° Closed Tuesday, November 17, 1964. (1
performance)

Bert Andrews Photo
**Right: Pirie MacDonald, Jered Barclay
Below: Robert Hooks, Jennifer West**

David O. Petersen, Joyce Jillson, Victoria Rauch

CHERRY LANE THEATRE

Opened Tuesday, November 24, 1964.°
Theater 1964 (Richard Barr, Clinton Wilder, Edward Albee) presents:

THE ZOO STORY

By Edward Albee; Directed by Edward Parone; Production Designed by William Ritman.

CAST

Jerry	Jered Barclay
Peter	Pirie MacDonald†1

The action takes place at the present time on
a Sunday afternoon in Central Park.

DUTCHMAN

By LeRoi Jones; Directed by Edward Parone; Production Designed by William Ritman.

CAST

Clay	Robert Hooks
Lula	Jennifer West†2
Passengers	Sue Carol Davis, Peter DeAnda, Harvey Selsby, Richard Mansfield

The action takes place at the present time on
a subway train.

General Director: Michael Kasdan
Administrative Director: Barry Plaxen
Press: Howard Atlee, Michael Alpert,
David Roggensack
Stage Manager: Charles Kindl

° Closed Saturday, February 6, 1965, after 102
performances for "The Zoo Story" and 366
for "Dutchman" which opened March 24,
1964.
† Succeeded by: 1. Ted Tiller, 2. Beverlee Mc-
Kinsey

Alix Jeffry Photos

THEATRE DE LYS

Opened Wednesday, November 25, 1964.°
Lucille Lortel Productions, Inc. present:

I KNOCK AT THE DOOR

Adapted by Paul Shyre from Sean O'Casey's
autobiographical novel; Directed by Mr. Shyre;
Designed by Eldon Elder; Production Assistants, Dennis Helfend, David Harlan.

CAST

Rae Allen	Paul Shyre
Robert Walker	Stephen Elliott
Jessie Royce Landis	Staats Cotsworth

Standbys: Jen Jones, Dermot McNamara

Presented in two parts.

General Manager: Joseph Beruh
Company Manager: Mike Weinberg
Press: Lawrence Witchel, David Lipsky,
Marian Graham, Lisa Lipsky
Stage Manager: Jacqueline Donnet

° Closed Friday, December 11, 1964 after a
limited engagement of 18 performances.

Bert Andrews Photo

**Paul Shyre, Jessie Royce Landis, Robert Walker,
Staats Cotsworth**

GRAMERCY ARTS THEATRE

Opened Tuesday, December 8, 1964.°
Manon Productions in association with
Persam Company present:

ON THE NECESSITY OF BEING POLYGAMOUS

By Silveira Sampaio; Translated by Roberto
Campos; Director, R. Martin; Designed by
Richard Shoemaker; Choreography, R. J. Lev-
ick; Consultant, William Hickey.

CAST

Marta	Liz Ingleson
Petunio	Robert Barend
Elvira	Maggie Shook
Daliacopulos	Stephen Strimpell
Government Official	Michael Henry
Professor	Jack Adams

A Comedy in three acts. The action takes
place at the present time in Rio de Janeiro,
before and during Carnival.

Press: Sol Jacobson, Lewis Harmon,
Earl Butler
Stage Manager: Judd Hirsch
° Closed Sunday, January 3, 1965. (31 per-
formances)

Bert Andrews Photo

WRITERS STAGE THEATRE

Opened Wednesday, December 9, 1964.°
Caroline Swann and Martin Lee present:

THE NEW PINTER PLAYS

By Harold Pinter; Directed by Word Baker;
Settings, Ed Wittstein; Lighting, Roger Morgan; Costumes, Caley Summers.

"The Room"

Burt Hudd	Clarence Felder†1
Rose	Frances Sternhagen
Mr. Kidd	Ralph Drischell†2
Mr. Sands	Ian Jenkins
Mrs. Sands	Margaret Linn†3
Riley	Robertearl Jones

"A Slight Ache"

Flora	Frances Sternhagen
Edward	Henderson Forsythe
Matchseller	Ralph Drischell†2

UNDERSTUDIES: Flora, Margaret Linn; Edward, Ralph Drischell; Matchseller, Clarence
Felder

General Manager: Paul Libin
Press: Bill Doll, Midori Tsuji, Shirley Herz,
Richard Spittel
Stage Managers: Bill Young, Ralph Drischell
° Still playing May 31, 1965.
† Succeeded by: 1. C. Thomas Blackwell, 2.
Jay Hampton, 3. Joan Kendall

Impact Photos

Maggie Shook, Robert Barend, Stephen Strimpell,
Liz Ingleson

Henderson Forsythe, Frances Sternhagen
in "A Slight Ache"

Frances Sternhagen, Robertearl Jones
in "The Room"

BOUWERIE LANE THEATRE

Opened Thursday, December 10, 1964.°
Matthew Stander presents:

HELEN

By Wallace Gray; Directed by Michael
Kahn; Settings and Lighting, Robert Darling;
Costumes, Willa Kim; Music, John Corigliano;
Assistant to the Producer, Melinda Page; Technical Director, Joe Guadagni; Dances Arranged by Richard Smithies.

CAST

Aphrodite	Sally Gracie
Telemachus	Nicolas Surovy
Peisistratos	Jack Burns
Helen	Katharine Balfour
Athena	Myra Carter
Menelaus	Ray Reinhardt

Understudy for Aphrodite, Helen, and Athena—Clorissa Kaye

A Comedy-Drama in two acts. The action takes place in and around the palace of Menelaus in Sparta on a Spring day.

Press: Betty Lee Hunt, Marie Pucci
Stage Managers: Don Gilliland, Bill
Mikulewicz

° Closed Sunday, December 27, 1965. (30 performances)

Friedman-Abeles Photo

Nicolas Surovy, Katharine Balfour,
Ray Reinhardt

Blair Nation, Vivian Nielsen

THEATRE DE LYS

Opened Wednesday, December 16, 1964.°
Lucille Lortel Productions, Inc. presents:

PICTURES IN THE HALLWAY

Adapted by Paul Shyre from Sean O'Casey's autobiographical novel; Directed by Mr. Shyre; Designed by Eldon Elder; Production Assistants, Dennis Helfend, David Harlan.

CAST

Rae Allen	Paul Shyre
Robert Walker	Stephen Elliott
Peggy Wood	Staats Cotsworth

Standbys: Jen Jones, Dermot McNamara

Presented in two parts.

General Manager: Joseph Beruh
Company Manager: Mike Weinberg
Press: Lawrence Witchel, David Lipsky,
Marian Graham, Lisa Lipsky
Stage Manager: Jacqueline Donnet

° Closed Sunday, January 3, 1965 after a limited engagement of 23 performances. Reopened Monday, January 18, 1965 at the Greenwich Mews Theatre with Wayne Maxwell succeeding Robert Walker, Nancy R. Pollock for Peggy Wood, Anne Meacham for Rae Allen, and Dermot McNamara for Staats Cotsworth. It ran for 24 performances and closed Sunday, February 28, 1965.

Bert Andrews Photo

ROYAL PLAYHOUSE

Opened Thursday, December 10, 1964.°
Rose Lynch presents:

THE EAGLE WITH TWO HEADS

By Jean Cocteau; English Version by Carl Wildman; Directed by Jonathan Tolliver; Scenery and Costumes, Franklin Gail Miller; Sound, Thomas Cole.

CAST

The Queen	Vivian Nielsen
Stanislas	Blair Nation
Edith von Berg	Sandra Kiersky
Duke von Willenstein	Edwin Byrd
Count von Foehn	Henry Coble
Tony	John Tisdale

A Romantic Melodrama in three acts. The action takes place in the Queen's bedroom and library at Krantz Castle in a mythical kingdom.

Press: Miss Beebe
Stage Manager: George Stahler

° Closed Sunday, January 24, 1965. (30 performances)

Stephen Elliott, Robert Walker, Peggy Wood,
Staats Cotsworth

ST. MARKS PLAYHOUSE

Opened Wednesday, December 16, 1964.°
Leo Garen and Stan Swerdlow in association with Gene Persson and Rita Fredricks present:

LE ROI JONES' 2 NEW PLAYS

By LeRoi Jones; Directed by Leo Garen; Designed by Larry Rivers; Associate Designer and Lighting by Harold Baldridge; Sound, Art Wolff; Presented in association with Theatre Vanguard.

"The Toilet"

CAST

Ora	James Spruill
Willie Love	Gary Bolling
Hines	D'Urville Martin
Johnny Holmes	Bostic Van Felton
Perry	Norman Bush
George Davis	Antonio Fargas
Donald Farrell	Gary Haynes
Knowles	Walter Jones
Skippy	Tony Hudson
Karolis	Jaime Sanchez[1]
Foots	Hampton Clanton

The action takes place at the present time in a high school boys' toilet.

"The Slave"

CAST

Walker Vessels, Very Old	Al Freeman, Jr.[2]
Walker Vessels	Al Freeman, Jr.[2]
Grace Easely	Nan Martin[3]
Bradford Easely	Jerome Raphel[4]

The action takes place some time in the future in the home of a college professor.

General Manager: Arthur Seidelman
Press: Lawrence Witchel, David Lipsky, Marian Graham
Stage Managers: Ed Cambridge, Oscar Jones

° Closed Sunday, April 25, 1965. (151 performances)
† Succeeded by: 1. Ramon Pabon, 2. Lincoln Kilpatrick, 3. Elizabeth Lawrence, 4. David Ford who was succeeded by Vincent Collins

Bert Andrews Photos

Right: Jerome Raphel, Al Freeman, Jr., Nan Martin in "The Slave". Above: Jaime Sanchez (RC) in "The Toilet"

Alan Mixon, Lester Rawlins, Alan Bunce, Paul McGrath

GARRICK THEATRE

Opened Monday, December 21, 1964.°
Theatre Guild Productions presents:

THE CHILD BUYER

By Paul Shyre; Adapted from John Hersey's Novel of the same name; Directed by Richard Altman; Setting and Lighting, Eldon Elder; Associate Producer, Don Herbert; Production Assistant, Mark Durand; Costume Supervision, Bill Collier.

CAST

Guard	Mark Durand
Mr. Broadbent	Alan Mixon
Court Stenographer	Barbara Alloway
Senator Canfield	Paul McGrath
Senator Skypack	Alan Bunce
Senator Voyolko	John C. Becher
Mrs. Paul Rudd	Marian Reardon
Dr. Gozar	Dee Victor
Charity Perrin	Jane Hoffman
Wissey Jones	Lester Rawlins
Paul Rudd	Charles Durning
Barry Rudd	Brian Chapin
Willard Owing	Wyman Pendleton
Mrs. Sloat	Nancy Cushman
Charles Perkonian	Christopher Votos

UNDERSTUDIES: Mrs. Sloat, Charity, Mrs. Rudd, Dr. Gozar, Kate Wilkinson; Voyolko, Skypack, Canfield, Owing, Wissey, Charles Durning; Broadbent, Mark Durand; Barry, Charles, Frank Hubert

A Drama in three acts. The action takes place in a Senate Hearing Room in a New England State Capitol.

General Manager: Ron Singer
Press: Nat and Irvin Dorfman
Stage Managers: Charles Durning, John Actman

° Closed Sunday, January 17, 1965. (32 performances)

Alix Jeffry Photo

FORTY-FIRST STREET THEATRE

Opened Saturday, December 26, 1964.°
DM Productions Inc. present:

HER MASTER'S VOICE

By Clare Kummer; Staged by Don Doherty; Sets and Lighting, Elmon Webb; Costumes, Lohr Wilson; Song "Only With You" by Clare Kummer.

CAST

Queena Farrar _____ Gloria Willis
Mrs. Martin _____ Doro Merande
Ned Farrar _____ Don Doherty
Craddock _____ William Hawley
Aunt Min _____ Elizabeth Kerr
Mr. Twilling _____ John Cecil Holm
Phoebe _____ Anne Ives

UNDERSTUDIES: Mr. Twilling, William Hawley; Mrs. Martin, Aunt Min, Anne Ives.

A Comedy in two acts and five scenes. The action takes place in 1933 in the living room of the Farrars' house in Homewood, N. J., and the sleeping porch of Aunt Min's home at Dewellyn.

Press: Robert Larkin, David Rothenberg
Stage Manager: William Hawley

° Closed Tuesday, January 12, 1965. (18 performances) Original production was presented by Max Gordon October 23, 1933 at the Plymouth Theatre and ran for 224 performances. In the cast were Elizabeth Patterson, Roland Young, and Laura Hope Crews.

Friedman-Abeles

Doro Merande, John Cecil Holm, Elizabeth Kerr

ORPHEUM THEATRE

Opened Monday, December 28, 1964.°
Sandy Farber and Aaron Schroeder present:

BABES IN THE WOOD

Lyrics, Music, Book and Direction by Rick Besoyan; Dances and Musical Numbers Staged by Ralph Beaumont; Costumes, Howard Barker; Sets and Lighting, Paul Morrison; Music Arranged and Orchestrated by Arnold Goland; Musical Direction, Natalie Charlson; Production Assistant, Abby Steinberg.

CAST

Oberon _____ Richard Charles Hoh
Robin Goodfellow _____ Elmarie Wendel
Titania _____ Carol Glade
Helena _____ Ruth Buzzi
Demetrius _____ Danny Carroll
Bottom _____ Kenneth McMillan
Lysander _____ Don Stewart
Hermia _____ Joleen Fodor
An Addition _____ Edward Miller

MUSICAL NUMBERS: "This State Of Affairs," "Titania's Philosophy," "A Lover Waits," "The Gossip Song," "I'm Not For You," "Mother," "Old Fashioned Girl," "Love Is Lovely," "Babes In The Wood," "Anyone Can Make A Mistake," "Cavorting," "There's A Girl," "Little Tear," "Helena's Solution," "Helena," "Midsummer Night," "Moon Madness," "The Alphabet Song," Finale.

A Musical in two acts. The action takes place in 300 B.C. on a midsummer night in a wood near Athens.

General Manager: David Lawlor
Company Manager: Paul Vroom
Press: Robert Larkin, David Rothenberg
Stage Managers: Edward Royce, Gary Farr

° Closed Sunday, February 7, 1965. (45 performances)

Friedman-Abeles Photos

Danny Carroll, Ruth Buzzi, Don Stewart

Center Left: Ruth Buzzi, Danny Carroll, Kenneth McMillan, Richard Charles Hoh, Carol Glade, Elmarie Wendel

RENATA THEATRE

Opened Wednesday. December 30, 1964.°
Bella Rosenberg, George Bellak, and Oscar Zurer present:

PLAY WITH A TIGER

By Doris Lessing; Directed by George Bellak; Production Designed by Kim Swados; Production Assistant, Zirel Handler.

CAST

Tom Lattimer	Leslie Redford
Anna Freeman	Janet Ward
Mary Jackson	Virginia Downing
Harry Payne	Frederick Rolf
Janet Stevens	Jenny O'Hara
Dave Miller	Barney Kates

A Drama in two acts. The action takes place in Anna Freeman's apartment on the second floor of a small house in London, during a single October night at the present time.

Press: Reginald Denenholz
Stage Managers: Ivan Uttal, Dick Bard

° Closed Sunday, January 17, 1965. (23 performances)

Bert Andrews Photo

Right: Leslie Redford, Virginia Downing, Janet Ward, Frederick Rolf

Peter Lombard, Adale O'Brien, Tom Wheatley, John Granger

GATE THEATRE

Opened Thursday, January 7, 1965.°
Theatre Guild Productions and Joseph E. Levine present:

ALL WOMEN ARE ONE

By Ben Kerner; Directed by Peter Kass; Setting and Lighting, James Nisbet Clark; Costumes, Peter Harvey; Associate Producer, Ron Singer; Production Assistant, June Rovenger; Hair Styles, Dorman Allison.

CAST

The Widow, Regina Bosco	Marian Seldes
The Professor, Gelati Trivelino	Paul E. Richards
The Wrestler, Cicerone Palpitini	Louis Zorin

A Play in two acts and four scenes.

General Manager: Ron Singer
Press: Nat and Irvin Dorfman, Harold Rand
Stage Manager: Robert Borod

° Closed Sunday, January 10, 1965. (6 performances)

Alix Jeffry Photo

STAGE 73

Opened Monday, January 4, 1965.°
The Whodunit Company (Robert D. Feldstein, Amnon Kabatchnik, Derek Mali) presents:

THE CAT AND THE CANARY

By John Willard; Directed by Amnon Kabatchnik; Designed by Paul Morrison; Assistant to the Producers, Doris Blum; Technical Assistant, Ken Starrett; Production Assistants, Robert Pollack, Ed Baram.

CAST

Maria Pleasant	Helen Martin†1
Roger Crosby	Bruce Kimes†2
Harry Blythe	Peter Lombard
Susan Sillsby	Beth Holland
Cecily Young	Mona Abboud
Charles Wilder	John Granger†3
Paul Jones	Tom Wheatley
Annabelle West	Adale O'Brien
Hendricks	Abe Vigoda
Patterson	Paul Andor

UNDERSTUDIES: Annabelle, Rowena Balos; Maria, Rosalind Mason; Cecily, Doris Medd; Crosby, Patterson, Robert Buchanan; Susan, Celia Howard; Charles, Harry, Duane Morris; Hendricks, Robert Gans; Paul, Ralph Goodman.

A Mystery Melodrama in three acts. The action takes place at Glencliff Manor on the Hudson, on September 27, 1921.

Press: David Lipsky, Lawrence Witchel, Marian Graham
Stage Manager: Robert Stevenson

° Closed Sunday, May 9, 1965. (143 performances)
† Succeeded by: 1. Fran Bennett, 2. Albert M. Ottenheimer, 3. Duane Morris.

Marian Seldes, Paul E. Richards

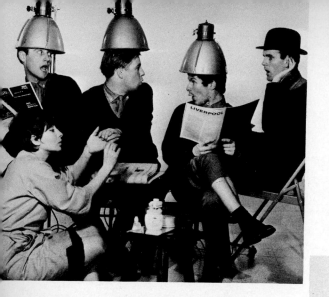

Jean Hart, David Hatch, Tim Brooke-Taylor,
Bill Oddie, John Cleese. Right: Jean Hart,
Bill Oddie

SQUARE EAST

Opened Thursday, January 14, 1965.°
Square East presents:

NEW CAMBRIDGE CIRCUS

Written by the cast with additional material
by John Cameron, Graham Chapman, Terry
Jones, and "Clap Hands" Company; Pianist
and Arranger, Sean Petran; Music, Bill Oddie;
Lighting, Peder Ness; Additional Arrangement,
John Cameron.

CAST
Jean Hart

Tim Brooke-Taylor   John Cleese
David Hatch   Bill Oddie

A Musical Revue in two parts.
General Manager: Felice Rose
Press: Merle Debuskey, Seymour Krawitz,
Lawrence Belling

° Closed Sunday, March 21, 1965. (78 performances)

Friedman-Abeles Photos

MAIDMAN PLAYHOUSE

Opened Tuesday, January 26, 1965.°
Cartoon Productions present:

THE FOURTH PIG
and
THE FISHERMAN

By Richard W. Harris; Directed by Bob
Scarpato; Scenery and Lighting, John J. Moore;
Costumes, Ed Fricke; Associate Producer, A.
M. Lucha; Production Assistants, Rea Turet,
Tom Gibson.

CAST

"The Fisherman"

The Lieutenant	Art Kassul
Officer Galvin	Steve Telman
Peter Mitchell	Peter Maloney

"The Fourth Pig"

Will	Don Becker
Min	Karen Johnson
Mary Werlin	Jayne Heller
Lotte Werlin	Norma Mindell
Ellen Louise	Diana Walker
Tyrone LaBlanche	Mel Gordon
Dr. Hans Ignoble	Tom Lacy
Fuller Merritt	Steve Telman
Goodfellow Pincher	Peter Maloney
Emily Dryline	Marion Present
Montague Formsworth	John Lemley
Herman Hunch	Art Kassul

Press: Howard Atlee, David Roggensack
Stage Manager: Carol Lucha

° Closed Wednesday, January 27, 1965. (2
performances)

Bert Andrews Photo

Mel Gordon, Diana Walker, Karen Johnson

Paul Collins, Nancy Andrews

JAN HUS PLAYHOUSE

Opened Wednesday, January 27, 1965.°
North-Wood Productions Ltd. presents:

SAY NOTHING

By James Hanley; Directed by William
Hunt; Sets and Lighting, David F. Segal; Costumes, David Rudish; Special Music, Jack
Hitchcock; Production Assistants, Eugene Taylor, James Boerlin.

CAST

Joshua	Rex O'Malley
Mrs. Baines	Nancy Andrews
Charlie Elston	Paul Collins
Winifred	Helen Stenborg

A Drama in two acts and five scenes. The
action takes place at the present time in the
Baines' house and Joshua's Backyard "Den" in
Garlston, a small industrial city in the north of
England, and in the Garlston cemetery.

Company Manager: Joseph Leberman
Press: Sol Jacobson, Lewis Harmon,
Earl Butler
Stage Manager: Gladys Riddle

° Closed Sunday, March 7, 1965. (47 performances)

SHERIDAN SQUARE PLAYHOUSE

Opened Thursday, January 28, 1965.°
Ulu Grosbard, Joseph E. Levine and
Katzka-Berne Corp. present:

A VIEW FROM THE BRIDGE

By Arthur Miller; Directed by Ulu Grosbard;
Designed by Robin Wagner; Lighting, John
McLain; Costumes, Doreen Ackerman; Sound,
Gigi Cascio; Assistant to the Director, Dustin
Hoffman; Production Assistant, Dean Delk.

CAST

Louis	Richard Castellano
Mike	Carmine Caridi
Alfieri	Mitchell Jason†
Eddie	Robert Duvall
Catherine	Susan Anspach
Beatrice	Jeanne Kaplan
Marco	Ramon Bieri
Tony	Gino Morra
Rodolpho	Jon Voight
1st Immigration Officer	Dan Priest
2nd Immigration Officer	Curt Dempster
Mr. Lipari	William Corio
Mrs. Lipari	Bea Brooks
"Submarines"	Noel Parente, Constantine Katsanos

UNDERSTUDIES: Eddie, James Tolkan; Alfieri, Gino Morra; Marco, Constantine Katsanos;
Rodolpho, Noel Parente; Beatrice, Bea Brooks;
Catherine, Jo Kelner.

A Drama in two acts. The action takes place
at the present time.

General Manager: Joseph Beruh
Company Manager: Jewel Howard
Press: David Lipsky, Lawrence Witchel,
Max Karper, Marian Graham
Stage Manager: Bud Schweich

° Still playing May 31, 1965.
† Succeeded by Val Bioglio

Henry Grossman Photos

**Robert Duvall, Jon Voight. Above: Robert Duvall
with Susan Anspach (R), Jeanne Kaplan (L)** **163**

POCKET THEATRE

Opened Monday, February 8, 1965.°
J. Alan Ornstein and James Mishler present:

FRIDAY NIGHT

By James Elward; Directed by Herbert Kenwith; Settings and Costumes, Jack H. Cornwell; Lighting, Roger Morgan; Production Manager, Harry Eno.

CAST

"Friday Night"

Terry	Jan Sterling
Yvonne	Margaret DePriest
The Girl	Eunice Brandon
The Man	Byron Sanders
Waitress	Elva Meehan

The action takes place last Friday night at 7 P.M. in the backroom of a bar, south of Fourteenth Street in New York City.

"Passport"

Charlie Meseger	Don Fellows

The action takes place at midnight in the livingroom of Charlie's apartment in the West 80's in New York City.

"Mary Agnes Is Thirty-Five"

Mary	Jan Sterling
Sam	Don Fellows

The action takes place at 3 A.M. in Mary's apartment east of Second Avenue in New York City.

General Manager: Jeff Britton
Press: Howard Atlee, Warren Pincus, David Roggensack

° Closed Sunday, February 28, 1965. (23 performances)

Bert Andrews Photo

Jan Sterling, Eunice Brandon, Margaret DePriest

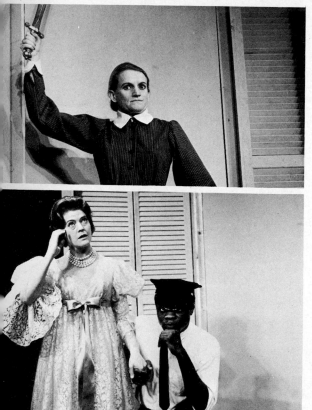

BOUWERIE LANE THEATRE

Opened Tuesday, February 9, 1965.°
Marge Sundgaard presents:

THE GREAT WESTERN UNION

By Ethan Ayer; Directed by Cyril Simon; Scenery and Costumes by Lloyd Burlingame; Lighting, Roger Morgan; Sound, New Sound Associates; Assistant to Producer, Robert Woods; Associate Set Designer, Milton Duke; Technical Director, Joe Guadagni.

CAST

Lavinia	Michaele Myers
Robert	Jon Cypher
Eminence	Ronald Weyand
Kubla	Yaphet Kotto
First Cop	Louis W. Waldon
Second Cop	Frederick Combs
Matron	Sudie Bond

Understudy: Morrie Peirce

Presented in three acts. The action takes place Now and Then, Here and Abroad.

General Manager: David Preston
Press: Arthur Cantor, Artie Solomon, Angela Nardelli, Betty Taylor
Stage Managers: Jerome Michael, Morrie Peirce

° Closed Saturday, February 13, 1965. (5 performances)

Michaele Myers, Yaphet Kotto
Above: Sudie Bond

CHERRY LANE THEATRE

Opened Wednesday, February 10, 1965.*
Theater 1965 (Richard Barr, Clinton Wilder, Edward Albee) presents:

FIRST EVENING OF NEW PLAYWRIGHTS
"Up To Thursday"

By Sam Shepard; Directed by Charles Gnys.
CAST

Young Man	Lee Kissman
First Man	Richard Mansfield
Second Man	Harvey Keitel
Terry	Stephanie Gordon
Sherry	Joyce Aaron
Larry	Robert F. Lyons
Harry	Kevin O'Connor

"Balls"

By Paul Foster; Directed by Syndey Schubert Walter; Original Music, Gary William Friedman.

CAST

"Commodore" Wilkinson	Paul Boesing
Beau Beau	James Barbosa
Miss McCutcheon	Shirley Stoler
Nasty Brat	Anthony Bastiano
Young Lovers	Shellie Feldman, Paul Boesing
Woman Who Had No Shadow	Claire Leyba
Military Commander	James Barbosa

The action takes place in a cemetery by the sea, an ancient place . . . the sea has washed away the land and claimed all the graves except two . . . Night.

"Home Free!"

By Lanford Wilson; Directed by Marshall W. Mason.

CAST

Lawrence	Michael Warren Powell
Joanna	Joanna Miles

The action takes place in early spring in the apartment of Joanna and Lawrence Brown.

General Director: Michael Kasdan
Administrative Director: Barry Plaxen
Press: Howard Atlee, Warren Pincus, David Roggensack
Stage Manager: Charles Kindl

* Closed Sunday, February 28, 1965. (23 performances)

Alix Jeffry Photos

Right: Joanna Miles, Michael Warren Powell in "Home Free!" Above: Harvey Keitel, Lee Kissman, Richard Mansfield in "Up To Thursday"

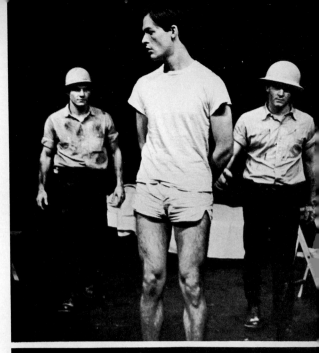

Mark Stone, Wayne Whitehill, Lynne Waggoner in "Once Upon A Mouse"

ROYAL PLAYHOUSE

Opened Thursday, February 11, 1965.*
Rose Lynch presents:

TWO BY PARKER

By Ken Parker; Directed by Steve Chernak; Lighting, Lynne Waggoner; Music, Ronnie Ward.

"ONCE UPON A MOUSE"
CAST

Hortensia	Arlene Sukoenig
Sylvanus	Wayne Whitehill
Osmund	Joe Picaro

A One Act Comedy-Drama. The action takes place at 7:30 P.M. at the present time in New York.

"THE KNOWING ONE"
CAST

Granny Raye	Dorothy N. S. Russell
Jill Raye	Sandra Rosenthal
Claire Raye	Reed Meredith Wolcott
David Raye	Tom Cole
Guest Star Spot	Johnnie Lee MacFadden
Mike	George Stahler

A Comedy-Drama in two parts with three scenes. The action takes place in the living room of the Raye family.

Press: Miss Beebe
Stage Manager: Lynne Waggoner

* Still playing May 31, 1965.

ACTORS PLAYHOUSE

Opened Monday, February 15, 1965.°
Richard R. Chandler and Bruce W. Stark present The Actors Studio Workshop Production of:

THE SWEET ENEMY

By Joyce Carol Oates; Directed by Frank Corsaro; Scenery and Costumes by Peter Harvey; Lighting, V. C. Fuqua.

CAST

Wolf	Bill Moor
Emanuel	Richard Ward
Eva	Alexandra Holland
Rhone Lee	Michael Hadge
Halloween Children	Larry Dove, Shelby Hiatt, Patrick Sullivan

UNDERSTUDIES: Emanuel, Arnold Johnson; Rhone, Larry Dove; Eva, Shelby Hiatt; Wolf, Patrick Sullivan.

A Play in two acts.

Press: Betty Lee Hunt
Stage Manager: D. S. Wilson

° Closed Sunday, February 21, 1965 (8 performances)

Martha Holmes Photo

Richard Ward, Alexandra Holland, Bill Moor

THE BLACKFRIARS' THEATRE

Opened Thursday, February 18, 1965.°
The Blackfriars' Guild presents:

PATRICK—THE FIRST

By Rev. Brendan Larnen; Directed by Walter Cool; Settings and Lighting, Allen Edward Klein; Costumes, Alice Merrigal; Dialogue Coordinator, Jerry Buckley.

CAST

King Eoghaidh	Reb Buxton, Joseph Cazalet
Princess Cynnia	Celia Howard, Carol Gutenberg
Nuala	Janeen Forest, Cindy Pigue
Cormack	Walter Hadler, Tom Baker
Patrick	Roderic Prindle, Ed Rombola

A Drama in three acts and four scenes. The entire action takes place in a room within the residence of King Eoghaidh, near Clogher, in Ulster, Ireland, more than fifteen and a half centuries ago.

Press: Rev. Thomas F. Carey
Stage Managers: Robert Charles, Judy Smith

° Closed Sunday, May 16, 1965. (90 performances)

Janeen Forest, Celia Howard, Roderic Prindle, Reb Buxton

GARRICK THEATRE

Opened Tuesday, February 23, 1965.°
David Fulford and William Dempsey present:

COLOMBE

By Jean Anouilh; Adpated by Denis Cannan; Directed by David Fulford; Sets, Lewis Stone Greenleaf III; Costumes, Margaretta Maganini; Lighting, V. C. Fuqua; Music Consultant, Crawford Wright; Technical Director, Stanley Rosenberg; Technical Coordinator, William A. Hominuke; Theme Music, Rack Godwin, George Lloyd.

CAST

Madame Alexandra	Cavada Humphrey
Julien	Marco St. John
Paul	George Reinholt
Colombe	Carol Teitel
Emile Robinet	Robert Ronan
Desfournettes	Walter Miller
Lagarde	George Lloyd
Madame Georges	Elizabeth Thurman
Surette	Lance Cunard
Hairdresser	Al Corbin
Manicurist	Peggy Osborne
Stagehands	James Marmon, Walter Brown

A Comedy in three acts with an epilogue. The action takes place at a theatre in Paris in 1900.

Press: Howard Atlee, Warren Pincus, David Roggensack
Stage Manager: Robert Trenour

° Closed Sunday, March 7, 1965. (13 performances)

Cavada Humphrey, Carol Teitel

Alix Jeffry Photo

THEATRE FOUR

Opened Thursday, February 25, 1965.°
Robert Fletcher and Richard Horner present:

THE QUEEN AND THE REBELS

By Ugo Betti; Directed by Paul Shyre; Scenery and Lighting, John Boyt; Costumes, Henry Heymann.

CAST

Porter	Rik Colitti
Engineer	Norman Barrs
Amos	Michael Higgins
Elisabetta	Clarice Blackburn
Argia	Tamara Geva
A Traveller	William Bush
Raim	Conrad Bain
Biante	Khigh Dhiegh
Maupa	George Sampson
Peasant Woman	Dorothy Stinnette
Peasant Man	Ed Penn
Peasant Boy	Jason Gero
Soldiers	Clay Johns, Bruce Monette
Travellers	David Jackson, Jud Davis, Thomas Smith
Peasants	Louise Stein, Beatrice Lunick, Robert Sinclair

A Drama in two acts and four scenes. The action takes place in the Town Hall of a European mountain village.

Company Manager: Robert Cherin
Press: Harvey Sabinson, Bob Ullman
Stage Managers: Chris Mahan, Clay Johns

° Closed Sunday, March 14, 1965. (22 performances)

Sam Siegel Photo

Top Right: Clarice Blackburn, Tamara Geva

CHERRY LANE THEATRE

Opened Wednesday, March 3, 1965.°
Theater 1965 (Richard Barr, Clinton Wilder, Edward Albee) presents:

SECOND EVENING OF NEW PLAYWRIGHTS "PIGEONS"

By Lawrence Osgood; Directed by Edward Parone.

CAST

First Woman	Charlotte Jones
Second Woman	Marian Reardon
Third Woman	Geraldine Fitzgerald

The action takes place on a bright fall afternoon inside a vacant lot in New York City at the present time.

"CONERICO WAS HERE TO STAY"

By Frank Gagliano; Directed by Melvin Bernhardt.

CAST

Yam	Mark Gordon
Woman	Vicki Blankenship
Voice	Charles Kindl
Blind Man	Willy Switkes
Girl With Cello	Linda Segal
Boy With Eye Patch	Jose M. Bonilla
His Friend	William Maner
Jesús	Jaime Sanchez
Another Friend	Harvey Selsby

The action takes place at the present time on a subway platform in New York City.

General Director: Michael Kasdan
Administrative Director: Barry Plaxen
Press: Howard Atlee, Warren Pincus, David Roggensack
Stage Manager: Charles Kindl

° Closed Saturday, March 20, 1965. (21 performances)

Alix Jeffry Photos

Jaime Sanchez, Mark Gordon
Above: Geraldine Fitzgerald

MAIDMAN PLAYHOUSE

Opened Monday, March 8, 1965.°
R. J. Productions presents:

A SOUND OF SILENCE

By Harold Willis; Directed by John Sillings;
Scenery and Lighting, Richard W. Segar; Costumes, Marsha L. Eck; Executive Producer,
Raymond A. League; Associate Producers, Jane
Cohen, Robert M. Holley.

CAST

Laura Northcutt	Lois Markle†
Clay Chandler	Howard Schell
Ollie	Evelyn Davis
Edward Northcutt	Michael McGuire
Cam Northcutt	John Pleshette
Louise Northcutt	Marie Masters
Mark Hendricks	Peter DeAnda
Marguerite Chandler	DeAnn Mears

UNDERSTUDIES: Bonnie Griffin, Marshal
Swerman

A Drama in two acts. The action takes place
at the present time in the Northcutt home in a
small town in Northern Louisiana.

General Manager: Raymond A. League
Press: Howard Atlee, Warren Pincus,
David Roggensack
Stage Managers: Iris Merlis, Bonnie Schwartz,
Annette Leiderman, Leonard Stephens

° Closed Sunday, May 23, 1965. (88 performances)
† Succeeded by Mary Bozeman Raines

Alix Jeffry Photos

Right: Lois Markle, John Pleshette, Marie Masters
Above: Peter DeAnda, Lois Markle

James Douglas, Muni Seroff, Phil Foster, Lou Gilbert,
Anthony Holland. Above: Lou Gilbert, Joseph Chaikin,
Royston Thomas

THE PLAYERS THEATRE

Opened Monday, March 15, 1965.°
Don Herbert and Russ Kaiser present:

TWO PLAYS BY
ARTHUR KOPIT

Directed by Gerald Freedman; Settings, Ed
Wittstein; Costumes, Willa Kim; Lighting, Tom
Skelton; Music Composed by John Morris;
Sound, Gigi Cascio.

SING TO ME THROUGH
OPEN WINDOWS

CAST

Andrew, The Boy	Royston Thomas
Ottoman, The Man	Lou Gilbert
The Clown	Joseph Chaikin

THE DAY THE WHORES
CAME OUT TO PLAY TENNIS

CAST

Old Gayve	Lou Gilbert
Alexander Ratscin	Muni Seroff
Franklin Delano Kuvl	Phil Foster
Herbert Hoover Kuvl	Anthony Holland
Duncan	John D. Irving
Rudolph	James Douglas

UNDERSTUDIES: Shimen Ruskin, Clyde Ventura, Ray Weston

The action takes place at the present time in
the nursery of the Cherry Valley Country Club.

General Managers: Joseph Beruh, Al Isaac
Company Manager: Myron Weinberg
Press: Samuel Lurie, Stanley F. Kaminsky
Stage Managers: Donald Wesley,
Clyde Ventura

° Closed Sunday, April 4, 1965. (24 performances)

GATE THEATRE

Opened Wednesday, March 17, 1965.°
Norma Frances and Robert Margulies present:

BILLY LIAR

By Keith Waterhouse and Willis Hall; Directed by Perry Bruskin; Scenery and Lighting, Karl Hueglin; Production Assistant, Joel Lawrence Thurm; Film Created and Directed by Ben Collarossi and Don Duga; Produced by Henry Traiman, Gerald Productions, Inc.; Narrated by Kathleen Roland.

CAST

Florence Boothroyd ....Ethel Griffies
Geoffrey Fisher..............................Donald Ewer
Alice Fisher ....Paddy Croft
Billy Fisher.........................Scott Hylands†
Arthur Crabtree..................Michael Berkson
Barbara....................................Margaret Linn
Rita ....Joy Gordon
Liz ....Cynthia BéBout

A Comedy in three acts. The action takes place in the Fisher home in Stradhoughton, an industrial town in the north of England today.

General Manager: Krone-Olim Management
Press: Harvey Sabinson, Robert Ullman
Stage Manager: Len Ross

° Closed Sunday, April 11, 1965. (30 performances)
† Played by Geoff Garland during Mr. Hylands' illness.

Sam Siegel Photos

Right: Ethel Griffies
Above: Scott Hylands, Margaret Linn

CHERRY LANE THEATRE

Opened Thursday, March 25, 1965.°
Theater 1965 (Richard Barr, Clinton Wilder, Edward Albee) presents:

A THIRD EVENING OF NEW PLAYWRIGHTS
"HUNTING THE JINGO BIRD"

By Kenneth Pressman; Directed by Charles Gnys.

CAST

Scoot ....Gene Scandur
J. R...John Zizak
Frazier..Paul Rufo
Walter...Jason Gero
Barney....................................Lawrence Pressman

The action takes place in a hunting cabin in the woods on a Friday evening in June of the present time.

"LOVEY"

By Joseph Morgenstern; Directed by Edward Parone.

CAST

Virginia Varnum.............................Ruth Ford
Roger Varnum................................ James Coco
Lovey ....Cynthia Belgrave
Duane Thompson.....................Victor Arnold

The action takes place in the interior of a motel on a secondary road in the South during a night of the present time.

General Director: Michael Kasdan
Administrative Director: Barry Plaxen
Press: Howard Atlee, Warren Pincus, David Roggensack
Stage Managers: Michael Kasdan, Charles Kindl, Harvey Selsby

° Closed Sunday, March 28, 1965. (6 performances)

Alix Jeffry Photo

Cynthia Belgrave, Ruth Ford

169

ORPHEUM THEATRE

Opened Monday, March 29, 1965.°
Jay Chase and James Walsh present:

MATTY AND THE MORON AND MADONNA

By Herbert Lieberman; Directed by José Quintero; Settings and Lighting, David Hays; Costumes, Noel Taylor; Musical Sound Effects, Doris Schwerin; Associate Producer, Gerald M. Ginsberg; Technical Director, Don McGovern; Assistant to the Producers, Melinda Page.

CAST

Matty Mollusca	Glenn Scimonelli
Rose Mollusca	Betty Miller
Dominick Mollusca	Felice Orlandi
Augie Henschel	Gregg Weir
Mr. Finnerty	James O'Connell
Alec Cushman	Frank Hubert
Gail	Viveca Tedesco
Twilight	Edward Espinosa
First Boy	Andrew Dunbar
Second Boy	Alan Zemel
Tommy Carbo	Louis Criscuolo
First Man	Edward Gustin
Second Man	James O'Connell
Third Man	Clifford A. Pellow
Beggar	George Petrarca
Rabbi Lichter	Leonardo Cimino
Lila Riker	Katherine Ross
Stella Rizzo	Sylvia Miles
Vito Tussi	Louis Criscuolo
Faceless	George Petrarca
Maria Esposito, Madonna	Miriam Colon
Juan Esposito	Dominick Cecala
Fantasies	Toby Glanternik, Dorothy Krooks, Leonora Landau, Lorraine Richman

A Drama in three acts. The action takes place at the present time in a New York City tenement building.

Press: Arthur Cantor, Artie Solomon, Angela Nardelli
Stage Managers: Don Garner, Edward Gustin
° Closed Sunday, April 25, 1965. (25 performances)

Right: Felice Orlandi, Katherine Ross
Above: Glenn Scimonelli, Betty Miller

THE BRIDGE

Opened Thursday, April 1, 1965.°
The Bridge Theatre presents:

TWO NEW PLAYS BY ARTHUR SAINER

Directed by Sydney Schubert Walter; Settings, Stephen Hendrickson; Costumes, Frieda Evans; Lights, Charles Norton; Music, Gary William Friedman; Production Coordinator, Brenda Steinberg.

CAST

"THE BITCH OF WAVERLY PLACE"

The Girl	Jean Armstrong

"THE BLIND ANGEL"

The Scholar	Paul Boesing
The Girl	Valerie Belden
The Little Man	Murray Paskin
The Blind Angel	Arlette Danton

UNDERSTUDIES: Dolores Welber, Murray Paskin

General Manager: Richard Volpe
Press: Roberta Weiner, Jerry Sternberg
Stage Manager: Margot Lewitin
° Closed Sunday, April 25, 1965. (50 performances)

Paul Boesing, Valerie Belden, Murray Paskin
Above: Jean Armstrong

170

Carl Bissinger Photos

Harold Lang, Elmarie Wendel, Kaye Ballard, Carmen Alvarez, William Hickey

SQUARE EAST

Opened Tuesday, March 30, 1965.°
Ben Bagley presents:

THE DECLINE AND FALL OF THE ENTIRE WORLD AS SEEN THROUGH THE EYES OF COLE PORTER REVISITED

Continuity, Special Vocal Arrangements, and Grand Finale written by Bud McCreery; Musical Numbers Directed by Vernon Lusby; Musical Direction, Arrangements, Skip Redwine; Collage Paintings, Shirley Kaplan; Projections Photographed by Wallace Litwin; Costumes and Gowns, Charles Fatone; Lighting, Jules Fisher; Cast and Material Assembled and Supervised by Ben Bagley, assisted by James Frasher.

CAST

Kaye Ballard	Harold Lang
Carmen Alvarez	William Hickey
Elmarie Wendel	

A Revue in two parts, using songs written by Cole Porter between the years 1929 and 1945.

General Manager: Felice Rose
Press: Merle Debuskey, Seymour Krawitz, Lawrence Belling
Stage Manager: James Frasher

° Still playing May 31, 1965.

Avery Willard and Friedman-Abeles Photos

Kaye Ballard   Elmarie Wendel
(also above)

Elmarie Wendel, Carmen Alvarez, Harold Lang, Kaye Ballard

171

RENATA THEATRE

Opened Monday, April 12, 1965.°
Lee Reynolds and Isobel Robins in association with Allan H. Mankoff present:

WET PAINT

Directed by Michael Ross; Musical Staging, Rudy Tronto; Scenery and Lighting, David Moon; Costumes, Mostoller; Musical Arrangement and Direction, Gerald Alters; Wigs and Hair Styling, Benjamin Murphree; Production Assistants, William Braufman, Judy Rosenthal; Material by Pat McCormick, Marc London, Judith Milan, Howard Schuman, Bob Rosenblum, Herbert Hartig, Sheldon Harnick, Lois Balk Korey, Tony Geiss, Stanley Handleman, Anne Croswell, Ed Scott, Pierre Berton, Martin Charnin, Bob Kessler, Paul Sand, Ronny Graham, David Panich, Dolly Jonah, Giles O'Connor, Stan Davis, Bob Hilliard, Johnny Myers, Paul Lynde, Jennifer Konecky, Lawrence B. Eisenberg, Betty Freedman.

CAST

Bill McCutcheon	Paul Sand
Gene Allen	Hank Garrett
Linda Lavin	Isobel Robins

General Understudy: William Braufman

PROGRAM

ACT I: "How's Elsie," "Walk Dog," "Red Moroccan Shoes," "Ventriloquy," "Concert Encore," "Potato Salad," "Neville," "No Tickee." "On The Phone," "Cantata," "Don't," "Little Woman," "Cream In My Coffee," "Shakespeare Revisited," "Love Affair," "Half-Way House," "Unrequited Love March."

ACT II: "Puns," "The Computer," "I Know He'll Understand," "The Well Boiled Icicle," "Canary," "Street Scene," "Showstopper," "It Takes A Heap," "These Things I Know Are True," "On The Phone," "Cryin' Shame," "I Spy," Finale.

A Musical revue in two acts and thirty scenes.

Manager: Lily Turner
Press: Robert Larkin, David Rothenberg
Stage Manager: George Martin

° Closed Saturday, April 24, 1965. (16 performances)

Friedman-Abeles Photos

Left: Linda Lavin, Paul Sand, Isobel Robins
Above: Bill McCutcheon, Linda Lavin, Paul Sand

CHERRY LANE THEATRE

Opened Monday, April 19, 1965.°
Theater 1965 (Richard Barr, Clinton Wilder, Edward Albee) presents:

DO NOT PASS GO

By Charles Nolte; Directed by Alan Schneider; Designed by William Ritman; Sound by Gary Harris; Production Assistants, Vicki Blankenship, Harvey Selsby.

CAST

Crawford	Charles Nolte
Lewis	Roberts Blossom

A Drama in three acts. The action takes place in the stockroom of a supermarket in California on the day before Christmas.

General Director: Michael Kasdan
Administrative Director: Barry Plaxen
Press: Howard Atlee, Warren Pincus, David Roggensack
Stage Managers: Michael Kasdan, Charles Kindl

° Closed Sunday, May 2, 1965. (16 performances)

Alix Jeffry Photo

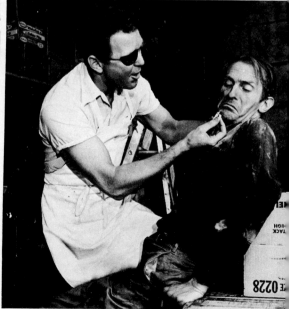

Charles Nolte, Roberts Blossom

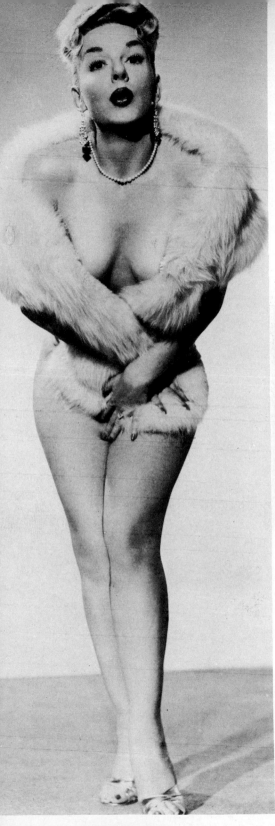

**Barbara Curtis in
"The Wonderful World Of Burlesque"**

MAYFAIR THEATRE

Opened Wednesday, April 28, 1965.°
LeRoy C. Griffith and William Berger present:

THE WONDERFUL WORLD OF BURLESQUE

Directed, Staged, and Supervised by LeRoy C. Griffith; Choreography, Guy Martin; Sets, Ed McDonnell; Costumes, Monique Starr; Lighting, Peter Xantho; Musical Director, Nick Aversano.

CAST

Yolanda Moreno

Julie Taylor	Barbara Curtis
Al Anger	Helena Jackman
Earl Van	Rosanna Faire
Bobbye Mack	Danny Jacobs
Rick Perri	

A Musical creation of the best in burlesque, past and present, presented in two parts.

PROGRAM: The Mayfairette, The M.C. and Mr. America, Strip, Love College, Mayfairette in Production Number with Rick Perri, The Telephone Scene, My Wedding Night, The Drunk Sketch, Songs by Helena Jackman, The School Room, The Grande Duchess of Burlesque, Finale.

Company Manager: Moses Baruch
Press: Richard Falk

° Still playing May 31, 1965.

Robert Blake, Lynn Bernay, David Huddleston

POCKET THEATRE

Opened Wednesday, May 5, 1965.°
Arthur Conescu and Paul Stoudt, Ltd. present:

HARRY, NOON AND NIGHT

By Ronald Ribman; Directed by David Eliscu; Designed by Charles Evans; Assistant to the Producers, Frank Geraci; Production Assistant, David Logan.

CAST

Harry	Robert Blake
Soldier	David Huddleston
Prostitute	Lynn Bernay
Archer	Gerald S. O'Loughlin
Immanuel	Jordan Charney
Woman	Lotte Stavisky
Policeman	Bruce Glover

UNDERSTUDIES: Cluney Dodge, Frank Geraci, Bruce Glover, Neal Parke.

A Dark Comedy in two parts and three scenes. The action takes place in December of 1955 in Munich, Germany in The Dolly Bar, and in Harry and Immanuel's room.

Company Manager: Arthur Conescu
Press: Joe Wolhandler, Mickie Mackay
Stage Manager: Richard Nesbitt

° Closed Sunday, May 9, 1965. (6 performances)

Friedman-Abeles Photo

MARTINIQUE THEATRE

Opened Thursday, May 6, 1965.°
Circle In The Square, Theodore Mann, and
Paul Libin present:

BAAL

By Bertolt Brecht; Adapted by Eric Bentley
and Martin Esslin; Directed by Gladys
Vaughan; Songs by Bertolt Brecht; Musical
Arrangements, Stefan Wolpe; Musical Direction, Will Holt; Setting, Robert Darling; Costumes, Noel Taylor; Lighting, Roger Morgan.

CAST

Mech	Herbert Nelson
Dr. Piller	Maury Cooper
Emily	Joan DeWeese
Baal	Mitchell Ryan
Pschierer	Leonard Hicks
Young Man	James Antonio
Young Lady	Bette Henritze
Johannes	Peter Gerety
Johanna	Kathleen Sullivan
Louise	Bette Henritze
Ekart	James Earl Jones
Horgauer	Maury Cooper
Truck Drivers	Ed Setrakian, David Gale, Lloyd Jollar, Alan Astredo, George McGrath
Elder Sister	Gilpin Oliver
Younger Sister	Lisa Weinstein
Landlady	Bette Henritze
Sophie Barger	Flora Elkins
Bum	Ed Setrakian
Chanteuse	Joan DeWeese
Lupu	James Antonio
Mjurk	Ed Setrakian
Pianist	Alan Astredo
Farmers	David Gale, George McGrath, Maury Cooper
Parson	Leonard Hicks
Teddy	Maury Cooper
Lumberjacks	Ed Setrakian, James Antonio, Herbert Nelson, Lloyd Hollar, David Gale
Bolleboll	Alan Astredo
Beggar	Leonard Hicks
Maja	Bette Henritze
Googoo	David Gale
Young Woman	Joan DeWeese
Watzmann	Ed Setrakian
Waitress	Flora Elkins
First Man	Leonard Hicks

A Drama in three acts.

Press: Lenny Traube, Marian Graham
Stage Manager: John Fenn

° Still playing May 31, 1965, in repertory with
"Othello."

Bert Andrews Photos

**Right: Mitchell Ryan, Kathleen Sullivan
Above: Bette Henritze, James Earl Jones,
Mitchell Ryan**

Kazimer Garas, Anne Meacham, Jon Cypher

STAGE 73

Opened Monday, May 17, 1965.°
Theatre: New York presents:

THE WIVES

By Lionel Abel; Directed by Herbert Machiz; Designed by Leo B. Meyer; Producers, Herbert Machiz, Leo B. Meyer; Production Assistant, Marti Knight.

CAST

First Woman	Avril Gentles
Second Woman	June Hunt
Third Woman	Jan Miner
Fourth Woman	Pegeen Lawrence
Deianeira	Anne Meacham
Hyllos	Alec Murphy
Likhas	Kazimer Garas
Iole	Fiddle Viracola
Herakles	Jon Cypher
Zeus	Leo Lucker

A Drama in two acts and three scenes. The
action takes place in the courtyard outside the
house of Deianeira.

Press: Phillip Bloom
Stage Manager: Gian Sciandra

° Still playing May 31, 1965.

174

Van Williams Photo

PLAYERS THEATRE

PLAYERS THEATRE

Opened Tuesday, May 18, 1965.°
Judith Rutherford Marechal and Paul Libin
present:

IN WHITE AMERICA

By Martin B. Duberman; Directed by Harold
Stone; Designed by Robin Wagner; Lighting,
George Blanchard; Costumes, Patricia Quinn
Stuart; Musical Director, Oscar Brand; Pro-
duction Associates, Susan Richardson, Larry
Goossen.

CAST

Elizabeth Franz	Richard Levy
Philip Baker Hall	Novella Nelson
Robert Jackson	Fred Pinkard

Music Performed by Happy Traum

A Documentary of Negro History presented
in two acts.

Stage Manager: Dale E. Whitt

° Still playing May 31, 1965. Original production opened Oct. 31, 1963 at the Sheridan
Square Playhouse and closed Jan. 3, 1965
after 499 performances. See THEATRE
WORLD, Vol. 20.

Adger Cowans Photo

Elizabeth Franz, Happy Traum, Fred Pinkard,
Novella Nelson, Robert Jackson, Richard Levy,
Philip Baker Hill

Morgan Paull, JoAnne Worley, Gloria Bleezarde,
Evelyn Russell, Ben Kukoff

CHERRY LANE THEATRE

Opened Tuesday, May 18, 1965.°
Theater 1965 presents:

THAT THING AT THE
CHERRY LANE

By Jeff Steve Harris; Additional Material by
Lesley Davison, Michael McWhinney, Jerry
Powell, Ira Wallach; Directed by Bill Penn;
Scenery, Lighting, Costumes by Fred Voelpel;
Musical Supervision, Abba Bogin; Musical Con-
ductor, Natalie Charlson; Sculptured Figures
by Charles Loubier; Sound by Garry Harris.

CAST

John C. Becher	Hugh Hurd
Gloria Bleezarde	Morgan Paull
Conard Fowkes	Evelyn Russell
Ben Kukoff	Jo Anne Worley

Understudy: Jayme Mylroie

PROGRAM: "The Long Song," "Beat This!,"
"Lady Bird," "Ragtime," "Tears," "Olympics,"
"Scotch On The Rocks," "You Won't Believe
Me," "Minnesota," "Blues," "Safety In Num-
bers," "Communication," "To Belong," "Jer-
sey," "The New York Coloring Book."

A Revue in three acts and fifteen scenes.

Administrative Director: Barry Plaxen
Press: Howard Atlee, Warren Pincus,
David Roggensack
Stage Managers: Charles Kindl, Hugh Hurd

° Closed Saturday, May 22, 1965. (6 performances)

Alix Jeffry Photos

Evelyn Russell, JoAnne Worley, Gloria Bleezarde
Above: John C. Becher, JoAnne Worley, Ben Kukoff,
Gloria Bleezarde

"H.M.S. Pinafore"

"The Mikado"

"The Gondoliers"

JAN HUS PLAYHOUSE

Opened Tuesday, May 18, 1965.°
J. G. Britton in association with M. J.
Boyer presents the sixth season of:

THE AMERICAN SAVOYARDS

Dorothy Raedler, Producer-Director.

Libretto, W. S. Gilbert; Music, Arthur Sulli-
van; Staged by Dorothy Raedler; Musical Di-
rection, Simon Sargon; Associate Producer,
Ronald Bush; Sets, Frank Wicks; Lighting,
Chuck Eisler; Associate Musical Director, Ju-
dith Somogi; At the Hammond Organ, Simon
Sargon; At the Piano, Judith Somogi; Technical
Director, Don Sims.

"IOLANTHE"

CAST

The Lord Chancellor	Robert Fields
Earl of Mountararat	John Campbell
Earl Tolloller	Edwin Sholz
Private Willis	Bruce Lawrence
Strephon	David Bennett
Queen of The Fairies	Artis Lewis
Iolanthe	Ellen Shade
Celia	Peg Dearden
Leila	Elaine Kraut
Fleta	Anne Bloch
Phyllis	Dolores Leffingwell

"H.M.S. PINAFORE"

CAST

Sir Joseph Porter	Robert Fields
Captain Corcoran	David Bennett
Tom Tucker	Susan Goeppinger
Ralph Rackstraw	Edwin Sholz
Dick Deadeye	John Campbell
Bob Bobstay	Bruce Lawrence
Bob Becket	Dan Kingman
Josephine	Dolores Leffingwell
Hebe	Ellen Shade
Mrs. Cripps (Buttercup)	Artis Lewis

"THE MIKADO"

CAST

The Mikado	John Campbell
Nanki-Poo	Edwin Sholz
Ko-Ko	Robert Fields
Pooh-Bah	Bruce Lawrence
Pish-Tush	David Bennett
Yum-Yum	Estella Munson
Pitti-Sing	Ellen Shade
Peep-Bo	Peg Dearden
Katisha	Artis Lewis

"THE GONDOLIERS"

CAST

Duke of Plaza-Toro	Robert Fields
Luiz	Jack Lines
Don Alhambra del Bolero	John Campbell
Marco Palmieri	Edwin Sholz
Giuseppe Palmieri	David Bennett
Antonio	Bruce Lawrence
Francesco	Don Derrow
Giorgio	Dan Kingman
Annibale	Don Derrow
Duchess of Plaza-Toro	Artis Lewis
Casilda	Dolores Leffingwell
Gianetta	Estella Munson
Tessa	Ellen Shade
Fiametta	Peg Dearden
Vittoria	Elaine Kraut
Giulia	Susan Goeppinger
Inez	Anne Bloch
Solo Cachucha Dancers	Anne Bloch, Kermit Klein

CHORUS: Anne Bloch, Peg Dearden, Don
Derrow, Fred-Munro Ferguson, Adrienne Fog-
ler, Susan Goeppinger, Dan Kingman, Elaine
Kraut, Bruce Lawrence, Craig Palmer, Andrea
Peters, Rhonda Saunders, Lauren Scott, Jules
Small.

Press: David Lipsky
Stage Manager: Chuck Eisler

° Still playing in repertory May 31, 1965.

Alix Jeffry Photos

THEATRE DE LYS

Opened Wednesday, May 19, 1965.°
The Establishment Theatre Co., Inc. (Directors: Ivor David Balding, Peter Cook, Joseph E. Levine) by arrangement with Lucille Lortel Productions Inc. presents:

SQUARE IN THE EYE

By Jack Gelber; Directed by Ben Shaktman; Scenery by Kim Swados; Costumes, Ruth Morley; Lighting, Jules Fisher; Film Sequences, Leonard Glasser; Sound Effects, Gigi Cascio; Executive Producer, Ivor David Balding; Production Assistant, Trisha Mortimer.

CAST

Ed Stone	Philip Bruns
Luis	Jose Perez
Sandy Stone	Carol Rossen
Al Jaffe	Gene Rupert
Jane Jaffe	Dixie Marquis
Bill, Jr.	Alan Howard
Sarah	Kerrie Lynn
Hy Becker	Alfred Dennis
Sally Becker	Eda Reiss Merin
Doc	Conrad Bain

Understudy: Bernard Passeltiner

A Drama in two acts and five scenes. The action takes place in 1962 in the Stones' workroom, a hospital, and funeral parlor.

General Manager: Thomas B. Burrows
Company Manager: Paul B. Berkowsky
Press: John Springer Associates,
Walter Alford, Mary Ward
Stage Managers: Wilder M. Snodgrass,
Brian Syron, Charles Yingling

° Still playing May 31, 1965.

Bert Andrews Photos

Alfred Dennis, Conrad Bain, Eda Reiss Merin,
Philip Bruns (also above)

Philip Bruns, Carol Rossen

GREENWICH MEWS THEATRE

Opened Thursday, May 20, 1965.°
Greenwich Players Inc. presents a Beverly
Landau, Stella Holt, Henrietta Stein pro-
duction of:

THE EXCEPTION AND
THE RULE

By Bertolt Brecht; Adapted by Eric Bentley;
Directed by Isaiah Sheffer; Music Composed by
Stefan Wolpe; Music Directed by Arnold Black;
Sets, Peter Wingate; Costumes, Eve Gribbin;
Lighting, Jim Gore; Associate Producers, Steph-
anie Sills, Yanna Brandt; Piano, Frank
Groseclose; Trumpet, Charles Sullivan; Per-
cussions, Willard Bond.

CAST

Merchant	Paul E. Richards
Coolie	Joseph Chaikin
Guide	Richard Hamilton
Leader of Second Caravan	Gary Farr
Members of Second Caravan	Johnny Harris, Joseph Attles
First Policeman	Willard Bond
Second Policeman	Charles Sullivan
Innkeeper	Joseph Attles
Guard	Johnny Harris
Coolie's Widow	Jeannette Hodge
Judge	Frank Groseclose
Associate Judge	Willard Bond

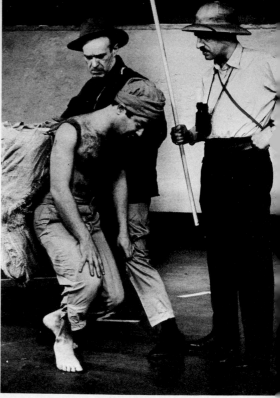

Richard Hamilton, Joseph Chaikin, Paul E. Richar
in "The Exception And The Rule"

THE PRODIGAL SON

By Langston Hughes; Directed by Vinnette
Carroll; Sets, Peter Wingate; Costumes, Eve
Gribbin; Lighting, Jim Gore; Music Arranged
and Directed by Marion Franklin; Choreography, Syvilla Fort; Piano, Marion Franklin; Organ, Robert McCann; Percussion, Willard Bond.

CAST

Sister Lord	Dorothy Drake
Brother Callius	Robert Pinkston
Prodigal Son	Philip A. Stamps
Exhorter	Joseph Attles
Father	Ronald Platts
Mother	Jeannette Hodge
Jezebel	Glory Van Scott
Brother John	Marion Franklin
Brother Alex	Johnny Harris
Sister Anna	Jean Perry
Sister Waddy	Sylvia Terry
Brother Jacob	Teddy Williams
Brother Joseph	Jeffrey Wilson
Sister Fatima	Hattie Winston

SONGS: Wade In The Water, Take The Lord
God, Rock With Jezebel, I Look Down The
Road, Devil Take Yourself Away, How I'm
Gonna Make It, Feast At The Welcome Table,
When I Touch His Garment, Fly Away
(Wings), You Better Take Time To Pray, I'm
Waiting For My Child, Done Found My Lost
Sheep, Come On In The House.

General Manager: Stella Holt
Press: Max Eisen
Stage Manager: James Gore

° Still playing May 31, 1965.

Bert Andrews Photos

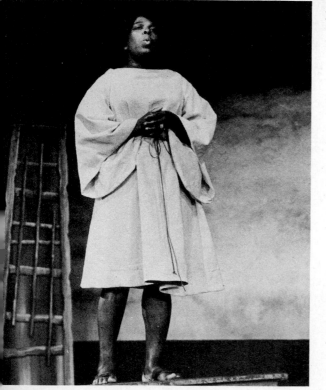

**Dorothy Drake
in "The Prodigal Son"**

BOUWERIE LANE THEATRE
Opened Wednesday, May 26, 1965.°
Waverly Productions presents:

THE UMBRELLA

By Bertrand Castelli in collaboration with Jack Raphael Guss; Directed by Robert Ellis Miller; Production Designed by Jack Lindsay; Hair Styling, Pierre Henri.

CAST

Cornelius V. Stolts_____J. D. Cannon
Sister Bonaventure_____Jan Farrand
Wango_____Reni Santoni

A Drama in two acts and four scenes. The action takes place on a desert on a lovely summer day of a post-war year.

Press: Robert W. Larkin, David P. Rothenberg
Stage Manager: Joel Thurm

° Closed Friday, May 28, 1965. (3 performances)

Friedman-Abeles Photo

Right: J. D. Cannon, Reni Santoni, Jan Farrand

OFF-BROADWAY PLAYS FROM OTHER SEASONS THAT CLOSED DURING THIS SEASON

Play	Opened	Closed	Performances
The Blacks	May 4, 1961	Sept. 27, 1964	1408
The Trojan Women	Dec. 23, 1963	May 30, 1965	600
Six Characters In Search Of An Author	March 8, 1963	June 28, 1964	529
The Boys From Syracuse	Apr. 15, 1963	June 28, 1964	500
In White America	Oct. 31, 1963	Jan. 3, 1965	497
Dutchman	March 24, 1964	Feb. 6, 1965	366
Cindy	March 19, 1964	May 2, 1965	318
The Streets Of New York	Oct. 29, 1963	Aug. 2, 1964	318
The Blood Knot	March 2, 1964	Sept. 27, 1964	239
The American Dream	Apr. 21, 1964	Nov. 8, 1964	232
The Third Ear	May 28, 1964	Oct. 4, 1964	150
Association of Producing Artists (in repertory)	March 4, 1964	June 28, 1964	135
Home Movies with "Softly, And Consider The Nearness"	May 11, 1964	July 12, 1964	72
Two By Ionesco: (The New Tenant, Victims Of Duty)	May 24, 1964	June 14, 1964	27

Van William

Ellis Rabb, Nancy Marchand, Clayton Corzatte, Rosemary Harris
in
"MAN AND SUPERMAN"

PHOENIX THEATRE

Opened Sunday, December 6, 1964.*
Phoenix Theatre with the Association of
Producing Artists presents:

MAN AND SUPERMAN

By George Bernard Shaw; Directed by Stephen Porter; Setting by Judith Haugan; Costumes, Nancy Potts; Lighting, Gilbert Hemsley.

CAST

Roebuck Ramsden	Richard Woods, Ronald Bishop
Parlormaid	Jennifer Harmon
Octavius Robinson	Donald Moffat, Gordon Gould
Jack Tanner	Ellis Rabb, Donald Moffat
Ann Whitefield	Nancy Marchand, Rosemary Harris
Mrs. Whitefield	Joanna Roos, Paddy Croft
Miss Ramsden	Paddy Croft
Violet	Rosemary Harris, Christine Pickles
Henry Straker	Keene Curtis
Hector Malone	Clayton Corzatte, John Allan Macunovich
Mendoza	Paul Sparer, Sydney Walker
The Anarchist	Joseph Bird
Duval	Gordon Gould, Michael McCarthy
The Social Democrat	John Allan Macunovich
Rowdy Social Democrat	Mark White
Goatherd	Robert Lumish
Policemen	Ron Bly, Ed Levey, Michael McCarthy, Leonard Peters
Don Juan	Ellis Rabb, Donald Moffat
Dona Ana	Nancy Marchand, Rosemary Harris
The Devil	Paul Sparer, Sydney Walker
The Commander	Richard Woods, Ronald Bishop
Hector Malone, Sr.	Ronald Bishop, Joseph Bird

A Comedy in three acts and four scenes.

General Manager: Norman Kean
Press: Ben Kornzweig, Robert Ganshaw, Reginald Denenholz, Paul Solomon
Stage Managers: Robert Moss, Bruce A. Hoover, Sean Gillespie

* Still playing May 31, 1965, in repertory with "War and Peace" and "Judith". First New York production at the Hudson Theatre, Sept. 5, 1905, and played 192 performances. Last revival was with Maurice Evans Oct. 8, 1947 and played 295 performances. (See THEATRE WORLD, Vol. 4)

Van Williams Photos

Nancy Marchand, Ellis Rabb (also above),
Richard Woods, Paul Sparer. Top: Richard Woods,
Ellis Rabb, Nancy Marchand

PHOENIX THEATRE

Opened Monday, January 11, 1965.°
Phoenix Theatre with the Association of
Producing Artists presents in repertory:

WAR AND PEACE

After the Novel by Leo Tolstoy; Adapted
for the Stage by Alfred Neumann, Erwin Pisca-
tor, and Guntram Prufer; English Version by
Robert David MacDonald; Directed by Ellis
Rabb; Platform, Ceiling, and Battle of Boro-
dino Designed by Peter Wexler; Decor by
Judith Haugan; Costumes, Nancy Potts; Lighting, Gilbert Hemsley.

CAST

The Narrator	Clayton Corzatte
Andrei	Donald Moffat
Lisa, Andrei's wife	Jennifer Harmon
Prince Bolkonski, Andrei's father	Sydney Walker
Maria, Andrei's sister	Christine Pickles
Natasha	Rosemary Harris
Nicolai Rostov, Natasha's brother	Mark White
Countess Rostova, Natasha's mother	Joanna Roos
Pierre	Ronald Bishop
Dolokhov	Paul Sparer
Anatol Kuragin	Richard Jordan
Kusmich	Gordon Gould
Alpatich	Joseph Bird
Karatayev	Richard Woods
Napoleon Bonaparte	Keene Curtis
Tzar Alexander I	John Allan Macunovich
Kutusov	Richard Woods
Marshall Soult	Robert Lumish
Soldiers, Peasants, Servants	Al Hill, Ed Levey, Robert Lumish, Michael McCarthy, Leonard Peters, David Prass, Barry Bonner, George Addis, Richard Netzband, William Shorr

A Drama in three acts. The action takes
place in Europe between the Rhine and the
Mitishchi between 1805 and 1812.

General Manager: Norman Kean
Press: Ben Kornzweig, Robert Ganshaw,
Reginald Denenholz, Paul Solomon
Stage Managers: Robert Moss, Bruce A.
Hoover, Sean Gillespie

° Still playing May 31, 1965, in repertory with
"Man and Superman" and "Judith."

Van Williams Photos

Christine Pickles, Donald Moffat, Rosemary Harris,
and top with Sydney Walker
Above: Ronald Bishop

Rosemary Harris, Donald Moffat

Donald Moffat, Rosemary Harris

Van Williams Phot

Rosemary Harris
in
"JUDITH"

PHOENIX THEATRE

Opened Wednesday, March 24, 1965.°
The Phoenix Theatre with the Association
of Producing Artists presents:

JUDITH

By Jean Giraudoux; English version, John K.
Savacool; Directed by Ellis Rabb; Scenery,
Judith Haugan; Costumes, Nancy Potts; Light-
ing, Gilbert Hemsley; Music Composed by Con-
rad Susa; Movement Consultant, Rhoda Levine;
Hair Styling, Thomas Pazik.

CAST

Joseph	Ronald Bishop
A Servant	Mark White
Prophet	Gordon Gould
John	Richard Jordan
Joachim	Sydney Walker
Paul, First Cantor	Joseph Bird
Judith	Rosemary Harris
Little Jacob	Paul Pimsler
Susanna	Nancy Marchand
Egon	Keene Curtis, Richard Woods
Otta	Michael McCarthy
Assur	David Mogek
Yami	Robert Lumish
Sarah	Dee Victor
Holofernes	Paul Sparer
Daria	Jennifer Harmon
The Guard	Clayton Corzatte

SERVANTS, SOLDIERS, GUARDS, CAN-
TORS, TOWNSPEOPLE: George Addis, Jen-
nifer Harmon, Al Hill, Ed Levey, Robert Lum-
ish, John Allan Macunovich, Michael McCarthy,
Richard Netzband, Leonard Peters, William
Shorr, David Stewart, Mark White.

A Drama in two parts and four scenes. The
action takes place in a room in Judith's house,
and an ante-chamber in Holofernes' tent.

General Manager: Norman Kean
Press: Ben Kornzweig, Reginald Denenholz
Stage Managers: Robert Moss, Buce A.
Hoover, Sean Gillespie

° Still playing May 31, 1965 in repertory with
"War and Peace" and "Man and Superman." This is the first professional production of "Judith" in the United States.

Van Williams Photos

Richard Jordan, Rosemary Harris, Nancy Marchand

Sydney Walker, Rosemary Harris

Paul Sparer, Rosemary Harris

NEW YORK SHAKESPEARE FESTIVAL
Delacorte Theatre, Central Park, New York
June 16 through August 29, 1964
Produced by Joseph Papp

DELACORTE THEATRE
Opened Tuesday, June 16, 1964.°

HAMLET

By William Shakespeare; Directed by Joseph Papp; Setting and Lighting, Ming Cho Lee; Costumes, Theoni V. Aldredge; Songs and Music, David Amram; Associate Producer, Bernard Gersten; Duels Staged by Christopher Tanner; Festival Stage by Eldon Elder.

CAST

Bernardo	Morris Erby
Francisco	Robin Gammell
Horatio	Tom Klunis
Marcellus	Stacy Keach, Jr.
Claudius	Howard Da Silva
Laertes	Clifford David
Polonius	Staats Cotsworth
Hamlet	Alfred Ryder†
Gertrude	Nan Martin
Ophelia	Julie Harris
Ghost of Hamlet's Father	Lou Polan
Reynaldo	Richard Smithies
Rosencrantz	Ian Cameron
Guildenstern	Chet London
First Player	Stacy Keach, Jr.
Second Player	Robin Gammell
Third Player	Michael Alaimo
Fortinbras	Michael M. Ryan
Norwegian Captain	Ray Stubbs
Sailor	Anthony Passantino
Gravedigger	John Randolph
Apprentice Gravedigger	Robin Gammell
Priest	LeRoi Operti
Osric	Norman MacDonald

MUSICIANS: John Perras, John Bergamo, Henry J. Nowak, Andrew J. Baron

LORDS, ATTENDANTS, SOLDIERS: Alexander Courtney, Tom Cunliffe, Charles Cyphers, T. J. Escott, William Jay, Joseph Kirk, Anthony Major, Arthur D. Roberts, Joseph Stern.

Presented in three parts.

Production Coordinator: Donald Koehler
Stage Managers: Russell McGrath, David Watrous, Vera Cochran
Press: Merle Debuskey, Seymour Krawitz, Madi Ross

° Closed Saturday, July 4, 1964. (24 performances)
† Succeeded after opening night by Robert Burr.

George E. Joseph Photos

Clifford David, Norman MacDonald, Robert Bur Nan Martin, Howard DaSilva, Staats Cotsworth Anthony Major. Top Left: Norman MacDonald, Alfred Ryder, Nan Martin, Howard DaSilva, Staats Cotsworth

Robert Burr, and above with Julie Harris

Julienne Marie, James Earl Jones
in
"OTHELLO"

DELACORTE THEATRE

Opened Wednesday, July 8, 1964.°
New York Shakespeare Festival in cooperation with the City of New York presents:

OTHELLO

By William Shakespeare; Directed by Gladys Vaughan; Setting, Ming Cho Lee; Lighting, Martin Aronstein; Costumes, Theoni V. Aldredge; Songs and Music, David Amram; Associate Producer, Bernard Gersten; Duels Staged by Christopher Tanner; Production Coordinator, Donald Koehler; Hair Styling, Ronald DeMann.

CAST

Roderigo	James Antonio
Iago	Mitchell Ryan
Brabantio	Herbert Nelson
Othello	James Earl Jones
Cassio	John Rayner†1
Duke of Venice	Maury Cooper
Gratiano	Leonard Hicks
Senator	Michael Prince
Desdemona	Julienne Marie†2
Montano	Ed Setrakian
Cyprus Gentlemen	Anthony Passantino, Dan Travanty, Maury Cooper
Emilia	Sada Thompson†3
Clown	Jaime Sanchez
Lodovico	David Gale†4
Musician	William Devane
Bianca	Joan DeWeese
Flutist	John Perras

SOLDIERS, SENATORS, MESSENGERS: Robert Anthony, Alexander Courtney, Tom Cunliffe, Charles Cyphers, T. J. Escott, William Jay, J. Adam Kirk, Tony Major, Anthony Passantino, Arthur David Roberts, Joseph Stern, Dan Travanty

A Drama presented in two parts. The action takes place in Venice and Cyprus.

General Manager: Hilmar Sallee
Press: Merle Debuskey, Seymour Krawitz
Stage Manager: John Fenn

° Closed Sunday, August 9, 1964. (25 performances) With few exceptions, same cast re-opened on Monday, October 12, 1964, at the Martinique Theatre, and still playing there May 31, 1965 in repertory with "Baal."
† Succeeded by: 1. David Gale, 2. Flora Elkins, 3. Bette Henritze, 4. Leonard Hicks

George E. Joseph, Friedman-Abeles, Bert Andrews Photo

Flora Elkins, James Earl Jones. Above: Julienne Marie, Mitchell Ryan, James Earl Jones

188

Flora Elkins, Mitchell Ryan, Bette Henritze

DELACORTE THEATRE

Opened Wednesday, August 5, 1964.°
The New York Shakespeare Festival, Produced by Joseph Papp in cooperation with the City of New York, presents:

ELECTRA

By Sophocles; Translation by H. D. F. Kitto; Directed by Gerald Freedman; Setting, Ming Cho Lee; Lighting, Martin Aronstein; Costumes, Theoni V. Aldredge; Music, John Morris; Choreography, Lee Becker Theodore; Associate Producer, Bernard Gersten; Hairstyling, Ronald DeMann.

CAST

Paedagogus	David Hurst
Orestes	Michael Baseleon
Electra	Lee Grant
Chorus Leader	Janet Dowd
Chrysothemis	Olympia Dukakis
Clytemnestra	Florence Stanley
Aegisthus	Alexander Panas
Pylades	J. R. Crawford
Attendants to Clytemnestra	Jody Carter, Vera Cochran

CHORUS OF WOMEN OF MYCENAE: Hope Arthur, Bonnie Brody, Sheridan Cogan, Tamara Daniel, Nancy Dawson, Betty Hellman, Ruby Holbrook, Sharon Laughlin, Margaret Linn, Mercedes Ospina, Dina Paisner, Frances Rainer, Laura Stuart, Rosemary Tory.

The action takes place before the royal palace of Mycenae in Argos.

Production Coordinator: Donald Koehler
General Manager: Hilmar Sallee
Press: Merle Debuskey, Seymour Krawitz
Stage Managers: Russell McGrath, David Watrous, Vera Cochran

° Closed Saturday, August 29, 1964, after a limited engagement of 22 performances.

George E. Joseph Photos

Chorus of Women, Richard Baseleon, Lee Grant
Top Left: Lee Grant

Lynn Hamilton, David C. Jones, Bill Fletcher,
Robert Nadder, Dennis Cooney, Kelly Jean Peters,
James Tripp, Susan Carr

DELACORTE MOBILE THEATRE
Opened Friday, June 26, 1964.°
The New York Shakespeare Festival in cooperation with the City of New York presents:

A MIDSUMMER NIGHT'S DREAM

By William Shakespeare; Directed by Jack
Sydow; Setting by William Ritman; Lighting,
Martin Aronstein; Costumes, Willa Kim; Music,
David Amram; Associate Producer, Bernard
Gersten; Producer, Joseph Papp; Dances Staged
by Jack Sydow; Technical Director, Tec Crans.

CAST

Theseus	Bill Fletcher
Hippolyta	Lynn Hamilton
Egeus	David C. Jones
Hermia	Kelly Jean Peters
Demetrius	James Tripp
Lysander	Dennis Cooney
Helena	Susan Carr
Peter Quince	Skedge Miller
Nick Bottom	Clifton James
Francis Flute	William Duell
Robin Starveling	Lance Cunard
Tom Snout	Frank Groseclose
Snug	Gilbert Price
Puck	Clyde M. Burton
First Fairy	Yolande Bavan
Oberon	Ted van Griethuysen
Titania	Ellen Holly
Peaseblossom	Margot Williams
Cobweb	Tana McClain
Moth	Ernesta Corvino
Mustardseed	Diane Gould
Attendants to Oberon	Morris Donaldson, Raymond Sawyer

LORDS, LADIES, GUARDS: Arthur Berwick,
Joetta Cherry, Robert Corpora, Robert Craner,
Lauren Frost, Robert Jundelin.

Presented in two parts. The action takes
place in Athens and in a nearby wood.

General Manager: Hilmar Sallee
Press: Merle Debuskey, Seymour Krawitz
Stage Managers: Nathan E. Caldwell, Jr.,
Hal DeWindt, Arthur Berwick

° Closed Saturday, August 29, 1964. This
company toured New York City's five bor-
oughs, performing in 39 parks and play-
grounds.

Ellen Holly, Ernesta Corvino, Margot Williams,
Diane Gould

George E. Joseph Photos

AMERICAN SHAKESPEARE FESTIVAL
Stratford, Connecticut
May 30 through September 13, 1964
Tenth Season

THE TRAGEDY OF KING RICHARD THE THIRD

By William Shakespeare; Directed by Allen Fletcher; Scenery and Costumes by Will Steven Armstrong; Lighting, Tharon Musser; Music, Conrad Susa; Musical Director, Charles Wilson; Duels Staged by Christopher Tanner.

CAST

Richard, Duke of Gloucester ... Douglas Watson
George, Duke of Clarence...............Tom Sawyer
Sir Robert Brakenbury ....Ted Graeber
William Hastings ....John Devlin
Sir William Catesby ....Nicholas Martin
Sir Richard Ratcliffe...................Robert Benedict
Lord Lovel .... Theodore Sorel
Lady Anne ....Patricia Peardon
Elizabeth,
    Queen to Edward IV ....Jacqueline Brookes
Lord Rivers.................................Josef Sommer
Lord Grey.....................................Todd Drexel
Marquis of Dorset ....Terence Scammell
Duke of Buckingham......................Patrick Hines
Lord Stanley...................................David Byrd
Margaret,
    Widow of Henry VI...............Margaret Phillips

Two Murderers ....Rex Everhart, Donald Gantry
Edward IV...............................Philip Bosco
Duchess of York.........................Anne Draper
Bishop of Ely ....Harry Frazier
Princess Elizabeth..................Marisa Joffrey
Richard, Duke of York...............Billy Partello
Edward, Prince of Wales ....Richard Thomas
The Lord Mayor of London ....David Sabin
Cardinal Bouchier...................Geddeth Smith
Messenger from Lord Stanley........David Grimm
Sir James Tyrrel ....Richard Mathews
Henry, Earl of Richmond......Frank G. Converse
Earl of Oxford...........................Ted Graeber
Sir James Blunt ....David Sabin
Duke of Norfolk ....Donald Gantry

SOLDIERS, SERVANTS, LADIES, CITIZENS: Richard Bowden, Mona Feit, Jon Gold, David Grimm, Peter Haig, Kenneth Happe, Michael Holmes, Marisa Joffrey, Dennis Jones, Ray Laine, Janet League, Stephen Levi, William MacAdam, Jon Renn McDonald, Wayne Maunder, Irene Roseen, Edward Rudney, Gilbert Spevack, Robert Sullivan, William Vines.

Friedman-Abeles Photos

Douglas Watson

Douglas Watson, Patricia Peardon

Philip Bosco, Douglas Watson, Frank Converse,
Patrick Hines

MUCH ADO ABOUT NOTHING

By William Shakespeare; Directed by Allen
Fletcher; Scenery and Costumes, Will Steven
Armstrong; Lighting, Tharon Musser; Music,
Conrad Susa; Choreography, William Burdick;
Musical Director, Charles Wilson.

CAST

Leonato	Patrick Hines
Balthasar	Robert Benedict
Antonio	Josef Sommer
Beatrice	Jacqueline Brookes
Hero	Anne Draper
Don Pedro	Douglas Watson
Benedick	Philip Bosco
Claudio	Frank G. Converse
Don John	Nicholas Martin
Son to Antonio	Theodore Sorel
Conrade	Todd Drexel
Borachio	Donald Gantry
Margaret	Patricia Hamilton
Ursula	Patricia Peardon
Dogberry	Rex Everhart
Verges	Geddeth Smith
First Watch	David Sabin
Second Watch	Ted Graeber
Friar Francis	David Byrd
Sexton	Harry Frazier

SOLDIERS, SERVANTS, LADIES, MAIDS:
Mona Feit, Jon Gold, David Grimm, Peter
Haig, Michael Holmes, Marisa Joffrey, Dennis
Jones, Ray Laine, Janet League, Wayne Maunder, Irene Roseen, Edward Rudney, Robert
Sullivan.

Friedman-Abeles Photos

Philip Bosco, Jacqueline Brookes

192

HAMLET

By William Shakespeare; Costumes, Ray Diffen; Lighting, Tharon Musser; Music, John Duffy; Musical Director, Charles Wilson; Duels Staged by Christopher Tanner.

CAST

Bernardo	Donald Gantry
Francisco	Todd Drexel
Horatio	John Devlin
Marcellus	Frank G. Converse
Claudius	Philip Bosco
Cornelius	Edward Rudney
Voltemand	Harry Frazier
Laertes	Terence Scammell
Polonius	Patrick Hines
Hamlet	Tom Sawyer
Gertrude	Margaret Phillips
Ophelia	Anne Gee Byrd
Ghost of Hamlet's Father	David Byrd
Reynaldo	Ted Graeber
Rosencrantz	Richard Mathews
Guildenstern	Geddeth Smith
First Player	Josef Sommer
Fortinbras	Theodore Sorel
Norwegian Captain	David Sabin
A Sailor	William Vines
First Gravedigger	Rex Everhart
Second Gravedigger	Nicholas Martin
Osric	Todd Drexel
Player King	Josef Sommer
Player Queen	Patricia Hamilton
Lucianus	Todd Drexel

LORDS, LADIES, PLAYERS: Richard Bowden, Mona Feit, Jon Gold, David Grimm, Peter Haig, Kenneth Happe, Michael Holmes, Dennis Jones, Ray Laine, Janet League, Stephen Levi, William MacAdam, John Renn McDonald, Wayne Maunder, Irene Roseen, Robert Sullivan.

Producers: Joseph Verner Reed, Berenice Weiler
Company Manager: Ralph Roseman
Press: Sol Jacobson, Lewis Harmon, Peggy Reddy, Josephine Tocchi, Gary Kraut
Stage Managers: John Seig, Tom Hughes Sand, Mort Siegel, Meribeth Meacham

Friedman-Abeles Photos

Philip Bosco, Terence Scammell, Margaret Phillips, Patrick Hines, Anne Gee Byrd
Top: Tom Sawyer

RICHARD II

By William Shakespeare; Directed by Stuart Burge; Designed by Desmond Heeley; Music by John Cook; Fights Arranged by Patrick Crean.

CAST

King Richard II	William Hutt
John of Gaunt, Duke of Lancaster	Patrick Boxill
Henry Bolingbroke, Duke of Hereford	Leo Ciceri
Thomas Mowbray, Duke of Norfolk	Bruno Gerussi
Duchess of Gloucester	Mary Savidge
Duke of Surrey	Max Helpmann
Duke of Aumerle	Len Birman
Heralds	Joseph Rutten, Joseph Shaw
Sir Henry Green	Garrick Hagon
Sir John Bushy	Len Cariou
Sir John Bagot	Heath Lamberts
Edmund, Duke of York	Eric House
The Queen	Jackie Burroughs
Her Attendants	Suzanne Grossmann, Clare Coulter
Earl of Northumberland	Tony van Bridge
Lord Ross	Claude Bede
Lord Willoughby	Joseph Rutten
Servant To York	Al Kozlik
Henry Percy	Leon Pownall
Lord Berkeley	Hugh Webster
Captain of Welsh Force	Mervyn Blake
Earl of Salisbury	Patrick Crean
Sir Stephen Scroop	Joseph Shaw
Bishop of Carlisle	William Needles
Gardeners	Hugh Webster, Lewis Gordon
Lord Fitzwater	Edwin Stephenson
Another Lord	Richard Hogan
Abbot of Westminster	Claude Bede
Duchess of York	Amelia Hall
Sir Pierce of Exton	Joseph Shaw
His Accomplice	Ted Hodgeman
A Groom	Mervyn Blake
Keeper of The Prison	Joseph Rutten
Musicians	Clarence Brodhagen, Melvin Weitzel
Boys	Bruce Buxton, Tom Murray

STANDARD BEARERS, OFFICERS, SOLDIERS, SAILORS, ATTENDANTS: Larry Aubrey, Guy Bannerman, Maurice, Butler, Robert Ferguson, Vanya Franck, Mark Gilliland, John C. Juliani, Jack Lemon, Leslie Mulholland, Ken Pogue, Sylvia Shaffer, Cedric Smith.

Peter Smith Photos

William Hutt, Jackie Burroughs

Top: (L) William Hutt (C), (R) Claude Bede, Tony van Bridge, Leo Ciceri, Joseph Rutten

LE BOURGEOIS GENTILHOMME

By Moliere; Directed by Jean Gascon; Designed by Robert Prevost; Music and Songs, Gabriel Charpentier; Dances Staged by Alan Lund.

CAST

Monsieur Jourdain	Douglas Rain
Madame Jourdain	Diana Maddox
Lucile	Frances Hyland
Cleonte	Len Cariou
Dorimene	Martha Henry
Dorante	William Hutt
Nicole	Helen Burns
Covielle	Bruno Gerussi
Music Master	William Needles
Music Student	Heath Lamberts
Dancing Master	Eric House
Fencing Master	Leo Ciceri
Philosophy Master	Mervyn Blake
Master Tailor	Eric Christmas
His Assistant	Garrick Hagon
The Muphti	Hugh Webster
Lackeys	John C. Juliani, Kenneth Pogue

SINGERS: Vanya Franck, Heath Lamberts, Cedric Smith, Edwin Stephenson

DANCERS: Jackie Burroughs, Lewis Gordon, Garrick Hagon, Ted Hodgeman, Richard Hogan, Al Kozlik, Leon Pownall

MUSICIANS: Hubert Bedard, Robert Comber, Donald Hyder, Ronald Laurie, Earl Reiner

Peter Smith Photos

Seated at table: Douglas Rain, Martha Henry
Top: Martha Henry, William Hutt

KING LEAR

By William Shakespeare; Directed by Michael Langham; Designed by Leslie Hurry; Music and Effects by Louis Applebaum; Fights Staged by Patrick Crean.

CAST

King Lear	John Colicos
Goneril	Frances Hyland
Regan	Diana Maddox
Cordelia	Martha Henry
Duke of Albany	William Needles
Duke of Cornwall	Leo Ciceri
Earl of Kent	Tony van Bridge
Fool	Hugh Webster
Oswald	Eric Christmas
Earl of Gloucester	Mervyn Blake
Edgar	Douglas Rain
Edmund	Bruno Gerussi
King of France	Joseph Shaw
Duke of Burgundy	Len Birman
Curan	Garrick Hagon
A Gentleman	Len Birman
A Knight	Patrick Boxill
A Doctor	Joseph Shaw
Old Tenant of Gloucester's	Claude Bede
Cornwall Attendant	Joseph Rutten
Gloucester Servant	Max Helpmann
Cornwall Messenger	Heath Lamberts
French Messenger	John C. Juliani
Edmund Officer	Patrick Crean
Musician	Clarence Brodhagen

KNIGHTS, LORDS, ATTENDANTS, SOLDIERS: Larry Aubrey, Guy Bannerman, Lewis Gordon, Ted Hodgeman, Richard Hogan, Al Kozlik, Leslie Mulholland, Kenneth Pogue, Leon Pownall, Cedric Smith, Edwin Stephenson, Clare Coulter, Jackie Burroughs, Suzanne Grossman.

Peter Smith Photos

John Colicos (center and above) as King Lear

THE COUNTRY WIFE

By William Wycherley; Directed by Michael Langham; Designed by Desmond Heeley; Music by Godfrey Ridout; Dances Staged by Alan Lund.

CAST

Mr. Horner	John Colicos
Dr. Quack	Eric Christmas
Sir Jaspar Fidget	Eric House
Lady Fidget	Mary Savidge
Mistress Dainty Fidget	Frances Hyland
Mr. Harcourt	Heath Lamberts
Mr. Dorilant	Joseph Shaw
Mr. Sparkish	William Hutt
Mr. Pinchwife	Douglas Rain
Mrs. Margery Pinchwife	Helen Burns
Mistress Alithea	Amelia Hall
Lucy	Suzanne Grossmann
Mistress Squeamish	Martha Henry
Old Lady Squeamish	Edwin Stephenson
A Boy	Evan McCowan
A Bookseller	Max Helpmann
A Parson	Joseph Rutten
A Servant	Ted Hodgeman

MUSICIANS: Terry Helmer, Donald Hyder, Ronald Laurie, Earl Reiner

ATTENDANTS, SERVANTS, PEOPLE ON THE STREETS OF LONDON: Larry Aubrey, Jackie Burroughs, Len Cariou, Clare Coulter, Vanya Franck, Richard Hogan, John C. Juliani, Al Kozlik, Leslie Mulholland, Ken Pogue, Leon Pownall, Sylvia Shaffer, Cedric Smith.

Administrative Director: Victor Polley
Production Director: John Hayes
Company Manager: Bruce Swerdfager
Press: Jack Karr, Barbara Reid
Stage Managers: Jack Hutt, Thomas Bohdanetzky, Bill Kearns, Ronald Pollock, William Webster

Peter Smith Photos

Mary Savidge, John Colicos, Frances Hyland, Joseph Shaw, Martha Henry
Top Right: John Colicos, Helen Burns

MINNESOTA THEATRE COMPANY
Tyrone Guthrie Theatre
Minneapolis, Minnesota
May 11 through October 24, 1964
Second Season

George Grizzard (also above), Yvonne McElroy,
Kristina Callahan

VOLPONE

By Ben Jonson; Directed by Tyrone Guthrie;
Designed by Tanya Moiseiwitsch; Music by
Dominick Argento.

CAST

Volpone	Douglas Campbell
Mosca	George Grizzard
Nano	Sandy McCallum
Androgyno	Katherine Emery
Castrone	Graham Brown
Voltore	Ken Ruta
Corbaccio	Robert Pastene
Corvino	Claude Woolman
Celia	Kristina Callahan
Bonario	Thomas Slater
Sir Politic Wouldbe	Lee Richardson
Peregrine	Michael Levin
Lady Politic Wouldbe	Ruth Nelson
Maids	Yvonne McElroy, Sheila Goldes
Avocatores	Paul Ballantyne, John MacKay, John Cromwell, Charles Cioffi
Notario	Jordon Howard
First Merchant	John Lewin
Second Merchant	James Lineberger
Mountebank	William Pogue

MOUNTEBANKS, VENETIAN CITIZENS:
Richard Anderson, Edward Bach, Roger Beyer,
Ronald Boulden, Timothy Christie, Mary Dykhouse, Michael Harvey, Robert Haskin, Thornton Jones, Victor Koivumaki, Franklin Peters,
Barry Peterson, Richard Phillips, Ronald Rogo-
sheske, Theodore Rouse, Robert Spanabel, Alvah
Stanley, Ernest Stricklin, Donald Wallen, Jennifer Warren.

HENRY V

By William Shakespeare; Directed by Tyrone Guthrie; Designed by Lewis Brown; Music
by Herbert Pilhofer.

CAST

Chorus	Claude Woolman
Archbishop of Canterbury	Robert Pastene
Bishop of Ely	Michael Levin
Earl of Westmoreland	Michael Harvey
Humphrey, Duke of Gloucester	Thomas Slater
Duke of Exeter	John Cromwell
Lord Scroop	Harry Cronin
Earl of Cambridge	John MacKay
Sir Thomas Grey	Graham Brown
King Henry V	George Grizzard
Montjoy	William Pogue
Nym	Robert Spanabel
Bardolph	Charles Cioffi
Pistol	Ken Ruta
Mrs. Quickly	Ruth Nelson
Boy	Willis Sherman
Charles VI of France	Robert Pastene
Duke of Orleans	Alvah Stanley
Rambures	John Lewin
Constable of France	John MacKay
Lewis, the Dauphin	Michael Levin
Grandpre	Graham Brown
Fluellen	Ed Flanders
Gower	Claude Woolman
Jamy	Sandy McCallum
MacMorris	James Lineberger
Governor of Harfleur	John Lewin
Katherine	Kristina Callahan
Alice	Yvonne McElroy
Sir Thomas Erpingham	Sandy McCallum
Bates	Jordon Howard
Williams	Paul Ballantyne
Duke of York	Harry Cronin
Le Fer	Charles Cioffi
Queen of France	Sheila Goldes
Duke of Burgundy	Claude Woolman

LADIES, SOLDIERS, ARCHERS, MONKS:
Mary Dykhouse, Katherine Emery, Jennifer
Warren, Richard Anderson, Edward Bach, Rog-
er Beyer, Ronald Boulden, Curtis Carlson, Tim-
othy Christie, Ronald Kubler, Franklin Peters,
Richard Phillips, Darrell Ranum, Ronald Rogo-
sheske, Theodore Rouse, Allen Schulte, Charles
Stanley, Ernest Stricklin, Theodore Szymanski,
Donald Wallen.

**Douglas Campbell
as Volpone**

SAINT JOAN

By George Bernard Shaw; Directed by Douglas Campbell; Designed by Tanya Moiseiwitsch; Music by Dominick Argento.

CAST

Robert de Baudricourt	Douglas Campbell
Steward	Ed Flanders
Joan	Ellen Geer
Bertrand de Poulengy	John MacKay
Archbishop of Rheims	Ken Ruta
Mgr. de la Tremouille	John Lewin
French Sergeant	Sandy McCallum
Gilles de Rais	Michael Levin
Captain La Hire	Charles Cioffi
The Dauphin	George Grizzard
Duchess de la Tremouille	Yvonne McElroy
Dunois	Claude Woolman
His Page	Thomas Slater
Richard de Beauchamp	Robert Pastene
Chaplain de Stogumber	Paul Ballantyne
English Sergeant	Sandy McCallum
Peter Cauchon	Lee Richardson
The Inquisitor	Ed Flanders
D'Estivet	Graham Brown
De Courcelles	John Cromwell
Brother Martin Ladvenu	William Pogue
The Executioner	Charles Cioffi
An English Soldier	Douglas Campbell
A Gentleman of 1920	Thomas Slater

LADIES, GENTLEMEN, SOLDIERS: Mary Dykhouse, Katherine Emery, Sheila Goldes, Jennifer Warren, Graham Brown, Harry Cronin, Michael Harvey, John MacKay, William Pogue, Alvah Stanley, Richard Anderson, Timothy Christie, Theodore Szymanski, Donald Wallen, Ronald Boulden, Jordon Howard, Ronald Kubler, Charles Stanley, Ernest Stricklin, John Lewin, Robert Spanabel.

Left: Ellen Geer, George Grizzard, Ken Ruta, Claude Woolman. Above: Lee Richardson, Ellen Geer, George Grizzard

THE GLASS MENAGERIE

By Tennessee Williams; Directed by Alan Schneider; Designed by Lewis Brown; Music by Herbert Pilhofer.

CAST

The Son	Lee Richardson
The Mother	Ruth Nelson
The Daughter	Ellen Geer
The Gentleman Caller	Ed Flanders

Artistic Director: Tyrone Guthrie
Administrative Director: Barton H. Emmet
Press: Bradley G. Morison, Kay Fliehr, Anne Richards
Stage Managers: Rex Partington, Edward Payson Call, Gordon Smith

**Ruth Nelson, Lee Richardson, Ed Flanders
Left: Ellen Geer**

199

OLIVER!

Book, Music, and Lyrics by Lionel Bart; Freely adapted from Charles Dickens' "Oliver Twist"; Directed by Peter Coe; Designed by Sean Kenny; Orchestrations, Eric Rogers; Musical Director, Robert McNamee; Technical Supervisor, Ian Albery; Lighting, John Wyckham; Production Supervisor, Samuel Liff; Presented by David Merrick and Donald Albery. Opened Monday, November 16, 1964, at the Shubert Theatre in Cincinnati, Ohio, and still touring May 31, 1965.

CAST

Oliver Twist	Ronnie Kroll
Mr. Bumble	Alan Crofoot
Mrs. Corney	Dawna Shove
Old Sally	Ruth Maynard
Mr. Sowerberry	John Miranda
Mrs. Sowerberry	Ruth Maynard
Charlotte	Lynda Sturner
Noah Claypole	Terry Lomax
Fagin	Robin Ramsay
The Artful Dodger	David Jones
Nancy	Judy Bruce
Bet	Joan Lombardo
Bill Sikes	Danny Sewell
Mr. Brownlow	Bram Nossen
Dr. Grimwig	John Call
Mrs. Bedwin	Dortha Duckworth

WORKHOUSE BOYS AND FAGIN'S GANG: Joey Baio, Tommy Battreall, Paul Dwyer, Anthony Endon, Eugene Endon, Lee Koenig, Greg Lange, Mark Lonergan, Mark Novak, Jackie Perkuhn, George Priolo, Brett Smiley, Victor Stiles.

LONDONERS: Ted Bloecher, Dominic Chianese, Georgia Dell, Lee Howard, John M. Kimbro, Paul Kroll, Charlise Mallory, Richard Miller, Moose Peting, Sherill Price, Terry Robinson, Hugh Shine, Mary Ann Squitieri, Gretchen Van Aken, Richard Wulf, Virginia Sandifur.

UNDERSTUDIES: Fagin, Richard Miller; Nancy, Gretchen Van Aken; Bumble, John Call; Mrs. Corney, Georgia Dell; Brownlow, Hugh Shine; Grimwig, John Kimbro; Sikes, Richard Wulf; Mrs. Sowerberry, Sherill Price; Mr. Sowerberry, Dominic Chianese; Oliver, Victor Stiles and Eugene Endon; Artful Dodger, George Priolo and Joey Baio; Charlotte, Mary Ann Squitieri; Noah, Paul Kroll; Old Sally, Charlise Mallory; Bet, Mary Ann Sequitieri; Mrs. Bedwin, Georgia Dell.

MUSICAL NUMBERS: "Food, Glorious Food," "Oliver!," "I Shall Scream," "Boy For Sale," "That's Your Funeral," "Where Is Love?," "Consider Yourself," "You've Got To Pick A Pocket Or Two," "It's A Fine Life," "I'd Do Anything," "Be Back Soon," "Oom-Pah-Pah," "My Name," "As Long As He Needs Me," "Who Will Buy?," "Reviewing The Situation."

A Musical in two acts.

General Manager: Jack Schlissel
Manager: Emanuel Azenberg
Press: Lee Solters, Harvey B. Sabinson, Maurice Turet
Stage Managers: Edward Hastings, Geoffrey Johnson, Moose Peting
For original New York production, see THEATRE WORLD, Vol. 19.

Friedman-Abeles and Eileen Darby—Graphic House Photos

Top Left: Robin Ramsay, Danny Sewell, Judy Bruce
Below: John Call, Dortha Duckworth, Bram Nossen, Ronnie Kroll

Ronnie Kroll, Robin Ramsay, Judy Bruce

OLIVER!

Book, Music, and Lyrics by Lionel Bart; Freely adapted from Dickens' "Oliver Twist"; Directed by Edward Hastings; Scenic Design, James Hamilton; Costumes, Patton Campbell; Lighting, Peter Hunt; Musical Director, William Brohn; Orchestrations, Eric Rogers; Presented by Henry Guettel and Arthur Cantor by special arrangement with David Merrick and Donald Albery; Production Assistant, Leonard Majzlin. Opened Wednesday, September 30, 1964 at the Hershey, Pa. Community Theatre, and still touring May 31, 1965.

CAST

Oliver Twist	Christopher Spooner
Mr. Bumble	Dale Malone
Mrs. Corney	Lu Leonard
Old Sally	Patricia Drylie
Mr. Sowerberry	James Beard
Mrs. Sowerberry	Patricia Drylie
Charlotte	Yvonne Harvey
Noah Claypole	Robert Wexler
Fagin	Jules Munshin
The Artful Dodger	Chris Andrews
Nancy	Joan Eastman
Bet	Tina Month
Bill Sikes	Vincent Beck
Mr. Brownlow	Joseph Boland
Dr. Grimwig	James Beard
Mrs. Bedwin	Christine Thomas
Rose Girl	Tilda D'Andrea
Strawberry Girl	Lynn Carroll
Milkmaid	Joan Shepard
Knife Grinder	Evan Thompson
Hat Vendor	Ronn Carroll

WORKHOUSE BOYS and FAGIN'S GANG: Larry Victor, Arthur A-Zito, David Henesy, Christopher Month, Mark Month, Michael Month, Dean Paulin, Michael Paulin, Gavan Paulin, John Zizak, James Harvey.

LONDONERS: Jeanne Avery, Walter Blocher, Lynn Carroll, Ronn Carroll, Norma Crawford, Tilda D'Andrea, Joseph Della Sorte, Patricia Drylie, Gerald Nobles, Joan Shepard, Evan Thompson, Ralston Hill, Dugan Miller, Christine Thomas.

UNDERSTUDIES: Fagin, Brownlow, Sowerberry, Ralston Hill; Nancy, Tilda D'Andrea; Mrs. Corney, Norma Crawford; Grimwig, Ronn Carroll; Claypole, Joseph Della Sorte, Mrs. Sowerberry, Lynn Carroll; Dodger, James Harvey; Bet, Charlotte, Joan Shepard; Sikes, Evan Thompson; Sally, Mrs. Bedwin, Jeanne Avery; Oliver, Dean Paulin; Bumble, Walter Blocher.

MUSICAL NUMBERS: "Food, Glorious Food," "Oliver!," "I Shall Scream," "Boy For Sale," "That's Your Funeral," "Where Is Love?," "Consider Yourself," "You've Got To Pick A Pocket Or Two," "It's A Fine Life," "I'd Do Anything," "Be Back Soon," "Oom-Pah," "My Name," "As Long As He Needs Me," "Who Will Buy," "Reviewing The Situation," Finale.

A Musical in two acts. The action takes place in London in the past.

Company Manager: Boris Bernardi
Press: Zac Freedman, Roxy Horen
Stage Managers: Leonard Stein, J. P. Regan, Gerald Nobles

For original New York production, see THEATRE WORLD, Vol. 19.

Christopher Spooner. Above: Jules Munshin, Joan Eastman (top right)

Signe Hasso, Farley Granger in "Liliom"

THE NATIONAL REPERTORY THEATRE

Michael Dewell and Frances Ann Dougherty, Producers; Set Designer, Peter Larkin; Costumes, Alvin Colt; Lighting Designer, Tharon Musser; Production Supervisor, Robert Calhoun; Musical Director, Dean Fuller; Presented by The American National Theatre and Academy. Opened at the American Theatre, St. Louis, October 19, 1964, and closed at the Blackstone in Chicago, March 27, 1965.

LILIOM

By Ferenc Molnar; Translated by Benjamin Glazer; Directed by Eva LeGallienne; Music by Dean Fuller.

CAST

Liliom	Farley Granger
Mrs. Muskat	Signe Hasso
Julie	Dolores Sutton
Marie	Adrienne Hazzard
Servants	Patricia Guinan, Elizabeth Council
Police Captain	G. Wood
Policeman	Fred Ainsworth
Mother Hollunder	Paula Bauersmith
Sparrow	Thayer David
Wolf Berkowitz	Herbert Foster
Young Hollunder	Arthur Berwick
Mr. Linzman	Francis Bethencourt
Mounted Policemen	Patrick Farrelly, Richard Sterne
The Doctor	Richard Kronold
The Carpenter	Alan Becker
Heavenly Policemen	Fred Ainsworth, Miller Lide
The Old Guard	Richard Kronold
The Rich Man	Francis Bethencourt
The Poor Man	Richard Sterne
The Magistrate	G. Wood
Louise	Patricia Guinan

SHE STOOPS TO CONQUER

By Oliver Goldsmith; With a new epilogue by Marya Mannes; Directed by Jack Sydow; Music by Dean Fuller.

CAST

Diggory	Arthur Berwick
Roger	Fred Ainsworth
Thomas	Miller Lide
Pimple	Adrienne Hazzard
Mrs. Hardcastle	Paula Bauersmith
Mr. Hardcastle	G. Wood
Tony Lumpkin	Herbert Foster
Kate Hardcastle	Dolores Sutton
Miss Neville	Patricia Guinan
Tavern Guests	Alan Becker, Richard Sterne, Patrick Farrelly
Landlord	Richard Kronold
Barmaid	Elizabeth Council
Mr. Marlow	Farley Granger
Mr. Hastings	Francis Bethencourt
His Servant	Richard Sterne
Jeremy	Patrick Farrelly
Sir Charles Marlow	Thayer David

HEDDA GABLER

By Henrik Ibsen; Translated and Directed by Eva Le Gallienne; "Hedda's Waltz" Composed by Signe Hasso.

CAST

Berta	Elizabeth Council
Miss Julia Tesman	Paula Bauersmith
George Tesman	Thayer David
Hedda Gabler	Signe Hasso
Mrs. Elvsted	Dolores Sutton
Judge Brack	Francis Bethencourt
Ejlert Lovborg	Farley Granger

Company Manager: James Awe
Press: Robert W. Jennings, Mary Bryant, Mort Nathanson
Stage Managers: William Armitage, Helen Page Camp, Alan Becker

Van Williams Photos

Signe Hasso, Farley Granger in "Hedda Gabler"

Dolores Sutton, Farley Granger in
"She Stoops To Conquer"

Dolores Sutton, Farley Granger in "Liliom"

Paula Bauersmith, Herbert Foster, G. Wood,
Dolores Sutton in "She Stoops To Conquer"

Thayer David, Signe Hasso, Francis Bethencourt
in "Hedda Gabler"

Donald Marye, George Cotton, Alan Bergmann, William Countryman,
John Eames, Thomas Boyd, Gilbert Williams

LUTHER

By John Osborne; Staged by Mitchell Erickson; Scenery and Costumes, Jocelyn Herbert; Choral Director, Marvin Solley; Original Music, John Addison; Presented by Joel Spector, Julian Olney, and B. B. Randolph. Opened Friday, October 2, 1964 at the Center Theatre, Norfolk, Va., and closed Saturday, February 27, 1965 at the Royal Alexandra in Toronto, Canada.

CAST

Knight	Barry Snider
Prior	Alfred Sandor
Martin	Alan Bergmann
Hans	Herman Rudin
Lucas	John Eames
Reader	William Countryman
Weinand	Donald Marye
Tetzel	Sam Kressen
Staupitz	George Cotton
Cajetan	Alfred Sandor
Miltitz	Jay Gregory
Pope Leo X	Jack Hollander
Eck	John Eames
Katherine	Anne Countryman
Cantor	Marvin Solley

MONKS, SINGERS, LORDS, PEASANTS: Thomas Boyd, Gunnar Dahlberg, Dan Goggin, Jay Gregory, Gilbert Williams.

UNDERSTUDIES: Prior, Cajetan, Sam Kressen; Hans, Tetzel, Jack Hollander; Staupitz, Donald Marye; Luther, Barry Snider; Eck, Jay Gregory; Knight, Weinand, William Countryman; Lucas, Thomas Boyd; Pope, Gunnar Dahlberg; Miltitz, Gilbert Williams; Katherine, Francesca Gay Schulz.

A Drama in three acts and twelve scenes. The action takes place between 1506 and 1527.

General Manager: Monty Shaff
Company Manager: David Wyler
Press: Paul G. Anglim, Al Butler
Stage Managers: Irving Sudrow,
William Countryman
For original New York production, see THEATRE WORLD, Vol. 20.

Alan Bergmann

NEVER TOO LATE

By Sumner Arthur Long; Directed by George Abbott; Setting and Lighting, William and Jean Eckart; Costumes, Florence Klotz; "Never Too Late Cha-Cha" by Jerry Bock and Sheldon Harnick; Incidental Music, John Kander; Presented by Elliot Martin and Daniel Hollywood; Tour Direction by National Performing Arts Inc. Production Supervisor, Wally Peterson. Opened Saturday, October 3, 1964, in the Rajah Theatre. Reading, Pa., and closed at the Locust in Philadelphia on April 24, 1965.

CAST

Grace Kimbrough	Marjorie Nichols
Harry Lambert	Lyle Talbot
Edith Lambert	Penny Singleton
Dr. James Kimbrough	Robert Fitzsimmons
Charlie	Tom Connolly
Kate	Judith Barcroft
Mr. Foley	Charles Hohman
Mayor Crane	Larry Fletcher
Policeman	Don Fenwick

UNDERSTUDIES: Grace, Helen Bonstelle; Kate, Pamela Grey; Harry, Larry Fletcher; Edith, Marjorie Nichols; Charlie, Don Fenwick; Mayor, Robert Fitzsimmons; Doctor, Policeman, Charles Hohman.

A Comedy in three acts and five scenes. The action takes place in the living room of the Lambert home in Calverton, Massachusetts.

General Manager: C. Edwin Knill
Company Manager: James O'Neill
Press: Mary Bryant, Bernard Simon, Mae S. Hong
Stage Managers: Victor Straus, Charles Hohman

For original New York production, see THEATRE WORLD, Vol. 19.

Friedman-Abeles Photos

Penny Singleton, Lyle Talbot, Tom Connolly, Judith Barcroft (also at top right)
Center: Lyle Talbot, Penny Singleton

110 IN THE SHADE

By N. Richard Nash; Music, Harvey Schmidt; Lyrics, Tom Jones; Based on Play "The Rainmaker" by Mr. Nash; Dances and Musical Numbers Staged by Agnes De Mille; Directed by Joseph Anthony; Settings, Oliver Smith; Costumes, Motley; Lighting, John Harvey; Musical Director, Pembroke Davenport; Orchestrations, Hershey Kay; Dance Music by William Goldenberg; Vocal Arranger, Robert DeCormier; Hair Styles, Michel Kazan; Presented by David Merrick. Opened Monday, August 10, 1964 at the Curran Theatre in San Francisco, and closed in Louisville, Ky. on May 8, 1965.

CAST

Toby	George Church
File	Stephen Douglass
H. C. Curry	Will Geer
Noah Curry	John Carter
Jimmy Curry	Scooter Teague
Lizzie Curry	Inga Swenson†
Snookie	Lesley Warren
Mrs. Jensen	Addi Negri
Phil Mackey	David Cryer
Clem	Richard Barris
Tommy	Sean O. Leabo
Geshy Toops	Charles Scott
Gil Demby	Arthur Whitfield
Olive Barrow	Loi Leabo
Hannah	Jessie Foster
Wally Skacks, 3rd	Michael Harrison
Maurine Toops	Cathy Conklin
Bo Dollivan	Vernon Lusby
Mr. Curtis	Joe E. Hill
Bill Starbuck	Ray Danton
Wally Skacks	Joe Kirkland

TOWNSPEOPLE: Richard Barris, Cash Baxter, Amy Blaisdell, Cathy Conklin, Suzanne Crumpler, David Cryer, Leslie Daniel, Frank De Sal, Lesley Evans, Jessie Foster, Michael Harrison, Joe Hill, Doreen Kilmer, Joe Kirkland, Loi Leabo, Paula Lloyd, Joeanne Lotsko, Vernon Lusby, Addi Negri, Noel Parenti, Charles Scott, Joanne Shields, Barbara Sorensen, Gary Wales, Joel Warfield, Arthur Whitfield.

UNDERSTUDIES: Lizzie, Leslie Daniel; Starbuck, David Cryer; Curry, Joe E. Hill; Jimmie, Joel Warfield; Noah, Charles Scott; Snookie, Lesley Evans; Toby, Vernon Lusby.

MUSICAL NUMBERS: "Another Hot Day," "Lizzie's Coming Home," "Love, Don't Turn Away," "Poker Polka," "Hungry Men," "The Rain Song," "You're Foolin' Me," "Raunchy," "A Man and A Woman," "Old Maid," "Everything Beautiful Happens At Night," "Melisande," "Simple Little Things," "Little Red Hat," "Is It Really Me?," "Wonderful Music," Finale.

General Manager: Jack Schlissel
Company Manager: Irving L. Cone
Press: Lee Solters, Harvey Sabinson, Theresa Loeb Cone
Stage Managers: Charles Atkin, Paul Philips, Joe Hill

For original New York production, see THEATRE WORLD, Vol. 20.

† Succeeded by Leslie Daniel

Ray Danton, Inga Swenson, Stephen Douglass
Above: Will Geer, Inga Swenson

FROM THE SECOND CITY

A Comic Entertainment presented by Max Allentuck; Scenes and Dialogue Created by the Cast; Music Composed and Played by William Mathieu; Directed by Sheldon Patinkin with Bill Alton; Produced for the Second City by Bernard Sahlins and Sheldon Patinkin. Opened February 16, 1965 at the Fisher Theatre, Detroit, and closed at the Hanna in Cleveland on April 24, 1965.

CAST

Severn Darden	Robert Benedetti
Bill Alton	Sally Hart
Judy Graubart	David Steinberg

Scenes, games, and improvisations by the Second City Company.
Press: Seymour Krawitz, Merle Debuskey Harry Davies

Severn Darden

DEAR ME, THE SKY IS FALLING

By Leonard Spigelgass; Based on a Story by
Gertrude Berg and James Yaffe; Directed by
Herman Shumlin; Settings and Lighting, Will
Steven Armstrong; Costumes, Edith Lutyens Bel
Geddes; Presented by The Greek Theatre As-
sociation and The Theatre Guild. Opened
Saturday, September 12, 1964, at the Geary
Theatre, San Francisco, and still touring May
31, 1965.

CAST

Dr. Robert Evans	Jonathan Moore
Debbie Hirsch	Mary-Robin Redd
Libby Hirsch	Gertrude Berg
Mildred Feldman	Estelle Omens
Paul Hirsch	Roger DeKoven
Sophie	Mimi Randolph
Minnie	Mary Engel
Jessie	Berta Gersten
Robert Wolfe	Michael Baseleon
Mr. Schlinger	Sanford Seeger
Mrs. Schlinger	Dorothy Levine
Peter Nemo	Paul Vincent

UNDERSTUDIES: Libby, Estelle Omens;
Paul, Sanford Seeger; Debbie, Marguerite Tar-
rant; Robert, Evans, Peter, Schlinger, Chet
Leaming; Jessie, Minnie, Sophie, Dorothy Le-
vine; Mildred, Mimi Randolph; Mrs. Schlinger,
Marguerite Tarrant, Mary Engel;

A Comedy in three acts and seven scenes.
The action takes place in Dr. Evans' office,
and in the Hirsch home.

General Manager: Peter Davis
Press: Frank Liberman
Stage Manager: Karl Nielsen

For original New York production, see THE-
ATRE WORLD, Vol. 19.

**Right: Gertrude Berg, Paul Vincent,
Mary-Robin Redd, Roger DeKoven
Above: Jonathan Moore, Gertrude Berg**

Estelle Omens, Gertrude Berg, Roger DeKoven

Mary Engel, Mimi Randolph, Berta Gersten,
Gertrude Berg

H.M.S. PINAFORE

By W. S. Gilbert and Arthur Sullivan; Directed by Tyrone Guthrie; Musical Director and Conductor, Louis Applebaum; Sets and Costumes, Brian Jackson; Dances Staged by Douglas Campbell; Presented by Touring Theatre, Inc. Opened Monday, September 21, 1964, at the Huntington Hartford Theatre, Los Angeles, and closed December 20, 1965.

CAST

Boatswain	Donald Young
Buttercup	Irene Byatt
Dick Dead-Eye	Howard Mawson
Ralph Rackstraw	William Greene
Captain Corcoran	Grahame Laver
Josephine	Stephanie Augustine
Sir Joseph Porter	Michael Bates
Hebe	Maggie Bates
Carpenter's Mate	John Harcourt

SISTERS, COUSINS, AUNTS, AND SAILORS: Joy Alexander, Arthur Apy, Jamie Apy, Grant Cowan, David Geary, Genevieve Gordon, Robin Haddow, Maria Harris, Leslie J. Mackey, Helen Murray, Kathryn Newman, Marnie Patrick, Nasco Petroff, Roxolana Roslak, Terrence G. Ross, Ken Schultz, Arthur Sclater, Glen Stetson.

UNDERSTUDIES: Porter, Howard Mawson; Josephine, Helen Murray; Ralph, Nasco Petroff; Captain, Donald Young; Dick, Arthur Sclater; Buttercup, Kathryn Newman; Boatswain, Leslie J. Mackey; Carpenter's Mate, Robin Haddow.

An operetta in two acts. The action takes place aboard the H.M.S. Pinafore in nineteenth century England.

Company Manager: James Preston
Press: Dorathi Bock Pierre
Stage Managers: Leon Gersten, A. Marc Leventhal, Robin Haddow

Rothschild Photos

Right: Irene Byatt, Michael Bates, William Greene, Stephanie Augustine, Grahame Laver

Center: Michael Bates, Grahame Laver

HOW TO SUCCEED
IN BUSINESS
WITHOUT REALLY TRYING

Book, Abe Burrows, Jack Weinstock, Willie Gilbert; Based on Novel by Shepherd Mead; Music and Lyrics, Frank Loesser; Directed by Abe Burrows; Choreography, Hugh Lambert; Scenery and Lighting, Robert Randolph; Costumes, Robert Fletcher; Musical Direction, Fred Werner; Orchestrations, Robert Ginzler; Musical Staging, Bob Fosse; Presented by Feuer and Martin in association with Frank Productions Inc. Opened Monday, February 4, 1963 at the Hanna Theatre in Cleveland, Ohio, and still touring May 31, 1965.

CAST

Finch	Dick Kallman[1]
Gatch	Stanley Simmonds
Jenkins	I. W. Klein
Tackaberry	Larry Pool
Peterson	William Sisson
Kittridge	Larry Devon
J. B. Biggley	Willard Waterman[2]
Rosemary	Suzanne Menke
Bratt	Tom Batten
Smitty	Pat McEnnis
Frump	William Major
Miss Jones	Lilian Fields
Mr. Twimble	Joe Cowan
Hedy	Maureen Arthur
Scrubwomen	Carole Lindsey, Fayn LeVeille
Miss Krumholtz	Carole Lindsey
Toynbee	Lee Barry
Ovington	Larry Devon
Policeman	Bill Joyce
Womper	Joe Cowan

SINGERS: Lee Barry, Larry Devon, Joe Evans, William Sisson, I. W. Klein, Larry Pool, Stanley Simmonds, Jill Alexander, Eleanor Edie, Judith Leamon, Fayn LeVeille, Carole Lindsey, Anne Nathan

DANCERS: Ted August, Gene Foote, Curtis Hood, Bill Joyce, Ronald Stratton, Buddy Vest, Lou Zeldis, Felice Camargo, Natasha Grishin, Enid Hart, Diane Hull, Karen Miller, Renata Powers, Elyn Tia.

MUSICAL NUMBERS: "How To," "Happy To Keep His Dinner Warm," "Coffee Break," "The Company," "A Secretary Is Not A Toy," "Been A Long Day," "Grand Old Ivy," "Paris Original," "Rosemary," "Cinderella, Darling," "Love From A Heart Of Gold," "I Believe In You," "The Yo Ho Ho," "Brotherhood Of Man," Finale.

A Musical Comedy in two acts. The entire action takes place in the new Park Avenue office building of World Wide Wickets Company Inc.

General Manager: Donald Loze
Company Manager: Milton Pollack
Press: Merle Debuskey, Seymour Krawitz, Larry Belling
Stage Managers: Charles Durand, Hal Halvorsen, Larry Pool, Ted August

[†] Succeeded by: 1. Ronnie Welsh, 2. Jeff De-Benning
For original New York production, see THEATRE WORLD, Vol. 18.

Friedman-Abeles Photos

Center: Maureen Arthur, Jeff DeBenning, Ronnie Welsh

Pat McEnnis, Ronnie Welsh, Suzanne Menke
Above: Maureen Arthur

AFTER THE FALL

By Arthur Miller; Directed by Edward Parone; Setting and Lighting, Jo Mielziner; Costumes, Patton Campbell; Music Composed by David Amram; Production Assistants, Tosh Griner, Jean Hunt; A Martin Tahse Production; Presented by The American National Theatre and Academy. Opened October 21, 1964 at the Wilmington, Del., Playhouse, and closed May 29, 1965 at the Shubert in Boston.

CAST

Quentin	Charles Aidman
Felice	Susan Browning
Holga	Linda Geiser
Mother	Sylvia Gassell
Dan	Robert Baines
Father	Rudy Bond
Nurse	Ruth Tobin
Maggie	Judi West
Elsie	Heather Mackenzie
Louise	Patricia Falkenhain
Lou	Robert Gerringer[1]
Mickey	David Spielberg
Woman with parrot	Ruth Tobin
Man in park	John Swearingen
Homely Woman	Heather Mackenzie
Carrie	Lorna Thayer
Chairman	William Callan[2]
Rev. Harley Barnes	John Swearingen
Secretary	Ruth Tobin
Lucas	Carl Gabler

UNDERSTUDIES: Quentin, Robert Baines; Father, Lou, William Callan[2]; Mother, Lorna Thayer; Louise, Susan Browning; Maggie, Holga, Felice, Heather Mackenzie; Mickey, Dan, John Swearingen; Elsie, Carrie, Ruth Tobin.

A Drama in two acts. The action takes place in the mind, thought, and memory of Quentin, a contemporary man.

General Manager: Al Berr
Company Manager: Fred J. Cuneo
Press: Morton Langbord, Ruth Tobin, Ken Hinaman
Stage Managers: Thelma Chandler, Carl Gabler

† Succeeded by: 1. William Callan, 2. John Wardwell

For original New York production, see THEATRE WORLD, Vol. 20.

Top Left: Charles Aidman, Patricia Falkenhain. Right: Judi West. Charles Aidman (also below)

Linda Geiser, Patricia Falkenhain, Judi West, Charles Aidman

CAMELOT

Book and Lyrics, Alan Jay Lerner; Music, Frederick Loewe; Directed by Lawrence Kasha; Presented by Henry Guettell and Arthur Cantor by arrangement with Jenny Productions; Choreography and Musical Numbers by Hanya Holm; Scenic Production, Oliver Smith; Costumes, Stanley Simmons; Lighting, Feder; Orchestrations, Robert Russell Bennett and Philip J. Lang; Musical Directors, John Anderson, Edward Simons; Based on "The Once and Future King" by T. H. White. Opened Thursday, October 3, 1963 at the Masonic Temple, Scranton, Pa., and closed December 19, 1964.

CAST

Sir Dinadan	George Hearn
Sir Lionel	Ewel Cornett
Merlyn	Gwyllum Evans
Arthur	Biff McGuire†1
Guenevere	Jeannie Carson†2
Nimue	Jane Bergerman
A Page	Daryl Alford
Lancelot	Sean Garrison†3
Dap	Charles May
Pellinore	Melville Cooper
Clarius	Dennis Wayne
Lady Anne	Yvonne Lynn
Sir Sagramore	Edgar Mastin
Mordred	Brendan Burke
Tom	Daryl Alford

LADIES AND KNIGHTS: Sue Babel, Jane Bergerman, Sandra Brewer, Laura Graham, Barbara Gregory, Gracia Littauer, Peff Modelski, Eva Marie Sage, Susanne Whitcomb, Marjorie Wood, Daryl Alford, Paul Glover, Jay Gregory, Don Lawrence, Arnott Mader, Andre St. Jean.

UNDERSTUDIES: Arthur, George Hearn; Guenevere, Yvonne Lynn; Lancelot, Ewel Cornett; Pellinore, Gwyllum Evans; Mordred, Don Lawrence; Merlin, George Hearn; Nimue, Barbara Gregory; Sagramore, Lionel Dinadan, Jay Gregory.

MUSICAL NUMBERS: "I Wonder What The King Is Doing Tonight," "The Simple Joys of Maidenhood," "Camelot," "Follow Me," "C'est Moi," "The Lusty Month of May," "How To Handle A Woman," "The Jousts," "Before I Gaze At You Again," "If Ever I Would Leave You," "The Seven Deadly Virtues," "What Do The Simple Folk Do," "Fie On Goodness," "I Loved You Once In Silence," "Guenevere."

A Musical in two acts and eighteen scenes. The action takes place in Camelot a long time ago.

Company Manager: Charles Mooney
Press: Zac Freedman
Stage Managers: Eddie Dimond, Ruth Newton, Jay Gregory

† Succeeded by: 1. George Wallace, 2. Jan Moody, 3. Igors Gavon

For original New York production, see THEATRE WORLD, Vol. 17.

James J. Kriegsmann Photos

Top Left: Gwyllum Evans, Biff McGuire. Right: Melville Cooper, George Wallace. Below: Igors Gavon, Biff McGuire, Jeannie Carson

Melville Cooper, George Wallace, Jan Moody, Igors Gavon

WHO'S AFRAID OF VIRGINIA WOOLF?

By Edward Albee; Directed by Alan Schneider; Designed by William Ritman; Production Supervisor, Mona Lipp; Associate Director, Mark Wright; Presented by Richard Barr, Clinton Wilder, and Sometimes Inc. Opened August 17, 1964 at the Westport, Conn., Playhouse and closed at the Royal Alexandra, Toronto, Canada, April 3, 1965.

CAST

Martha	Vicki Cummings
George	Kendall Clark
Honey	Bryarly Lee
Nick	Donald Briscoe

UNDERSTUDIES: Martha, Fayne Blackburn; George, William Gibberson; Honey, Marian Clarke; Nick, Christopher Bernau.

A Drama in three acts. The action takes place at the present time in the home of Martha and George in a university town.

Company Manager: Herbert Cherin
Press: Arthur M. Brilant, Howard Atlee
Stage Managers: Elizabeth Caldwell, Christopher Bernau

For original New York production, see THEATRE WORLD, Vol. 19.

Right: Vicki Cummings, Bryarly Lee, Kendall Clark, Donald Briscoe

Vicki Cummings, Kendall Clark

Bryarly Lee, Donald Briscoe

A FUNNY THING HAPPENED ON THE WAY TO THE FORUM

Book by Burt Shevelove and Larry Gelbart; Based on Plays of Plautus; Music and Lyrics, Stephen Sondheim; Directed by George Abbott; Choreography and Musical Staging, Jack Cole; Settings and Costumes, Tony Walton; Lighting, Jean Rosenthal; Musical Director, Joseph D. Lewis; Orchestrations, Irwin Kostal and Sid Ramin; Dance Music Arranged by Hal Schaefer; Presented by Martin Tahse by arrangement with Harold Prince. Opened at the Forrest, Philadelphia, December 25, 1963, and closed August 31, 1964 at the Shubert in Chicago.

CAST

Prologus	Jerry Lester
The Proteans	David Neuman, Scott Hunter[1], Eric Kelly[2]
Senex	Paul Hartman
Domina	Justine Johnston
Hero	Bert Stratford
Hysterium	Arnold Stang[3]
Lycus	Erik Rhodes
Pseudolus	Jerry Lester
Tintinabula	Tisa Chang
Panacea	Gloria Mills
The Geminae	Helen Levit, Pamela Hayford
Vibrata	Helen Sylvia
Gymnasia	Ricki Covette
Philia	Donna McKechnie
Erronius	Edward Everett Horton
Miles Gloriosus	Adair McGowen[4]

UNDERSTUDIES: Erronius, Senex, Ross Hertz; Lycus, Miles Gloriosus, Alan Louw; Hysterium, David Neuman; Domina, Gymnasia, Emily Ruhberg; Hero, Proteans, Don Fleming; Panacea, Vibrata, Tintinabula, Jo Ann Tenney; Philia, Geminae, Carol Fox.

MUSICAL NUMBERS: "Comedy Tonight," "Love, I Hear," "The House of Marcus Lycus," "Lovely," "Pretty Little Picture," "Everybody Ought To Have A Maid," "I'm Calm," "Impossible," "Bring Me My Bride," "That Dirty Old Man," "That'll Show Him," "Funeral Sequence and Dance," "Comedy Tonight."

A Musical Comedy in two acts. The action takes place on a street in Rome in front of the houses of Erronius, Senex, and Lycus, on a day in spring, two hundred years before the Christian era.

General Manager: Al Berr
Company Manager: Carl Abraham
Press: George Deber, Ken Hinaman
Stage Managers: Henry Garrard, Ross Hertz, Don Fleming

† Succeeded by: 1. Dan Goff, 2. Keith Stewart, 3. Gil Lamb, 4. Robert Brooks.

For original New York production, see THEATRE WORLD, Vol. 18.

Top: (L) Helen Sylvia, Tisa Chang, Jerry Lester, Pamela Hayford, Ricki Covette, Helen Levit, Gloria Mills. (R) Jerry Lester, Ricki Covette, Arnold Stang. **Below:** Gil Lamb, Edward Everett Horton, Erik Rhodes, Paul Hartman, Jerry Lester

Bert Stratford, Donna McKechnie. **Above:** Arnold Stang, Justine Johnston

213

ANY WEDNESDAY

By Muriel Resnik; Directed by Henry Kaplan; Scenery Designed by Robert Randolph; Costumes, Theoni V. Aldredge; Lighting, Tharon Musser; Production Assistant, Nelle Nugent; Technical Supervisor, Ralph O. Willis; Presented by George W. George and Frank Granat and Howard Erskine, Edward Specter Productions, and Peter S. Katz. Opened Wednesday, September 9, 1964 at the Rochester, N. Y., Auditorium, and still touring May 31, 1965.

CAST

John Cleves	Larry Parks
Ellen Gordon	Monica Moran
Cass Henderson	Richard Roat
Dorothy Cleves	Patricia Cutts

STANDBYS: John, Warren Brown; Ellen, Loretta Swit; Dorothy, Jean LeBouvier; Cass, Warren Brown.

A Comedy in two acts and four scenes. The action takes place in a garden apartment in Manhattan's East Sixties at the present time.

General Manager: Edward H. Davis
Company Manager: Abe Cohen
Press: Lee Solters, Harvey B. Sabinson, Mary Ward
Stage Managers: Joe Calvan, Warren Brown

For original New York production, see THEATRE WORLD, Vol. 20.

Friedman-Abeles Photos

Top: (L) Monica Moran, Richard Roat
(R) Monica Moran, Larry Parks

Monica Moran, Patricia Cutts, Larry Parks

HERE'S LOVE

Book, Music, and Lyrics by Meredith Willson; Based on "Miracle On 34th St"; Story by Valentine Davies; Directed by Stuart Ostrow; Dances and Musical Numbers Staged by Michael Kidd; Settings by William and Jean Eckart; Costumes, Alvin Colt; Lighting, Tharon Musser; Musical Direction and Vocal Arrangements, Elliot Lawrence; Orchestrations, Don Walker; Dance Music Arranged by Peter Howard; Orchestra Conducted by Don Smith; Presented by Stuart Ostrow. Opened Monday, August 3, 1964 in the Los Angeles Philharmonic Auditorium, and closed at the Curran in San Francisco on December 19, 1964.

CAST

Mr. Kris Kringle	Laurence Naismith
Fred Gaily	John Payne
Susan Walker	Diane Higgins
Marvin Shellhammer	Bill Hinnant
Doris Walker	Lisa Kirk
Clerks	Catherine Collins, Gary Crabbe, Grace Mitchell, Betty Rosebrock, Sally Ransone, Ron L. Steinbeck, Kent Thomas
R. H. Macy	Howard I. Smith
Harry Finfer	Jeffrey Golkin
Hendrika	Donna Conforti
Hendrika's New Mother	Penny Gaston
Miss Crookshank	Betty Rosebrock
Mrs. Finfer	Lisa Carroll
Mr. Sawyer	Phil Leeds
Governor	Charles Dunn
Mayor	Russell Goodwin
Mr. Gimbel	Spencer Davis
Policeman	Bob McClure
Clara	Sally Ransone
Judge Martin Group	Cliff Hall
District Attorney Mara	Charles Braswell
Tammany O'Halloran	Robert Shafer
Nurse	Penny Gaston
Marines	Ed Becker, Charles Cagle, Bob McClure
Girl Scout Leader	Lita Terris
Bailiff	Charles Dunn
Mailman	Russell Goodwin
Thomas Mara, Jr.	Dewey Golkin
Thompson	Spencer Davis

CHILDREN: Dewey Golkin, Donna Conforti, Jeffrey Golkin, Bridget Knapp, Perry Golkin.

DANCERS: Arlene Ancona, Ron Bostick, Catherine Collins, Gary Crabbe, Patrick Cummings, Patrick Heim, Cheri Ingram, Grace Mitchell, Gary Ramback, Sally Ransone, Betty Rosebrock, Sandy Richardson, Salicia Smith, Bill Stanton, Ron L. Steinbeck, Kent Thomas.

SINGERS: Ed Becker, Charles Cagle, Lisa Carroll, Spencer Davis, Charles Dunn, Penny Gaston, Russell Goodwin, Barbara Gregory, Bob McClure, Carol Richards, Lita Terris.

UNDERSTUDIES: Fred, Charles Braswell; Doris, Lisa Carroll; Kris, Spencer Davis; Macy, Robert Shafer; Shellhammer, Russell Goodwin; D.A., Charles Dunn; Susan, Bridget Knapp; Sawyer, Russell Goodwin; Judge, Spencer Davis; Tammany, Edward Becker.

MUSICAL NUMBERS: "The Big Clown Balloons," "Arm In Arm," "You Don't Know," "The Plastic Alligator," "The Bugle," "Here's Love," "My Wish," "Pine Cones and Holly Berries," "Look, Little Girl," "Expect Things To Happen," "Love Come Take Me Again," "She Hadda Go Back," "That Man Over There," "My State," "Nothing In Common," Finale.

A Musical Play in two acts and twenty-four scenes. The action takes place at the present time between Thanksgiving and Christmas.

General Manager: Joseph Harris
Company Manager: Sam Pagliaro
Press: Harvey B. Sabinson, Harry Nigro, Hal Wiener
Stage Managers: Henri Caubisens, Tom Porter, Edward Becker

For original New York production, see THEATRE WORLD, Vol. 20.

Friedman-Abeles Photos

Right: John Payne, Lisa Kirk, Laurence Naismith, ane Higgins. Below: Howard I. Smith, Lisa Kirk, Cliff Hall, Bill Hinnant, Robert Shafer

Diane Higgins, Lisa Kirk

BAREFOOT IN THE PARK

By Neil Simon; Directed by Mike Nichols;
Setting Designed by Oliver Smith; Lighting,
Jean Rosenthal; Costumes, Donald Brooks;
Presented by Saint Subber. Opened Monday,
July 27, 1964 in Central City, Colo., Opera
House, and still touring May 31, 1965.

CAST

Corie Bratter	Joan Van Ark
Telephone Man	Lou Tiano
Delivery Man	Paul Haney
Paul Bratter	Richard Benjamin
Mrs. Banks	Myrna Loy
Victor Velasco	Sandor Szabo

UNDERSTUDIES: Mrs. Banks, Carolyn Bren-
ner; Paul, Jerry Mickey; Corie, Millee Taggart;
Victor, Paul Haney.

A Comedy in three acts and four scenes.
The action takes place at the present time in
the Bratter's apartment on East 48th Street in
New York City.

General Manager: C. Edwin Knill
Company Manager: Morry Efron
Press: Harvey B. Sabinson, Robert Reud
Stage Managers: Scott Jackson, Paul Haney
For original New York production, see THE-
ATRE WORLD, Vol. 20.

Friedman-Abeles Photos

Richard Benjamin, Joan Van Ark, Myrna Loy, Sandor Szabo
Top: (L) Myrna Loy, Joan Van Ark (R) Joan Van Ark, Richard Benjamin

George Blanchard

IN WHITE AMERICA

By Martin Duberman; Presented by Judith Rutherford Marechal; Directed by Harold Stone; Designed by Robin Wagner; Costumes, Patricia Quinn Stuart; Lighting, George Blanchard; Musical Director, Oscar Brand. Opened Wednesday, Jan. 27, 1965 in Plainfield, N.J., and closed May 15, 1965 in Mount Vernon, N.Y.

CAST

Elizabeth Franz	Novella Nelson
Moses Gunn†1	Anthony Palmer†2
Philip Baker Hall	Fred Pinkard

Music performed by George Blanchard

A Documentary of Negro History presented in two acts.

Stage Managers: Patricia Carmichael†3, George Blanchard

† Succeeded by: 1. Robert Jackson, 2. Richard Levy, 3. Dale E. Whitt

For original New York production, see THEATRE WORLD, Vol. 20.

Top: Moses Gunn, Novella Nelson, Philip Baker Hall, Fred Pinkard, Anthony Palmer, Elizabeth Franz

217

Harry Secombe

PICKWICK

Book, Wolf Mankowitz; Based on Charles Dickens' posthumous papers of the Pickwick Club; Music, Cyril Ornadel; Lyrics, Leslie Bricusse; Directed by Peter Coe; Settings and Lighting, Sean Kenny; Costumes, Roger Furse and Peter Rice; Choreography, Gillian Lynne; Musical Direction and Vocal Arrangements, Ian Fraser; Orchestrations, Eric Rogers; Presented by David Merrick in association with Bernard Delfont. Opened April 19, 1965, at the Curran Theatre, San Francisco, and still touring May 31, 1965.

CAST

Hot Toddy Seller	Jim Connor
Cold Toddy Seller	Stanley Simmonds
Bird Seller	Roger LePage
Hot Potato Man	Gerrit de Beer
Turnkey	Allan Lokos
Pickwick	Harry Secombe
Augustus Snodgrass	Julian Orchard
Tracy Tupman	John Call
Nathaniel Winkle	Oscar Quitak
Roker	Peter Costanza
Sam Weller	David Jones
Mr. Wardle	Michael Logan
Rachel	Helena Carroll
Isabella	Nancy Haywood
Emily	Sybil Scotford
Fat Boy	Joe Richards
Mr. Jingle	Anton Rodgers
Mary	Nancy Barrett
Mrs. Bardell	Charlotte Rae
Dr. Slammer	Stanley Simmonds
Bardell, Jr.	Sheldon Golomb
Major Domo	Jim Connor
First Officer	Richard Neilsen
Second Officer	Haydon Smith
Dodson	Michael Darbyshire
Fogg	Tony Sympson
Mrs. Leo Hunter	Elizabeth Parrish
Slumkey	Taylor Reed
Wicks	Haydon Smith
Judge	Richard Neilsen
Usher	Taylor Reed
Sgt. Snubbins	Allan Lokos
Sgt. Buzfuz	Brendan Barry
Jackson	Keith Perry
Sgt. Skimpkin	Clyde Laurents

CHILDREN: Michael Easton, Richard Easton, Tracy Evans, Leslie Ann Mapes, Bonnie Turner

PASSERS-BY, OSTLERS, DEBTORS, MAIDS, ETC.: Jill Alexander, Michael Amber, Julie Anderson, Bill Black, Bill Coppola, Ann Tell, Edmond Varrato, Larry Whiteley, Bruce Becker, Susan Cartt, Marilyn Charles, Bill Earl, Jo Freilich, Mary Keller, Don Lawrence, Frank Shepard, Nancy Stevens, Don Strong

UNDERSTUDIES: Messrs. Secombe, Taylor Reed; Jones, Roger LePage; Orchard, Keith Perry; Quitak, Larry Whitely; Call, Taylor Reed; Mrs. Bardell, Ann Tell; Mrs. Hunter, Selma Marcus; Wardle, Larry Pool; Dodson, Keith Perry; Mary, Mary Keller; Fogg, Gerrit de Beer; Buzfuz, Peter Costanza; Jingle, Richard Neilsen; Rachel, Elizabeth Parrish.

MUSICAL NUMBERS: "Business Is Booming," "Debtors Lament," "That's What I'd Like For Christmas," "The Pickwickians," "A Bit Of A Character," "Learn A Little Something," "There's Something About You," "You Never Met A Feller Like Me," "I'll Never Be Lonely Again," More Of Everything," "A Hell Of An Election," "Very," "If I Ruled The World," "Talk," "That's The Law," "Do As You Would Be Done By."

A Musical Comedy in two acts and thirteen scenes. The action takes place in and around London and Rochester in 1827.

General Manager: Jack Schlissel
Company Manager: Richard Highley
Press: Harvey Sabinson, Lee Solters, Lila King
Stage Managers: George Eckert, Larry Pool, Peter Stern

Friedman-Abeles

Mary Martin
in
"HELLO, DOLLY!"

HELLO, DOLLY!

Book by Michael Stewart; Music and Lyrics, Jerry Herman; Based on Play "The Matchmaker" by Thornton Wilder; Directed and Choreographed by Gower Champion; Settings, Oliver Smith; Costumes, Freddy Wittop; Lighting, Jean Rosenthal; Dance and Incidental Music Arrangements, Peter Howard; Musical Direction, Jay Blackton; Orchestration, Philip J. Lang; Vocal Arrangements, Shepard Coleman; Assistant to the Director, Lucia Victor; Dance Assistant, Lowell Purvis; A David Merrick and Champion Five Inc. Production; Presented by David Merrick. Opened April 19, 1965 at the Orpheum Theatre, Minneapolis, and still touring May 31, 1965.

CAST

Mrs. Dolly Gallagher Levi	Mary Martin
Ernestina	Judith Drake
Ambrose Kemper	Mark Alden
Horse	Eileen Barbaris, Debra Lyman
Horace Vandergelder	Loring Smith
Ermengarde	Beverlee Weir
Cornelius Hackl	Carleton Carpenter
Barnaby Tucker	Johnny Beecher
Irene Malloy	Marilynn Lovell
Minnie Fay	Coco Ramirez
Mrs. Rose	Charlise Mallory
Rudolph	Robert Hocknell
Judge	Skedge Miller

TOWNSPEOPLE, WAITERS, ETC: Eileen Barbaris, Alberta Barry, Eileen Casey, Polly Dawson, Elisa De Marko, Susan Freeman, Barbara Gregory, Caryl Hinchee, Kathryn Humphreys, Debra Lyman, Charlise Mallory, Ellen Mitchell, Susan Mora, Diane Nels, Jane Quinn, Julie Sargent, Robert Avian, Alvin Beam, Wayne Boyd, Gene Cooper, Byron Craig, Norman Fredericks, Ed Goldsmid, Mickey Hinton, Jim Hovis, Robert L. Hultman, Robert Lenn, Alexander Orfaly, Rudy Rajkovich, Bob Remick, Ross-Miles, Ree Russel, Kirby Smith, Charles Vick, Lou Zeldis.

MUSICAL NUMBERS: "I Put My Hand In," "It Takes A Woman," "Put On Your Sunday Clothes," "Ribbons Down My Back," "Motherhood," "Dancing," "Before The Parade Passes By," "Elegance," "The Waiters' Gallop," "Hello Dolly!," "It Only Takes A Moment," "So Long, Dearie," Finale.

A Musical Comedy in two acts and fifteen scenes. The action takes place during the past in Yonkers and Manhattan.

General Manager: Jack Schlissel
Company Manager: Fred Cuneo
Press: Lee Solters, Harvey B. Sabinson, Gertrude Bromberg
Stage Managers: Ben D. Kranz, Alan Hall, Richard Via, Skedge Miller

For original New York production, see THEATRE WORLD, Vol. 20.

Friedman-Abeles Photo

Loring Smith, Mary Martin

RICH LITTLE RICH GIRL

By Hugh Wheeler; Based on a Play by Miguel Mihura and Álvaro De Laiglesia; Directed by Noel Willman; Presented by Saint-Subber; Scenery by Peter Larkin; Costumes, Donald Brooks; Lighting, Martin Aronstein; Production Assistant, James Turner; Hairstyles, Ronald DeMann. Opened Monday, October 26, 1964 at the Walnut Street Theatre, Philadelphia, and closed there on Saturday, November 7, 1964.

CAST

Amelia Alton	Jean Simmons
Mae	Paddy Edwards
Liz Cantriss	Elizabeth Wilson
Fitzroy	Douglas Turner
Emery Alton	Larry Blyden
Raoul Orgaz	Raf Vallone
Pierre	Bruce Glover
Miss Brown	Joan Holloway

UNDERSTUDIES: Amelia, Wendy Mackenzie; Raoul, Bruce Glover; Emery, Jonathan Farwell; Liz, Miss Brown, Paddy Edwards; Fitzroy, Pierre, Roger Johnson, Jr.

A Comedy in three acts and four scenes. The action takes place at the present time in the Alton livingroom in Easthampton, Long Island.

General Manager: C. Edwin Knill
Company Manager: William Craver
Press: Harvey B. Sabinson, Lee Solters, Bernard J. Westman, Mel Kopp
Stage Managers: Ben D. Kranz, Roger Johnson, Jr.

Friedman-Abeles Photos

Raf Vallone, Jean Simmons, Larry Blyden
Above: Larry Blyden, Jean Simmons

221

EVERYBODY OUT, THE CASTLE IS SINKING

By Phoebe and Henry Ephron; Directed by Henry Ephron; Scenery and Lighting, George Jenkins; Costumes, Florence Klotz; Production Assistant, Cynthia Conroy; Title Song Composed by Elliot Lawrence; Presented by Lester Braunstein and Fred F. Finklehoffe. Opened at the Colonial Theatre, Boston, on Saturday, December 26, 1964, and closed there Saturday, January 9, 1965.

CAST

Jonathan Joy	Nigel Patrick
Marietta Joy	Marge Champion
Hilary Joy	Danny Fortus
Amanda Joy	Connie Scott
Nathaniel Joy	Jeff Conaway
Max	Richard Mulligan
Portia Joy	Audrey Price
Colin Joy	Phil Clark
Jenny Joy	Elizabeth Hartman
Elsa	Nancy Anderson
Albert Dennison	Hiram Sherman
Mr. Bonnard	Robert Dryden
Nick Ramo	Ryan MacDonald
Klara	Monica Lovett

UNDERSTUDIES: Jonathan, Dennison, John Beal; Marietta, Monica Lovett; Max, Nick, Bonnard, John Dutra; Jenny, Nancy Anderson; Hilary, Kenny Kealey; Colin, Nathaniel, Don Scardino.

A Comedy in two acts and five scenes. The action takes place in the living room of the Joy family in Switzerland at the present time.

General Managers: Joseph Harris, Ira Bernstein
Company Manager: Sam Pagliaro
Press: Bill Doll, Midori Tsuji, Shirley Herz, Richard Spittel
Stage Managers: Herman Shapiro, John Dutra

Impact Photos

Nigel Patrick, Marge Champion, Elizabeth Hartman, Phil Clark, Jeff Conaway, Connie Scott, Danny Fortus, Audrey Price. Above: Marge Champion, Ryan MacDonald

ROYAL FLUSH

Book by Jay Thompson and Robert Schlitt; Music and Lyrics, Jay Thompson; Sets and Costumes, Raoul Pene Du Bois; Lighting, Jules Fisher; Musical Direction, Skip Redwine; Orchestrations, Larry Wilcox; Dance Music Arranged by Hal Schaefer; Based on "The Green Bird" by Nino Savo; Presented by L. Slade Brown; Production Supervisor, Robert Linden; Production Associate, Mary Jean Parson. Opened Wednesday, December 30, 1964 at the Shubert Theatre, New Haven, Conn., and closed Saturday, January 23, 1965 at the Shubert Theatre in Philadelphia.

CAST

Mazocha	Mickey Deems
Pretty Girl	Jodi Williams
King Frederick	Louis Edmonds
Soldiers	Allen Knowles, Al De Sio, Fred Kimbrough
Queen Fredrika	Jane Connell
Ladies in Waiting	Judith Dunford, Renata Vaselle, Joyce Devlin, Donna Baccala
Dowager Queen Sadie	Kaye Ballard
Executioner	John Aristedes
Midwives	Altovise Gore, Meg Walter
Milkman	Allen Knowles
Banner Bearers	Ray Chabeau, Luigi Gasparinetti
Newsboy	Al De Sio
Babs	Jill O'Hara
Bob	Kenneth Nelson
Maxine	Charlotte Jones
Max	Dick O'Neill
Page	Al De Sio
Bird	Bernie Meyer
Bronzina	Beverly Todd
Alice	Kaye Ballard
Alvin	Mickey Deems
Albert	Allen Knowles
Radio Announcer	Al De Sio
Doorman	Ray Chabeau
Waiter	John Aristedes
Pianist	Allen Knowles
Maitre d'hotel	Mickey Deems
Miss Melba	Kaye Ballard
Willis	Mickey Deems
Wallace	Kaye Ballard
Announcer	Ray Chabeau
Miss Appleknocker	Kaye Ballard
Shirley	Renata Vaselle

UNDERSTUDIES: Sadie, Helen Gallagher; Mazocha, Allen Knowles; Bob, Al De Sio; Fredrika, Maxine, Jodi Williams; Babs, Bronzina, Donna Baccala; Frederick, Fred Kimbrough; Max, Bernie Meery; Bird, John Aristedes.

MUSICAL NUMBERS: "Caveat Emptor," "She's Sweet," "Bye Bye," "The Road To Hell," "For God, Home, Mother, and Country," "Think Up!," "It Could Be Worse," "Lotus Blossom," "You'll Be Something," "Being Quiet With You," "Oh, What An Island," "Just Reach Out And Touch Me," "The Edge Of The World," "Magic Time," "Try A Little," "No Happy Ending."

A Musical Comedy in two acts and sixteen scenes. The action takes place on Tuesday, June 31, in the Year of the Tarantula, on Cipango and that other island.

General and Company Manager: David Lawlor
Press: Bill Doll, Shirley Herz, Midori Tsuji, Richard Spittel
Stage Managers: James Frasher, Casey Walters, Fred Kimbrough

Friedman-Abeles Photos

Top Right: Jill O'Hara, Louis Edmonds
Below: Bernie Meyer, Jane Connell

Kaye Ballard, Mickey Deems

A SIGN OF AFFECTION

By Carolyn Green; Directed by Ron Winston; Scenery and Lighting, William and Jean Eckart; Costumes, Patricia Zipprodt; Presented by Gayle Stine; Production Supervisor, Ralph O. Willis; Production Assistant, Ann Hershey. Opened Wednesday, March 10, 1965, at the Shubert Theatre in New Haven, and closed Saturday, April 10, 1965 at the Walnut Theatre in Philadelphia.

CAST

Steve ....John Payne
Margo ....Nan Martin
Cassie ....Lesley Ann Warren

A comedy in three acts and five scenes. The action takes place in a broken-down carriage house on an old Long Island estate at the present time.

General Manager: Edward H. Davis
Company Manager: J. Ross Stewart
Press: Seymour Krawitz, Merle Debuskey, Ted Goldsmith
Stage Managers: John Maxtone-Graham, William H. Batchelder

Friedman-Abeles Photos

Left: Lesley Ann Warren, John Payne

Lesley Ann Warren, Nan Martin

Lesley Ann Warren, John Payne

PLEASURES AND PALACES

Music and Lyrics, Frank Loesser; Book by Sam Spewack and Frank Loesser; Based on Play "Once There Was A Russian" by Sam Spewack; Directed and Choreographed by Bob Fosse; Presented by Allen B. Whitehead in association with Frank Productions Inc.; Scenery and Lighting, Robert Randolph; Costumes, Freddy Wittop; Musical Director, Fred Werner; Orchestrations, Philip J. Lang; Hair Styles, Ronald DeMann; Production Manager, Ross Bowman. Opened Thursday, March 11, 1965, at the Fisher Theatre in Detroit, and closed there on Saturday, April 10, 1965.

CAST

Potemkin	Alfred Marks†
Bureyev	Leon Janney
Suslovski	Burt Bier
Minister	Darrell Notara
Catherine	Hy Hazell
John Paul Jones	John McMartin
Kollenovitch	Mort Marshall
Polgunov	Woody Romoff
First Villager	Michael Quinn
Second Villager	Burt Bier
Policeman	Stan Page
Sura	Phyllis Newman
Radbury	Eric Brotherson
Von Siegen	Sammy Smith
Captain Pasha	John Anania
Nun	Henrietta Valor
Father Feddor	Michael Quinn
Guard	David Gold
First Prisoner	John Anania
Second Prisoner	Michael Davis
Third Prisoner	Howard Kahl
Fourth Prisoner	Walter Hook

SINGERS: John Anania, Ken Ayers, Burt Bier, Michael Davis, Alice Evans, Laurie Franks, Walter Hook, Howard Kahl, Zona Kennedy, Stan Page, Michael Quinn, Dana Simmons, Henrietta Valor, Carole Woodruff.

DANCERS: Pat Cummings, Kathryn Doby, Don Emmons, Eddie Gasper, Gene Gavin, David Gold, Dick Korthaze, Darrell Notara, Leland Palmer, Renata Powers, Brooke Roma, Betty Rosebrock, Barbara Sharma, Ron L. Steinbeck

MUSICAL NUMBERS: "Salute," "I Hear Bells," "My Lover Is A Scoundrel," "To Marry," "Hail Majesty," "Thunder and Lightning," "To Your Health," "Turkish Delight," "Neither The Time Nor The Place," "In Your Eyes," "Truly Loved," "The Sins of Sura," "Hoorah For Jones," "Propaganda," "Barabanchik," "What Is Life?," "Ah To Be Home Again," "Pleasures and Palaces," "Tears of Joy," "Far, Far, Far Away."

A Musical Comedy in two acts. The action takes place in 1787 in the Russia of Catherine The Great.

General Manager: Joe Harris
Press: Reuben and Florence Rabinovitch
Stage Managers: Edward Preston, Michael Sinclair
† Succeeded by Jack Cassidy.

Friedman-Abeles Photos

Top: (L) Hy Hazell, Alfred Marks, Eric Brotherson, Leon Janney, Barbara Sharma (R) Alfred Marks (C) Below: John McMartin, Phyllis Newman

Hy Hazell, Phyllis Newman, Alfred Marks

Michael O'Sullivan
of
"TARTUFFE"

Carolyn Coates
of
"THE TROJAN WOMEN"

Keith Brian Staulcup Photo

Victor Spinetti
of
"OH, WHAT A LOVELY WAR"

228

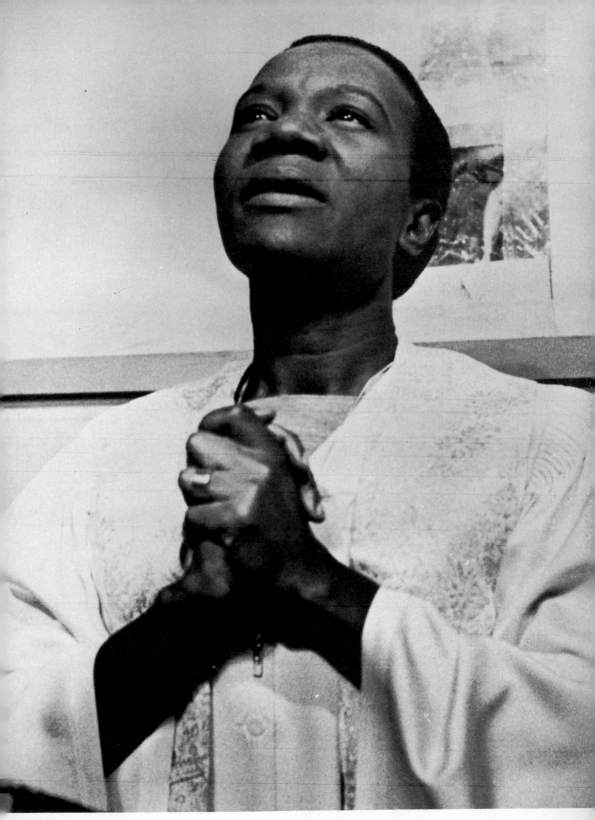

Bea Richards
in
"THE AMEN CORNER"

Joanna Pettet
of
"POOR RICHARD"

Jaime Sanchez
of
"CONERICO WAS HERE TO STAY" and "THE TOILET"

Clarence Williams III
of
"SLOW DANCE ON THE KILLING GROUND"

Linda Lavin
of
"WET PAINT"

Bert Andrews Photo

234

Robert Walker
in
"I KNOCK AT THE DOOR" and "PICTURES IN THE HALLWAY"

Joyce Jillson
of
"THE ROAR OF THE GREASEPAINT—THE SMELL OF THE CROWD"

Luba Lisa
of
"I HAD A BALL"

Nicolas Surovy
of
"HELEN"

PROMISING PERSONALITIES
THEATRE WORLD AWARD WINNERS

1944-45

Richard Davis
Judy Holliday
Bambi Linn

John Lund
Betty Comden
John Raitt

Margaret Phillips
Richard Hart
Charles Lang

Donald Murphy
Nancy Noland

1945-46

Burt Lancaster
Patricia Marshall
Bill Callahan

Barbara Bel Geddes
Wendell Corey

Marlon Brando
Mary James

Beatrice Pearson
Paul Douglas

1946-47

Patricia Neal
James Mitchell
Ellen Hanley

David Wayne
Marion Bell
Peter Cookson

Keith Andes
John Jordan
Dorothea MacFarland

Ann Crowley
George Keane

1947-48

Douglas Watson
Meg Mundy
James Whitmore

Valerie Bettis
Whitfield Connor
Patrice Wymore

Ralph Meeker
Peggy Maley
Edward Bryce

June Lockhart
Mark Dawson
Estelle Loring

1948-49

Carol Channing
Tod Andrews
Mary McCarty

Gene Nelson
Allyn Ann McLerie
Byron Palmer

Julie Harris
Richard Derr
Doe Avedon

Cameron Mitchell
Jean Carson
Bob Scheerer

1949-50

Charlton Heston
Priscilla Gillette
Rick Jason

Grace Kelly
Don Hanmer
Marcia Henderson

Charles Nolte
Lydia Clarke
Roger Price

Nancy Andrews
Phil Arthur
Barbara Brady

1950-51

Richard Burton
Barbara Ashley
Russell Nype

Maureen Stapleton
Eli Wallach
Isabel Bigley
William Smithers

Jack Palance
Marcia Van Dyke
Martin Brooks

Pat Crowley
James Daly
Cloris Leachman

1951-52

Audrey Hepburn
Tony Bavaar
Patricia Benoit

Ronny Graham
Virginia de Luce
Charles Proctor
Marian Winters

Kim Stanley
Conrad Janis
Diana Herbert
Dick Kallman

Eric Sinclair
Helen Wood
Peter Conlow

1952-53

Paul Newman
Eileen Heckart
John Stewart

Geraldine Page
Ray Stricklyn
Edie Adams
Rosemary Harris

John Kerr
Gwen Verdon
Peter Kelley
Penelope Munday

Sheree North
Richard Kiley
Gloria Marlowe

1953-54

Eva Marie Saint
Leo Penn
Elizabeth Montgomery

James Dean
Kay Medford
Orson Bean

Harry Belafonte
Carol Haney
Jonathan Lucas

Ben Gazzara
Joan Diener
Scott Merrill

1954-55

Anthony Perkins
Jacqueline Brookes
Page Johnson

Julie Andrews
Dennis Patrick
Shirl Conway

Christopher Plummer
Loretta Leversee
David Daniels

Barbara Cook
Jack Lord
Mary Fickett

1955-56

Jayne Mansfield
Anthony Franciosa
Susan Strasberg

Laurence Harvey
Susan Johnson
John Michael King
Al Hedison

Sarah Marshall
Andy Griffith
Diane Cilento
Dick Davalos

Fritz Weaver
Gaby Rodgers
Earle Hyman

1956-57

George Grizzard
Carol Lynley
Sydney Chaplin

Peggy Cass
Peter Palmer
Inga Swenson

Cliff Robertson
Pippa Scott
Jason Robards, Jr.

Bradford Dillman
Sylvia Daneel
Peter Donat

1957-58

Anne Bancroft
George C. Scott
Colleen Dewhurst

Robert Morse
Joan Hovis
Eddie Hodges

Carol Lawrence
Warren Berlinger
Jacqueline McKeever

Timmy Everett
Wynne Miller
Richard Easton

1958-59

Rip Torn
Dolores Hart
Lou Antonio

Paul Roebling
France Nuyen
Ben Piazza
Pat Suzuki

Tammy Grimes
William Shatner
Ina Balin
Richard Cross

Larry Hagman
Susan Oliver
Roger Mollien

1959-60

Carol Burnett
Donald Madden
Eileen Brennan

Jane Fonda
John McMartin
Elisa Loti

Warren Beatty
Anita Gillette
Dick Van Dyke

George Maharis
Patty Duke
Lauri Peters

1960-61

Robert Goulet
Joyce Bulifant

James MacArthur
June Harding
Ron Husmann

Dennis Cooney
Joan Hackett

Bruce Yarnell
Nancy Dussault

1961-62

Barbara Harris
John Stride
Brenda Vaccaro

Peter Fonda
Karen Morrow
Don Galloway

Janet Margolin
Sean Garrison
Elizabeth Ashley

Robert Redford
James Earl Jones
Keith Baxter

1962-63

Dorothy Loudon
Stuart Damon
Julienne Marie

Alan Arkin
Estelle Parsons
Robert Drivas

Liza Minnelli
Bob Gentry
Diana Sands

Swen Swenson
Melinda Dillon
Brandon Maggart

1963-64

Gilbert Price
John Tracy
Claude Giraud

Barbara Loden
Philip Proctor
Gloria Bleezarde

Alan Alda
Ketty Lester
Jennifer West

Imelda De Martin
Lawrence Pressman

238

| Ben Aliza | Anne Bancroft | Alan Bates | Barbara Baxley | Linda Bennett |

BIOGRAPHIES

ADLER, LUTHER. Born in New York City, May 4, 1903. Attended Lewis Inst. Made first appearance in 1908 in "Schmendrick." Other performances include "Night Over Taos," "Success Story," "Alien Corn," "Men In White," "Gold Eagle Guy," "Awake And Sing," "Paradise Lost," "Johnny Johnson," "Golden Boy," "Rocket To The Moon," "The Russian People," "Two On An Island," "Common Ground," "Beggars Are Coming To Town," "Dunnigan's Daughter," "A Flag Is Born," "The Merchant of Venice," "A Month In The Country," "A Very Special Baby," "The Passion of Josef D.," "The Three Sisters," "Fiddler On The Roof."

ALCALDE, MARIO. Born in Key West, Fla., Sept. 6, 1926. Attended Theatre School of Dramatic Arts and American Theatre Wing. Made first appearance in City Center's 1950 revival of "Captain Brassbound's Conversion," followed by "Bullfight," "The Flowering Peach," "The Lovers," "Diamond Orchid."

ALDA, ALAN. Born in New York City, Jan. 28, 1936. Attended Fordham Univ. and Cleveland Playhouse. Broadway credits include "Only In America," "Purlie Victorious," "Fair Game For Lovers" for which he won a THEATRE WORLD Award, and "Cafe Crown." Off-Broadway credits: "Darwin's Theories," "A Whisper In God's Ear," and "Second City" (1963 edition), "The Owl and The Pussycat."

ALDA, ROBERT. Born in New York City, Feb. 26, 1914. Attended New York U. Made many motion pictures and appeared in night clubs before making Broadway bow in 1950 in "Guys and Dolls." Has appeared since in "Harbor Lights," "What Makes Sammy Run."

ALDERMAN, JOHN. Born in Syracuse, N.Y., June 6, 1937. Attended Syracuse U. Made Broadway bow in 1957 in "The Cave Dwellers," followed by "The Sign in Sidney Brustein's Window."

ALIZA, BEN. Born in Brooklyn, March 22, 1938. Graduate of Brooklyn College. Appeared Off-Bdwy in "Witches' Sabbath" before making Broadway bow in 1963 in "Andorra," followed by "The Sign In Sidney Brustein's Window."

ALLEN, ELIZABETH. Born in Jersey City, N.J., Jan. 25, 1934. Attended Rutgers U. Made Broadway debut in 1957 in "Romanoff and Juliet," followed by "The Gay Life," "Do I Hear A Waltz?"

ALLEN, NORMAN. Born in London, Dec. 24, 1939. Attended Royal Academy of Dramatic Art. Played in English productions before making New York bow in 1963 in "Chips With Everything," followed by "Half A Sixpence."

ALLEN, RAE. Born in Brooklyn, July 3, 1926. Attended Hunter College, American Academy of Dramatic Arts. Has appeared in "Where's Charley?," "Alive and Kicking," "Call Me Madam," "Pajama Game," "Damn Yankees," "Pictures In The Hallway" and "I Knock At The Door" (Off-Bdwy), "Oliver," "Traveller Without Luggage."

ANDERSON, JUDITH. Born in Adelaide, Australia, Feb. 10, 1898. Made NY debut in 1923 in "Peter Weston," followed by "Cobra," The Dove," "Strange Interlude," "As You Desire Me," "Firebird," "The Mask and The Face," "Come of Age," "The Old Maid," "Family Portrait," "Hamlet," "Macbeth," "The Three Sisters," "Medea," "Tower Beyond Tragedy," "John Brown's Body," "In The Summer House," "The Chalk Garden," "Comes A Day," and toured in a one-woman show.

ANDREWS, NANCY. Born in Minneapolis, Dec. 16, 1924. Studied at Pasadena Playhouse. Has appeared in "Hilarities," "Touch and Go," for which she received a THEATRE WORLD Award, "Gentlemen Prefer Blondes," "Hazel Flagg," "Plain and Fancy," "Pipe Dream," "Juno," "Christine," "The Threepenny Opera," "Tiger Rag," "Flower Drum Song," "Madame Aphrodite," "Little Me," "Say Nothing" (Off-Bdwy).

ANTONIO, LOU. Born in Oklahoma City, Jan. 23, 1934. Attended U. of Okla. Appeared in stock before NY bow (off-Bdwy) in 1959 in "The Buffalo Skinner" for which he received a THEATRE WORLD Award. Has appeared since in "The Power of Darkness," "The Good Soup," "Cry of The Raindrop," "Garden of Sweets," "Andorra," "Lady of The Camellias," "The Ballad of The Sad Cafe," "Dr. Faustus," "Ready When You Are C. B."

ARKIN, ALAN. Born in NYC, March 26, 1934. Attended Los Angeles Junior College, and Bennington College. Won 5 acting scholarships, including Brandeis Arts Inst. Appeared off-Bdwy in "Heloise," "Man Out Loud," and on Bdwy in "From The Second City" (1962), and "Enter Laughing" for which he received a THEATRE WORLD Award, "Luv."

ARMUS, SIDNEY. Born in the Bronx, Dec. 19, 1924. Attended Brooklyn College. Has appeared in "South Pacific," "Wish You Were Here," "The Flowering Peach," "A Hole In The Head," "The Cold Wind and The Warm," "Harold," "A Thousand Clowns," "Never Live Over A Pretzel Factory," "The Odd Couple."

ARTHUR, BEATRICE. Born in NYC, May 13. Attended The New School. Has appeared in "Seventh Heaven" (1954), "Nature's Way," "The Threepenny Opera," "Shoestring Revue," "Ulysses in Nighttown," "The Gay Divorce," "Fiddler On The Roof."

BAIN, CONRAD. Born in Lethbridge, Canada, Feb. 4, 1923. Attended Banff School of Fine Arts, American Academy of Dramatic Arts. Has appeared in "Sixth Finger In A Five Finger Glove," "Candide," "The Makropoulos Secret," "Hot Spot," "Advise and Consent," "The Queen and The Rebels" (off-Bdwy).

BALLARD, KAYE. Born in Cleveland, Ohio, Nov. 20. Appeared in stock, vaudeville, and night clubs before making NY bow in "The Golden Apple," followed by "Carnival," "The Beast In Me," "Cole Porter Revisited" (Off-Bdwy).

| Stanley Beck | Tom Bosley | Carol Burnett | Robert Burr | Mary Grace Can... |

BANCROFT, ANNE. Born in NYC, Sept. 17, 1931. Attended American Academy of Dramatic Art. Made Bdwy debut in 1958 in "Two For The Seesaw" for which she received a THEATRE WORLD Award, followed by "The Miracle Worker," "Mother Courage and Her Children."

BANKHEAD, TALLULAH. Born in Huntsville, Ala., Jan. 31, 1902. Made Bdwy debut in 1918 in "The Squab Farm," followed by "39 East," "Footloose," "Nice People," "Her Temporary Husband," "The Exciters." Appeared in London from 1923-30. Returned in 1933 in "Forsaking All Others," followed by "Dark Victory," "Something Gay," "Reflected Glory," revivals of "Rain," "The Circle," "Antony and Cleopatra," "Private Lives," and "A Streetcar Named Desire," in "The Little Foxes," "Clash By Night," "The Skin Of Our Teeth," "The Eagle Has Two Heads," "Dear Charles," "Eugenia," "Crazy October" and "Here Today" on tour, "Midgie Purvis," "The Milk Train Doesn't Stop Here Anymore."

BARRS, NORMAN. Born in London, Nov. 6, 1917. Appeared with Dublin Gate Co. in "John Bull's Other Island," "The Old Lady Says No!," and "Where Stars Walk," and in "Now I Lay Me Down To Sleep," "The Little Glass Clock," "The Apple Cart," "The Little Moon of Alban," "Kwamina," "Poor Bitos."

BATES, ALAN. Born in Derbyshire, Eng., Feb. 17, 1934. Attended Royal Academy of Dramatic Art. Made Broadway bow in 1957 in "Look Back In Anger," followed by "The Caretaker," "Poor Richard."

BAXLEY, BARBARA. Born in Porterville, Cal., Jan. 1, 1925. Trained at Neighborhood Playhouse. Has appeared in "Private Lives" (1948), "Out West of Eighth," succeeded Jean Arthur in "Peter Pan," Julie Harris in "I Am A Camera," and Kim Stanley in "Bus Stop," "Camino Real," "The Frogs of Spring," "Oh, Men! Oh, Women!," "The Flowering Peach," "Period of Adjustment," "Brecht on Brecht," "She Loves Me," "The Three Sisters."

BEAN, ORSON. Born in Burlington, Vt., July 22, 1928. Appeared in night clubs before making Bdwy bow in 1953 in "Men of Distinction," followed by "John Murray Anderson's Almanac" for which he received a THEATRE WORLD Award, "Will Success Spoil Rock Hunter?," "Nature's Way," City Center revivals of "Mister Roberts" and "Say, Darling," "Subways Are For Sleeping," "Never Too Late," "Home Movies," "I Was Dancing."

BECK, STANLEY. Born in NYC, June 5, 1936. Has appeared in "Mr. Roberts," and Off-Bdwy in "The Balcony," "There Is No End," "The Days and Nights of Beebee Fenstermaker," and with the Lincoln Center Repertory Co. in "The Changeling" and "Incident At Vichy."

BEDFORD, BRIAN. Born in Morley, Yorkshire, Eng., Feb. 16, 1935. Attended Royal Academy of Dramatic Arts. Made NY bow Dec. 2, 1960, in "Five Finger Exercise." Has appeared since in "Lord Pengo," "The Private Ear" and "The Public Eye," "The Knack."

BENNETT, LINDA. Born June 19, 1942 in Salt Lake City, Utah. Appeared in stock and television before making New York debut Dec. 23, 1964 in City Center revival of "Brigadoon."

BLACKBURN, CLARICE. Born in San Francisco. Graduate of Texas State College. Appeared Off-Bdwy in "The Grass Harp" and "American Gothic" before making Bdwy debut in 1955 in "The Desk Set," followed by "The Happy Time," Juno," "The Miracle Worker," "The Queen And The Rebels."

BOAZ, CHARLES. Born in Massena Springs, N.Y., June 19, 1919. Attended American Theater Wing, and American Academy of Dramatic Art. Made Bdwy bow in 1946 in "A Joy Forever," followed by "Mr. Roberts," "A Flag Is Born," "The Big Two," "Gramercy Ghost," "The Male Animal" (1952), "The Last Analysis."

BOOTH, CAROL. Born in Manchester, Eng., Feb. 24, 1941. Studied at Royal Academy of Dramatic Arts. Appeared Off-Bdwy in "The Knack" before making Broadway debut Oct. 7, 1964 in "Beekman Place."

BOSLEY, TOM. Born in Chicago, Oct. 1, 1927. Made Bdwy bow in 1959 in "Fiorello!," followed by "Nowhere To Go But Up," "Natural Affection," "A Murderer Among Us," "Catch Me If You Can."

BRUCE, CAROL. Born in Great Neck, L.I., Nov. 15, 1919. Made Broadway debut in "George White's Scandals of 1939," followed by "Nice Goin'," "Louisiana Purchase," "Show Boat" (1946), "Along Fifth Avenue," "A Family Affair," "Pal Joey" (City Center), "Do I Hear A Waltz?"

BURNETT, CAROL. Born in San Antonio, Tex., April 26, 1935. Attended UCLA. Made NY debut in 1959 in "Once Upon A Mattress" for which she received a THEATRE WORLD Award. Has appeared since in "Fade Out—Fade In."

BURNS, DAVID. Born in NYC, June 22, 1902. Has appeared in "Polly Preferred," "Wonder Boy," "Face The Music," "The Man Who Came To Dinner," "Pal Joey," "My Dear Public," "Billion Dollar Baby," "Make Mine Manhattan," "Out Of This World," "Two's Company," "Men of Distinction," "A Hole In The Head," "The Music Man," "A Funny Thing Happened On The Way To The Forum," "Hello, Dolly!"

BURR, ROBERT. Born in Jersey City, N.J. Attended Colgate U. Has appeared in "The Cradle Will Rock," "Mister Roberts," "Romeo and Juliet" (de Haviland revival), "Picnic," "The Lovers," "Anniversary Waltz," "Top Man," "Remains To Be Seen," "The Wall," "Andersonville Trial," "A Shot In The Dark," "A Man For All Seasons," "Luther," "Hamlet" (1964), "Bajour."

BURTON, RICHARD. Born in Pontrhydyfen, South Wales, Nov. 10, 1925. Attended Exeter College, Oxford. Made Bdwy bow in 1950 in "The Lady's Not For Burning" for which he received a THEATRE WORLD Award, followed by "Legend of Lovers," "Time Remembered," "Camelot," "Hamlet."

CANFIELD, MARY GRACE. Born Sept. 3, 1926 in Rochester, N.Y. Graduate of Harley School. Has appeared in "The Frogs of Spring," "The Waltz of The Toreadors," "Beekman Place," and Off-Bdwy in "Galileo," "The Immortal Husband" and "In The Summerhouse."

CARNEY, ART. Born in Mt. Vernon, N.Y., Nov. 4, 1918. Appeared in vaudeville, night clubs, stock and television before making Bdwy bow in 1957 in "The Rope Dancers," followed by "Take Her, She's Mine," "The Odd Couple."

Nancy Carroll   Judy Cassmore   Barbara Cook   Grover Dale   Cathryn Damon

CARROLL, DANNY. Born May 30, 1940 in Maspeth, L.I. Graduate of High School of Performing Arts. Made Broadway bow in 1957 in "The Music Man," followed by "The Boys From Syracuse" and "Babes In The Wood" (Off-Bdwy), "Flora, The Red Menace."

CARROLL, NANCY. Born in NYC, Nov. 19, 1906. Made Broadway debut in "The Passing Show of 1923," followed by "Topics Of 1923," "The Passing Show of 1924," "Mayflowers," ten years in films, "Undesirable Lady," "I Must Love Someone," "For Heaven's Sake, Mother," "Cindy" (Off-Bdwy).

CASSMORE, JUDY. Born in San Francisco, March 27, 1942. Attended Hollywood Professional School. Appeared with Los Angeles Civic Light Opera and in stock before making Bdwy debut in "Fade Out —Fade In."

CHANNING, CAROL. Born in Seattle, Wash., Jan. 31. 1921. Attended Bennington College. Has appeared in "No For An Answer," "Let's Face It," "So Proudly We Hail," "Lend An Ear" for which she received a THEATRE WORLD Award, "Gentlemen Prefer Blondes," "Wonderful Town," "The Vamp," "Show Girl," "Hello Dolly!"

CHAPLIN, SYDNEY. Born in Los Angeles, Mar. 31, 1926. Attended Lawrenceville School. Managed, directed, and acted in Circle Theatre, Hollywood. Made several films before Bdwy bow in 1956 in "Bells Are Ringing" for which he received a THEATRE WORLD Award, followed by "Goodbye, Charlie," "Subways Are For Sleeping," "In The Counting House," "Funny Girl."

CHEVALIER, MAURICE. Born Sept. 12, 1893 in Paris. Made NY bow in 1928 at the New Amsterdam Roof, followed by several years in Hollywood films. Returned to Broadway in one-man shows in 1934, 1947, 1948, 1963, and 1965.

CLARK, ALEXANDER. Born in NYC, May 2, 1904. Has appeared in "Merton Of The Movies," "Excess Baggage," "Biography," "Too True To Be Good," "Victoria Regina," "Abe Lincoln In Illinois." "Margin For Error," "In Time To Come," "Sheppy," "Legend Of Lovers," "The Captains and The Kings," "Calculated Risk," "Brigadoon" (1964 City Center).

CLARK, FRED. Born in Lincoln, Calif., March 9, 1914. Attended Stanford U. and American Academy of Dramatic Art. Has appeared in "School House On The Lot," "What A Life," "See My Lawyer," "Mister Roberts" (1956 City Center), "Romanoff and Juliet," "Viva Madison Avenue," "Absence Of A Cello."

CONVY, BERT. Born in St. Louis, Mo., July 23, 1935. Graduate of UCLA. Made NY bow in 1959 in "Billy Barnes Revue," followed by "Nowhere To Go But Up," "Morning Sun," "Love and Kisses," "Fiddler On The Roof"

COOK, BARBARA. Born in Atlanta, Ga., Oct. 25, 1927. Has appeared in "Flahooley," "Plain and Fancy" for which she received a THEATRE WORLD Award, "Candide," "The Music Man," City Center revivals of "Carousel" and "The King and I," "The Gay Life," "She Loves Me," "Something More," "Any Wednesday."

COPELAND, JOAN. Born in NYC, June 1, 1922. Attended Brooklyn College and American Academy of Dramatic Arts. Has appeared in "How I Wonder," "Sundown Beach," "Detective Story," "A Handful Of Fire," "Tovarich," "Something More."

CORNELL, KATHARINE. Born Feb. 16, 1898 in Berlin, Ger. Has appeared in "Nice People," "A Bill of Divorcement," "Will Shakespeare," "The Enchanted Cottage," "Candida," "The Green Hat," "The Letter," "The Age of Innocence," "The Barretts of Wimpole Street," "Romeo and Juliet," "St. Joan," "Wingless Victory," "No Time For Comedy," "The Doctor's Dilemma," "The Three Sisters," "Lovers and Friends," "Antigone," "Antony and Cleopatra," "That Lady," "The Constant Wife," "The Prescott Proposals," "The Dark Is Light Enough," "The Firstborn," "Dear Liar."

COTSWORTH, STAATS. Born in Oak Park, Ill., Feb. 17, 1908. Received training with Eva Le-Gallienne's Civic Repertory Theatre. Has appeared in "Romeo and Juliet," "Alice In Wonderland," "Rain From Heaven," "Murder At The Vanities," "Madame Capet," "Macbeth" (1941), "She Stoops To Conquer" (1949 City Center), "Richard III" (1953), "Advise and Consent," "Hamlet" (Central Park), "I Knock At The Door" and "Pictures In A Hallway" Off-Bdwy.

COULOURIS, GEORGE. Born in Manchester, Eng., Oct. 1, 1903. Made NY bow in 1929 in "The Novice and The Duke," followed by "The Apple Cart." "The Late Christopher Bean," "Best Sellers," "Mary of Scotland," "Valley Forge," "Blind Alley," "Saint Joan," "Julius Caesar," "The Shoemaker's Holiday," "Madame Capet," "The White Steed." "Richard III," "The Alchemist," "The Insect Comedy," "Beekman Place."

CRONYN, HUME. Born in London, Ont. Can., July 18, 1911. Attended Ridley College, McGill U., American Academy of Dramatic Art. Has appeared in "Hipper's Holiday," "High Tor," "Escape This Night," "Three Men On A Horse," "Boy Meets Girl," "Room Service," "The Three Sisters," "Mr. Big," "Retreat To Pleasure," "The Fourposter," "The Honeys," "A Day By The Sea," "The Man In The Dog Suit," "Triple Play," "Big Fish, Little Fish," "Hamlet" (Burton revival), "The Physicists."

CUSHMAN, NANCY. Born in Brooklyn, April 26, 1913. Graduate of Rollins College. Has appeared in "White Man," "Storm Over Patsy," "Gloriana," "Janie," "Be Your Age," "J.B.," "Little Me," and Off-Bdwy in "The American Dream" and "The Child Buyer."

DAILEY, IRENE. Born in NYC, Sept. 12, 1920. Attended Sacred Heart Convent. Has appeared in "Nine Girls," "Truckline Cafe," "Miss Lonely Hearts," "Andorra." "The Good Woman of Setzuan" (Phoenix), "The Subject Was Roses."

DALE GROVER. Born in Harrisburg, Pa., July 22, 1935. Made Bdwy bow in 1956 in "Li'l Abner," followed by "West Side Story," "Greenwillow," Off-Bdwy in "Fallout" and "Too Much Johnson," "Sail Away," "Half A Sixpence."

DAMON, CATHRYN. Born Sept. 11, in Seattle, Wash. Studied at Met Opera Ballet School. Made Bdwy debut in 1954 in "By The Beautiful Sea," followed by "The Vamp," "Shinbone Alley," "A Family Affair," "Foxy," Off-Bdwy in "The Boys From Syracuse" and "The Secret Life Of Walter Mitty," "Flora, The Red Menace."

DAMON, STUART. Born in Brooklyn, Feb. 5, 1937. Graduate of Brandeis U. Made Bdwy bow in 1959 in "First Impressions," followed by "From A To Z," "Entertain A Ghost," Off-Bdwy revival of "The Boys From Syracuse" for which he received a THEATRE WORLD Award, "Do I Hear A Waltz?"

241

| John Devlin | Brandon DeWilde | Alice Drummond | James Dybas | Michael Enser |

DANA, LEORA. Born in NYC, April 1, 1923. Attended Barnard College and Royal Academy of Dramatic Arts, London. Has appeared in "The Madwoman of Chaillot," "The Happy Time," "Point of No Return," "Sabrina Fair," "The Best Man," "In The Summer House" (Off-Bdwy), "Beekman Place."

DANIELS, CAROLAN. Born May 16, 1940 in Fullerton, Calif. Graduate of USC. Appeared in stock and television, and Off-Bdwy in "Telemachus Clay" before making Broadway debut Nov. 30, 1964 in "Slow Dance On The Killing Ground."

D'ANTONAKIS, FLEURY. Born in Athens, Greece, May 11, 1939. Graduate of Brandeis U. Studied at Neighborhood Playhouse. Made Broadway debut March 18, 1965 in "Do I Hear A Waltz?"

DAVIS, SAMMY, JR. Born in NYC, Dec. 8, 1925. Played in vaudeville, burlesque, and night clubs before making Broadway bow in 1956 in "Mr. Wonderful" followed by "Golden Boy."

DAYKARHANOVA, TAMARA. Born in Moscow, Russia, Jan. 14, 1894. Trained at Moscow Art Theatre, with Stanislavsky. Has appeared in "The House of Bernarda Alba," "The Emperor's Clothes," "Bullfight," "The Three Sisters."

DE LAPPE, GEMZE. Born in Portsmouth, Va., Feb. 28, 1925. Attended Hunter College and Peabody Conservatory. Has appeared in "Oklahoma," "The King and I," "Paint Your Wagon," "Juno," "Brigadoon" (1964 City Center).

DELL, GABRIEL. Born in Barbados, B.W.I., Oct. 7, 1930. Has appeared in "Dead End," "Tickets, Please," "Ankles Aweigh," "Fortuna," City Center revivals of "Can-Can," "Wonderful Town," and "Oklahoma," "Marathon '33," "Anyone can Whistle," "The Sign In Sidney Brustein's Window."

De MARTIN, IMELDA. Born in Merano, Italy, Sept. 16, 1936. Has appeared in "Plain and Fancy," "My Fair Lady," "Goldilocks," "Gypsy," "Girls Against The Boys," "The Sound of Music," "Jenny," "South Pacific" (City Center), and Off-Bdwy in "The Amorous Flea" for which she received a THEATRE WORLD Award, "Brigadoon" (1964 City Center).

DEVLIN, JOHN. Born in Cleveland, Ohio, Jan. 26, 1937. Graduate of Carnegie Tech. Appeared in stock and with American Shakespeare Festival before making Broadway bow Nov. 14, 1964 in "Poor Bitos."

DE WILDE, BRANDON. Born in NYC, April 9, 1942. Made Broadway bow in 1950 in "The Member Of The Wedding," followed by "Mrs. McThing," "The Emperor's Clothes," "A Race Of Hairy Men."

DRAKE, ALFRED. Born in NYC, Oct. 7, 1914. Attended Brooklyn College. Has appeared in "Two Bouquets," "White Horse Inn," "Babes In Arms," "One For The Money," "Straw Hat Revue," "Two For The Show," "Out Of The Frying Pan," "As You Like it," "Oklahoma," "Sing Out Sweet Land," "Beggar's Holiday," "The Cradle Will Rock," "Joy To The World," "Kiss Me, Kate," "The Gambler," "Kismet," "Kean," "Lorenzo," "Hamlet" (1964).

DRIVAS, ROBERT. Born in Coral Gables, Fla. Attended U. of Miami, U. of Chicago. Trained with Greek National Theatre, Athens, and Coconut Grove Playhouse, Fla. Made Bdwy bow in 1958 in "The Firstborn," followed by "Mrs. Dally Has A Lover" (Off-Bdwy) for which he received a THEATRE WORLD Award, "Lorenzo," "The Irregular Verb To Love," "And Things That Go Bump In The Night."

DRUMMOND, ALICE. Born in Pawtucket, R.I., May 21, 1929. Attended Pembroke College. Made Bdwy debut in 1963 in "The Ballad of The Sad Cafe" after appearing with the Phoenix Co., and Off-Bdwy in "Royal Gambit," "Go Show Me A Dragon," "Gallows Humor," "The American Dream," and "The Giants' Dance."

DUNNOCK, MILDRED. Born in Baltimore, Md. Attended Goucher College, Johns Hopkins U., and Columbia. Made Bdwy debut in 1932 in "Life Begins," followed by "The Corn Is Green," "Richard III," "Only The Heart," "Foolish Notions," "Lute Song," "Another Part Of The Forest," "The Hallams," "Death Of A Salesman," "Pride's Crossing," "The Wild Duck" (1951), "In The Summer House," "Cat On A Hot Tin Roof," "Child of Fortune," "The Milk Train Doesn't Stop Here Anymore," "The Trojan Women" (Off-Bdwy), "Traveller Without Luggage."

DUSSAULT, NANCY. Born in Pensacola, Fla., June 30. Attended Northwestern U. Made Broadway debut in 1960 in "Do Re Mi" for which she received a THEATRE WORLD Award, followed by "The Sound of Music," "Bajour."

DYBAS, JAMES. Born Feb. 7, 1944 in Chicago. Had experience in stock before making Broadway bow March 18, 1965 in "Do I Hear A Waltz?"

ENSERRO, MICHAEL. Born in Soldier, Pa., Oct. 5, 1918. Attended Allegheny College, and Pasadena Playhouse. Has appeared in "Molly and Me," "The Passion of Josef D.," and Off-Bdwy in "Penny Change," "The Fantasticks," and "The Miracle."

EVANS, MAURICE. Born in Dorchester, Dorset, Eng., June 8, 1901. Made NY bow in 1935 as Romeo, followed by "St. Helena," "Richard II," "St. Joan," "Henry IV," "Hamlet," "Macbeth," "Man and Superman," "The Browning Version," "Harlequinade," "The Devil's Disciple," "The Wild Duck," "Dial 'M' For Murder," "The Apple Cart," "Heartbreak House," "Tenderloin," "The Aspern Papers," "Program For Two Players" on tour.

FELLOWS, DON. Born in Salt Lake City, Dec. 2, 1922. Attended U. of Wisc. Has appeared in "Mister Roberts," "South Pacific," "Only In America," "Marathon '33," "Friday Night" (Off-Bdwy).

FERRER, JOSE. Born in Santurce, P.R., Jan. 8, 1912. Attended Princeton. Has appeared in "A Slight Case of Murder," "Brother Rat," "In Clover," "Missouri Legend," "Mamba's Daughters," "Key Largo," "Charley's Aunt," "Vickie," "Let's Face It," "Othello," "Cyrano de Bergerac," "The Silver Whistle," "Twentieth Century," "Volpone," "The Shrike," "Angel Street" (City Center), "Richard III," "Edwin Booth," "The Girl Who Came To Supper."

| Jack Fletcher | Joleen Fodor | Paul Ford | George Gaynes | Ben Gazzara |

FIEDLER, JOHN. Born in Plateville, Wisc., Feb. 3, 1925. Studied at Neighborhood Playhouse. Made NY bow in 1954 in Phoenix revival of "The Sea Gull," followed by "Harold," "The Odd Couple."

FLETCHER, JACK. Born in Forrest Hills, L.I., April 21, 1921. Attended Yale. Has appeared in "Trial Honeymoon," "She Stoops To Conquer" (1950), "Romeo and Juliet" (1951), City Center revivals of "Can-Can," "Wonderful Town" and "Cyrano de Bergerac," Off-Bdwy in "Comic Strip," "The Way Of The World," "Thieves' Carnival," and "The Amorous Flea," "Ben Franklin In Paris."

FODOR, JOLEEN. Born Nov. 12, 1939 in Medina, Ohio. Attended Denison U. and U. of Colo. Appeared Off-Bdwy in "Leave It To Jane," "Little Mary Sunshine" and "Riverwind" before making Broadway debut in 1963 in "The Student Gypsy," followed by "A Funny Thing Happened On The Way To The Forum," "Babes In The Wood" (Off-Bdwy).

FONTANNE, LYNN. Born in London, Dec. 6, 1887. Made NY debut in 1910 in "Mr. Preedy and The Countess," followed by "Dulcy," "The Guardsman," "Goat Song," "At Mrs. Beam's," "The Second Man," "Strange Interlude," "Caprice," "Elizabeth The Queen," "Reunion In Vienna," "Design For Living," "Idiot's Delight," "The Sea Gull," "Amphitryon '38," "There Shall Be No Night," "The Pirate," "O Mistress Mine," "I Know My Love," "Quadrille," "The Great Sebastians," "The Visit."

FORD, DAVID. Brown in LaJolla, Calif., Oct. 30, 1929. Attended Arizona State College, U. of South Dakota, and Dramatic Workshop of New School. Made NY bow Off-Bdwy in "Billy Budd," followed by "The Physicists."

FORD, PAUL. Born in Baltimore, Nov. 2, 1901. Attended Dartmouth. Made NY bow in 1944 in "Decision," followed by "Lower North," "Kiss Them For Me," "Flamingo Road," "On Whitman Avenue," "Another Part of The Forest," "Command Decision," "The Teahouse of The August Moon," "Whoop-Up," "The Music Man," "A Thurber Carnival," "Never Too Late."

FORSYTHE, HENDERSON. Born in Macon, Mo., Sept. 11, 1917. Attended Iowa State U. Has appeared in "The Cellar and The Well," "Miss Lonelyhearts," "The Iceman Cometh" (Off-Bdwy), "Who's Afraid of Virginia Woolf?," Off-Bdwy in "The Collection," "The Room" and "A Slight Ache."

FRANCE, RICHARD. Born in Chicago, Jan. 6, 1930. Attended YMCA Professional School. Made NY bow in 1951 in "Seventeen," followed by "Wish You Were Here," "By The Beautiful Sea," "Pal Joey" in London, "Kiss Me, Kate" (1956 City Center), "What Makes Sammy Run?"

FRANCIS, ARLENE. Born in Boston in 1908. Attended Finch School. Has appeared in "One Good Year," "Horse Eats Hat," "The Women," "All That Glitters," "Michael Drops In," "Journey To Jerusalem," "The Doughgirls," "The Overtons," "The French Touch," "The Cup of Trembling," "My Name is Aquilon," "Metropole," "The Little Blue Light," "Late Love," "Once More, With Feeling," "Beekman Place."

FREY, NATHANIEL. Born in NYC, Aug. 3, 1918. Attended NYU and American Theatre Wing. Made Bdwy bow in 1947 in "Barefoot Boy With Cheek," followed by "High Button Shoes," "Touch and Go," "Call Me Madam," "A Tree Grows In Brooklyn," "Wonderful Town," "Damn Yankees," "Goldilocks," "Harold," "She Loves Me," "The Odd Couple."

GARRETT, BETTY. Born in St. Joseph, Mo., May 23, 1919. Has appeared in "Of V We Sing," "Let Freedom Ring," "Something For The Boys," "Jackpot," "Laffing Room Only," "Call Me Mister," "Bells Are Ringing," "Beg, Borrow or Steal," "Spoon River Anthology," "A Girl Could Get Lucky."

GAYNES, GEORGE. Born in Helsinki, Finland, May 3, 1917. Studied at Milan Conservatory. Sang opera in France, and City Center. Has appeared in "The Consul," "Out Of This World," "Wonderful Town," "The Beggar's Opera," "Can-Can" (City Center), "Lady Of The Camellias," "Dynamite Tonight" (Off-Bdwy), City Center Gilbert and Sullivan Co., "Any Wednesday."

GAZZARA, BEN. Born in NYC, Aug. 28, 1930. Attended CCNY, and Dramatic Workshop. Toured in "Jezebel's Husband" before making NY bow in 1956 in "End As A Man" for which he received a THEATRE WORLD Award, followed by "Cat On A Hot Tin Roof," "A Hatful of Rain," "Night Circus," "Strange Interlude" (1963), "Traveller Without Luggage."

GEVA, TAMARA. Born in Leningrad, Russia. Has appeared in "Whoopee," "Three's A Crowd," "Flying Colors," "A Divine Drudge," "The Red Cat," "On Your Toes," "Dark Eyes," "Pride's Crossing," "Misalliance," "The Queen and The Rebels" (Off-Bdwy).

GHOSTLEY, ALICE. Born in Eve., Mo., Aug. 14, 1926. Attended U. of Okla. Appeared Off-Broadway before making Broadway debut in "New Faces of 1952," followed by "Trouble in Tahiti," "Shangri-La," "Maybe Tuesday," "A Thurber Carnival," "The Beauty Part," "The Sign In Sidney Brustein's Window."

GIELGUD, JOHN. Born in London, Apr. 14, 1904. Attended Royal Academy of Dramatic Arts. Achieved great success in England before making NY bow in 1928 in "The Patriot," followed by "Hamlet," "The Importance of Being Earnest," "Love For Love," "Crime and Punishment," "The Lady's Not For Burning," "Medea," "Ages of Man," "School For Scandal," "Homage To Shakespeare," "Tiny Alice."

GILLETTE, ANITA. Born in Baltimore, Aug. 16, 1938. Made NY debut Off-Broadway in 1960 in "Russell Patterson's Sketchbook" for which she received a THEATRE WORLD Award, followed by "Carnival," "All American," "Mr. President," "Guys and Dolls" (1965 City Center).

GINGOLD, HERMIONE. Born in London, Dec. 9. Had long career on English stage before making Bdwy debut in 1953 in "John Murray Anderson's Almanac," followed by "The Sleeping Prince," "First Impressions," "From A To Z," "Milk and Honey," "Oh, Dad, Poor Dad, Mama's Hung You In The Closet and I'm Feelin' So Sad."

Lillian Gish

George Grizzard

Rosemary Harris

Mel Haynes

Eileen Hecka

GISH, DOROTHY. Born in Massilon, Ohio, Mar. 11, 1898. Made stage debut in 1903 in "East Lynn." After eminent career in films, returned to stage in 1928 in "Young Love," followed by "The Inspector General," "Getting Married," "The Streets of New York," "Pillars of Society," "The Bridge The Sun Shines On," "Foreign Affair," "Brittle Heaven," "Missouri Legend," "Life With Father," "The Great Big Doorstep," "The Magnificent Yankee," "The Story of Mary Surratt," "The Man."

GISH, LILLIAN. Born in Springfield, Ohio, Oct. 14, 1896. Made stage debut at 6. After long film career, returned to Bdwy in 1930 in "Uncle Vanya," followed by "Camille," "Nine Pine Street," "The Joyous Season," "Hamlet," "The Star Wagon," "Dear Octopus," "Life With Father," "Mr. Sycamore," "Crime and Punishment," "The Curious Savage," "The Trip To Bountiful," "Family Reunion," "All The Way Home," "Too True To Be Good," "American Shakespeare Festival (1965).

GORDON, RUTH. Born in Wollaston, Mass., Oct. 30, 1896. Studied at American Academy of Dramatic Art. Made Stage debut with Maude Adams in 1915 in "Peter Pan," followed by "Seventeen," "Clarence," "Saturday's Children," "Serena Blandish," "Hotel Universe," "A Church Mouse," "Three Cornered Moon," "Ethan Frome," "The Country Wife," "A Doll's House," "The Three Sisters," "Over 21," "The Leading Lady," "The Smile of The World," "The Matchmaker," "The Good Soup," "My Mother, My Father and Me."

GRAHAM, RONNY. Born in Philadelphia, Aug. 26, 1919. Appeared in nightclubs before making Broadway bow in "New Faces of 1952" for which he received a THEATRE WORLD Award, followed by "The Tender Trap," "Something More."

GRAVET, FERNAND. Born in Brussels, Belgium, Dec. 25, 1905. Attended London's St. Paul's College, and Paris U. Appeared in 63 French plays and 109 films before making Broadway bow Oct. 7, 1964 in "Beekman Place."

GRAY, CHARLES D. Born in Hampshire, Eng., Aug. 29, 1928. After appearing with London's Old Vic, made Broadway bow in 1956 with them in "Romeo and Juliet," "Macbeth," "Richard II," and "Troilus and Cressida," followed by "Kean," "Poor Bitos."

GREENHOUSE, MARTHA. Born in Omaha, Neb., June 14. Attended Hunter College and American Theatre Wing. Has appeared in "Sons and Soldiers," Off-Bdwy in "Clerambard" and "Our Town," "Dear Me, The Sky Is Falling," "The Family Way."

GRIMES, TAMMY. Born in Lynn, Mass., Jan. 30, 1934. Attended Stephens College and Neighborhood Playhouse. Appeared Off-Broadway in "The Littlest Revue" and "Clerambard," "The Lark," on tour, made Broadway debut in 1959 in "Look After Lulu" for which she received a THEATRE WORLD Award, followed by "The Unsinkable Molly Brown," "Rattle Of A Simple Man," "High Spirits."

GRIZZARD, GEORGE. Born in Roanoke Rapids, N.C., April 1, 1928. Attended U. of NC. Made Broadway bow in 1955 in "The Desperate Hours," followed by "The Happiest Millionaire" for which he received a THEATRE WORLD Award, "The Disenchanted," "Big Fish, Little Fish," APA Repertory 1961-2, "Who's Afraid Of Virginia Woolf?," "The Glass Menagerie" (1965).

GROUT, JAMES DAVID. Born in London, Oct. 22, 1927. Attended Royal Academy of Dramatic Art. Appeared in several British productions before making Broadway bow in 1965 in "Half A Sixpence."

GUINNESS, ALEC. Born in London, Apr. 2, 1914. Attended Pembroke Lodge, Southbourne and Roxborough Schools. Studied for stage with Martita Hunt and Fay Compton. Made Broadway bow in 1942 in "Flare Path," followed by "The Cocktail Party," "Dylan."

HACKETT, BUDDY. Born in Brooklyn, Aug. 31, 1924. Appeared in nightclubs, films, and television before making Broadway bow in 1954 in "Lunatics and Lovers," followed by "I Had A Ball."

HACKETT, JOAN. Born in NYC. Has appeared in "Much Ado About Nothing" (1959), Off-Bdwy in "A Clearing In The Woods" and "Call Me By My Rightful Name" for which she received a THEATRE WORLD Award, "Peterpat."

HARRIS, JULIE. Born in Grosse Point, Mich., Dec. 2, 1925. Attended Yale. Made Bdwy debut in 1945 in "It's A Gift," followed by "Henry V" and "Oedipus" with Old Vic, "The Playboy Of The Western World," "Alice In Wonderland," "Macbeth," "Sundown Beach" for which she received a THEATRE WORLD Award, "The Young and The Fair," "Magnolia Alley," "Montserrat," "The Member Of The Wedding," "I Am A Camera," "Mlle. Colombe," "The Lark," "The Country Wife," "The Warm Peninsula," "The Little Moon of Alban," "A Shot In The Dark," "Marathon '33," "Hamlet" (NY Shakespeare Festival), "Ready When You Are C. B."

HARRIS, ROSEMARY. Born in Ashby, Suffolk, Eng., Sept. 19, 1930. Made Bdwy debut in 1952 in "The Climate of Eden" for which she received a THEATRE WORLD Award, followed by Old Vic's "Troilus and Cressida," "Interlock," "The Disenchanted," "The Tumbler," and in repertory with APA this season in "War and Peace," "Man and Superman," and "Judith."

HAYES, HELEN. Born in Washington, D.C., Oct. 10, 1900. Attended Sacred Heart Academy. Made stage debut in 1908 in "Babes In The Woods," Broadway bow in 1909 in "Old Dutch," followed by "The Summer Widowers," "Penrod," "Dear Brutus," "Clarence," "To The Ladies," "We Moderns," "Dancing Mothers," "Caesar and Cleopatra," "What Every Woman Knows," "Coquette," "Mary of Scotland," "Victoria Regina," "Twelfth Night," "Candle In The Wind," "Happy Birthday," "The Wisteria Trees," "Mrs. McThing," "The Glass Menagerie" (City Center), "The Skin Of Our Teeth," "Time Remembered," "A Touch Of The Poet," "A Program For Two Players," "The White House."

HAYNES, MEL. Born Feb. 18, 1921 in Brooklyn. Appeared Off-Bdwy in "Titus Andronicus," "Trial Of Dmitri Karamazov," "Legend Of Lovers" and "Purple Canary" before making Broadway bow Feb. 10, 1965 in "Diamond Orchid."

Pat Hingle

Hal Holbrook

Tresa Hughes

William Hughes

Anne Jackson

HECKART, EILEEN. Born in Columbus, O., March 29. Attended Ohio State U. and American Theatre Wing. Made NY debut in City Center's "Our Town," followed by "They Knew What They Wanted," "The Traitor," "Hilda Crane," "In Any Language," "Picnic" for which she received a THEATRE WORLD Award, "The Bad Seed," "A View From The Bridge," "The Dark At The Top Of The Stairs," "Invitation To A March," "Pal Joey" (City Center), "Everybody Loves Opal." "A Family Affair," "Too True To Be Good," "And Things That Go Bump In The Night."

HEFLIN, FRANCES. Born in Oklahoma City. Attended Barnard College. Made Bdwy debut in revival of "Charley's Aunt," followed by "The Walrus and The Carpenter," "The Skin Of Our Teeth," "The World's Full Of Girls," "Sheppy," "I Remember Mama," "The Tempest," "The Dark At The Top Of The Stairs," "A Streetcar Named Desire" (City Center), "The Physicists."

HEPBURN, KATHARINE. Born in Hartford, Conn., Nov. 9, 1909. Attended Bryn Mawr. Made Bdwy debut in 1928 in "Night Hostess," followed by "A Month In The Country," "Art and Mrs. Bottle," "The Warrior's Husband," "The Lake," "The Philadelphia Story," "Without Love," "As You Like It," "The Millionairess," Stratford productions of "The Merchant of Venice," "Much Ado About Nothing," "Twelfth Night," and "Antony and Cleopatra."

HERLIE, EILEEN. Born in Glasgow, Scot., March 8, 1920. Starred on London stage before making Broadway debut in 1955 in "The Matchmaker," followed by "The Makropoulos Secret" (Phoenix), "Epitaph For George Dillon," "Take Me Along," "All American," "Photo Finish," "Hamlet" (1964).

HIGGINS, MICHAEL. Born in Brooklyn, Jan. 20, 1922. Attended Manhattan College and American Theatre Wing. Made Bdwy bow in 1946 in "Antigone," followed by "Our Lan'," "Romeo and Juliet" (1951), "The Crucible," "The Lark," with the NY Shakespeare Festival, and Off-Bdwy in "The White Devil," "The Carefree Tree," "Easter," "The Queen and The Rebels."

HIKEN, GERALD. Born in Milwaukee, May 23, 1927. Attended U. of Wisc. Has appeared Off-Bdwy in "The Cherry Orchard," "The Sea Gull," "The Good Woman of Setzuan," "The Misanthrope" and "The Iceman Cometh." and on Bdwy in "The Lovers," "The Cave Dwellers," "The Nervous Set," "The Fighting Cock," "The 49th Cousin," "Gideon," "Foxy," "The Three Sisters."

HILL, ARTHUR. Born in Melfort, Can., Aug. 1, 1922. Attended U. of British Col. Has appeared in "The Matchmaker," "Look Homeward, Angel," "The Gang's All Here," "All The Way Home," "Who's Afraid Of Virginia Woolf?" (NY and London), "Something More."

HINGLE, PAT. Born in Denver, Colo., July 19, 1923. Attended Texas U. Has appeared in "End As A Man," "Festival," "Cat On A Hot Tin Roof." "Girls Of Summer," "The Dark At The Top Of The Stairs," "J.B.," "The Deadly Game," "Strange Interlude (1963)," "Blues For Mr. Charlie," "A Girl Could Get Lucky," "The Glass Menagerie" (1965).

HOFFMAN, FERDI. Has appeared in "Judgement Day," "Pride and Prejudice," "Masque of Kings," "The Fabulous Invalid," "Candle In The Wind," "Angel Street," "The Firebrand of Florence," "Dear Judas," "Seventh Heaven," "Becket," "Take Her, She's Mine," "And Things That Go Bump In The Night."

HOFFMAN, JANE. Born July 24 in Seattle, Wash. Attended U. of Calif. Has appeared in "'Tis Of Thee," "Crazy With The Heat," "Something For The Boys," "One Touch Of Venus," "Calico Wedding," "The Mermaids Singing," "The Rose Tattoo," "The Crucible," "Witness For The Prosecution." "Mother Courage and Her Children," "The American Dream," "Fair Game For Lovers," "A Murderer Among Us," "The Child Buyer" (Off-Bdwy).

HOLBROOK, HAL. Born in Cleveland, O., Feb. 17, 1925. Attended Denison U. Toured world in his one-man show "Mark Twain Tonight!," and played it Off-Broadway in 1959. Made Bdwy bow in 1961 in "Do You Know The Milky Way?," followed by "Abe Lincoln In Illinois" (Phoenix), "Marco Millions," "Incident at Vichy," "Tartuffe." (Lincoln Center Rep).

HOWES, SALLY ANN. Born in London. Has appeared in New York in "My Fair Lady," "Kwamina," "Brigadoon" (City Center), "What Makes Sammy Run?"

HUGHES, TRESA. Born in Washington, D.C., Sept. 17, 1929. Attended Wayne U. Has appeared in "Electra" and "The Crucible" Off-Bdwy, and in "The Miracle Worker," "The Devil's Advocate," "Dear Me, The Sky Is Falling," "The Last Analysis."

HUGHES, WILLIAM. Born in Altoona, Pa., July 19, 1924. Graduate of Harvard. Made Bdwy bow in 1944 in "The Last Stop," followed by "Oedipus Rex," and Off-Bdwy in "Mummers and Men," "The Anvil," and "Shout From The Rooftops."

IRVING, GEORGE S. Born in Springfield, Mass., Nov. 1, 1922. Has appeared in "Oklahoma," "Call Me Mister." "Along Fifth Avenue." "Two's Company," "Me and Juliet," "Can-Can," "Shinbone Alley," "Bells Are Ringing," "The Good Soup," "Tovarich," "A Murderer Among Us," "Alfie."

JACKSON, ANNE. Born in Alleghany, Pa., Sept. 3, 1926. Attended Neighborhood Playhouse. Made Bdwy debut in 1945 in "Signature," followed by "Yellow Jack," "John Gabriel Borkman," "The Last Dance," "Summer and Smoke," "Magnolia Alley," "Love Me Long," "The Lady From The Sea." "Never Sav Never," "Oh, Men! Oh. Women!," "Rhinoceros," Off-Broadway in "Brecht On Brecht" and "The Tiger" and "The Typists," "Luv."

JAMES, CLIFTON. Born in Spokane, Wash., May 29, 1921. Attended U. of Oregon, and Actors Studio. Has appeared in "The Time Of Your Life" (City Center revival), "The Cave Dwellers," "Great Day In The Morning," "Andorra," "And Things That Go Bump In The Night."

JAMES, POLLY. Born in Lancashire, Eng., July 8, 1941. Attended Royal Academy of Dramatic Art. Appeared in repertory and other British productions before making Broadway debut in 1965 in "Half A Sixpence."

Page Johnson   Jack Kelly   Clinton Kimbrough   Bert Lahr   Jessie Royce La

JANNEY, LEON. Born in Ogden, Utah, Apr. 1, 1917. Child film star. Made Bdwy bow in 1934 in "Every Thursday," followed by "The Simpleton Of The Unexpected Isle," "Parade," "Mulatto," "Foreigners," "Ghost For Sale," "The Flowering Peach," "Madam, Will You Walk," "Measure For Measure," "The Country Wife," "Damn Yankees," "The Gazebo," "Summer Of The 17th Doll," "Nobody Loves An Albatross," "The Last Analysis."

JEANMAIRE, ZIZI. Born in Paris. Danced with Monte Carlo Ballet and Ballet Russe before making Broadway debut with Roland Petit's "Ballets de Paris," Has since starred in "The Girl In Pink Tights," "Zizi."

JENS, SALOME. Born in Milwaukee, May 8, 1936. Attended Northwestern U. Has appeared in "The Disenchanted," "A Far Country," "Night Life," and Off-Broadway in "The Bald Soprano," "Deirdre Of The Sorrows," "U.S.A.," "The Balcony," "Shadow Of Heroes," "Desire Under The Elms," "After The Fall," "But For Whom Charlie," "Tartuffe" with Lincoln Center Repertory Co.

JOHNSON, PAGE. Born in Welch, W. Va., Aug. 25, 1930. Graduate of Ithaca College. Made Broadway bow in 1951 in "Romeo and Juliet," followed by "Electra," "Oedipus," "Camino Real," "In April Once" for which he received a THEATRE WORLD Award, "Red Roses For Me," "The Lovers," and Off-Bdwy in "The Enchanted," "Guitar," "4 In 1."

JOHNSTON, JUSTINE. Born June 13 in Evanston, Ill. Appeared Off-Bdwy in "Little Mary Sunshine," City Center revival of "The Time Of Your Life," and on Broadway in "The Pajama Game," "Milk And Honey."

JONES, JAMES EARL. Born in Tate County, Miss., Jan. 17, 1931. Graduate of U. of Mich. Has appeared in "The Egghead," "Sunrise At Campobello," "The Cool World," and Off-Broadway in "The Pretender," "The Blacks," "Clandestine On The Morning Line," "The Apple," "A Midsummer Night's Dream," "Moon On A Rainbow Shawl" for which he received a THEATRE WORLD Award, "P.S. 193," "The Last Minstrel," "The Love Nest," "The Bloodknot," "Othello," "Baal."

JONES, NEIL. Born in Boston, May 6, 1942. Attended Boston Conservatory of Music. Has appeared in summer stock, and in "The Music Man," "Hello, Dolly!"

JORDAN, RICHARD. Born in NYC, July 19, 1938. Attended Sherbourne School, Eng., and Harvard. Made Bdwy bow in 1961 in "Take Her, She's Mine," followed by NY Shakespeare Festival productions of "A Midsummer Night's Dream," "Romeo and Juliet" and "Richard II," "Bicycle Ride To Nevada," APA's "War and Peace," "Judith."

KARNILOVA, MARIA. Born in Hartford, Conn., Aug. 3, 1920. Has appeared in "Call Me Mister," "Miss Liberty," "Out Of This World," "Gypsy," "Bravo Giovanni," "Fiddler On The Roof."

KASZNAR, KURT. Born in Vienna, Aug. 12, 1913. Studied with Max Reinhardt. Made NY bow in "The Eternal Road," followed by "The Army Play By Play," "Joy To The World," "Make Way For Lucia," "The Happy Time," "Waiting For Godot," "Look After Lulu," "Sound Of Music," "Barefoot In The Park."

KELLY, JACK. Born in Astoria, L.I., Sept. 16, Attended UCLA. Has appeared in "The Ghost of Yankee Doodle," "Swing Your Lady," "Schoolhouse On The Lot," "Stopover," "St. Helena," "Night Life," "The Family Way."

KILEY, RICHARD. Born in Chicago, Mar. 31, 1922. Attended Loyola U. and Barnum Dramatic School. Toured in "A Streetcar Named Desire" before making Bdwy bow in 1953 in "Misalliance" for which he received a THEATRE WORLD Award, followed by "Kismet," "Sing Me No Lullaby," "Time Limit!," "Redhead," "Advise and Consent," "No Strings," "Here's Love," "I Had A Ball."

KIMBROUGH, CLINTON. Born in Sandusky, O., Feb. 14, 1935. Appeared Off-Broadway in "Our Town" and "Camino Real" before making Bdwy bow in 1961 in "Look, We've Come Through," followed by "After The Fall," "But For Whom Charlie," "The Changeling," "Incident At Vichy."

KING, DENNIS. Born in Coventry, Eng., Nov. 2, 1897. Made NY bow in 1921 in "Claire De Lune," followed by "Romeo and Juliet," "Antony and Cleopatra," "The Vagabond King," "The Three Musketeers." "I Married An Angel," "A Doll's House," "The Three Sisters," "Dunnigan's Daughter," "He Who Gets Slapped," "Medea," "Edward, My Son," "The Devil's Disciple," "Billy Budd," "Music In The Air," "The Strong Are Lonely," "Lunatics and Lovers," "A Day By The Sea," "Affair Of Honor," "Shangri-La," "The Hidden River," "The Greatest Man Alive," "Love and Libel," "Photo Finish."

LAHR, BERT. Born in NYC Aug. 13, 1895. Appeared in vaudeville and burlesque before making Bdwy bow in 1927 in "Delmar's Revels," followed by "Hold Everything," "Flying High," "Hot-Cha," "George White's Varieties," "The Show Is On," "DuBarry Was A Lady," "Seven Lively Arts," "Burlesque," "Make Mine Manhattan," "Two On The Aisle," "Waiting For Godot," "Hotel Paradiso," "Romanoff and Juliet," "A Midsummer Night's Dream," "The Boys Against The Girls," "The Beauty Part," "Foxy."

LANDIS, JESSIE ROYCE. Born in Chicago, Nov. 25, 1904. Made Bdwy debut in 1926 in "The Honor Of The Family," followed by "Solid South," "Merrily We Roll Along," "Love From A Stranger," "Brown Danube," "Dame Nature," "Love's Old Sweet Song," "Papa Is All," "Kiss and Tell," "The Winter's Tale," "The Last Dance," "Little A," "Magnolia Alley," "Richard III," "Sing Me No Lullaby," "Someone Waiting," "I Knock At The Door" (Off-Bdwy).

LANG, HAROLD. Born in Daly City, Calif., Dec. 21, 1923. Appeared with Ballet Russe and Ballet Theatre before making Bdwy bow in 1945 in "Mr. Strauss Goes To Boston," followed by "Three To Make Ready," "Look, Ma, I'm Dancin'," "Kiss Me, Kate," "Make A Wish," "Pal Joey," "Shangri-La," "Ziegfeld Follies" (1957), "I Can Get It For You Wholesale," and Off-Bdwy in "On The Town" and "Cole Porter, Revisited."

LaROSA, JULIUS. Born Jan. 2, 1930 in Brooklyn. After radio, television, and stock, made Broadway bow in 1962 in "Come Blow Your Horn," followed by "Kiss Mama" Off-Bdwy.

ohn Phillip Law	Bethel Leslie	Hal Linden	Laurence Luckinbill	Julienne Marie

LAVIN, LINDA. Born Oct. 15, 1939 in Portland, Maine. Graduate of William and Mary College. Made Broadway debut in 1962 in "A Family Affair," followed by "The Riot Act," "Wet Paint."

LAW, JOHN PHILLIP. Born in Hollywood, Calif., Sept. 7, 1937. Attended Calif. Polytechnic College, U. of Hawaii, and Neighborhood Playhouse. Made Broadway bow in 1962 in "Come On Strong," followed by Lincoln Center Rep. productions of "After The Fall," "Marco Millions," "The Changeling," and "Tartuffe."

LEE, SONDRA. Born in New Jersey. Has appeared in "High Button Shoes," "Peter Pan," "Hotel Paradiso," "Sunday In New York," "Hello, Dolly!"

LeGALLIENNE, EVA. Born in London, Jan. 11, 1899. Attended Royal Academy of Dramatic Arts. Made Bdwy debut in 1915 in "Mr. Boltay's Daughters." Organized Civic Repertory Co. in 1926 and presented many notable productions before disbanding in 1936. Has appeared in "Lilliom," "The Swan," "The Master Builder," "L'Aiglon," "Madame Capet," "Uncle Harry," "The Cherry Orchard," "Therese," "What Every Woman Knows," "Alice In Wonderland," "Ghosts," "Hedda Gabler," "The Corn Is Green" (City Center), "The Southwest Corner," Phoenix productions of "Mary Stuart" and "Elizabeth The Queen," National Repertory Theatre revivals of "Ring Round The Moon," and "The Sea Gull."

LEIGH, VIVIEN. Born in Darjeeling, India, Nov. 1913. Attended Comedie Francaise, and Royal Academy of Dramatic Arts. Made Bdwy debut in 1940 in "Romeo and Juliet," followed by "Antony and Cleopatra," "Caesar and Cleopatra," "Duel of Angels," "Tovarich."

LeNOIRE, ROSETTA. Born in NYC. Has appeared in "Bassa Moona," "The Hot Mikado," "Marching With Johnny," "Janie," "Decision," "Three's A Family," "Destry Rides Again," City Center revivals of "Finian's Rainbow" and "South Pacific," Off-Bdwy in "The Bible Salesman," "Double Entry," "Clandestine On The Morning Line" and "Cabin In The Sky," "Sophie," "Tambourines To Glory," "Blues For Mister Charlie," "I Had A Ball."

LESLIE, BETHEL. Born in NYC, Aug. 3, 1929. Attended Breaney School. Has appeared in "Snafu," "Years Ago," "The Wisteria Trees," "Mary Rose," "The Brass Ring," "Inherit The Wind," "Catch Me If You Can."

LEVENE, SAM. Born in NYC in 1907. Attended American Academy of Dramatic Art. Has appeared in "Three Men On A Horse," "Dinner At Eight," "Room Service," "Margin For Error," "A Sound of Hunting," "Light Up The Sky," "Guys and Dolls," "The Hot Corner," "Fair Game," "Make A Million," "Heartbreak House," "The Good Soup," "The Devil's Advocate," "Let It Ride," "Seidman and Son," "Cafe Crown," "The Last Analysis."

LILLIE, BEATRICE. Born in Toronto, Can. Attended St. Agnes College. Made NY debut in 1924 in "Charlot's Revue," followed by "Oh, Please," "This Year Of Grace," "She's My Baby," "The Third Little Show," "Too True To Be Good," "At Home Abroad," "The Show Is On," "Set To Music," "Seven Lively Arts," "Inside U.S.A.," "An Evening With Beatrice Lillie," "Ziegfeld Follies," "Auntie Mame," "High Spirits."

LINDEN, HAL. Born in NYC, March 20, 1931. Attended CCNY, Queens College, and American Theatre Wing. Has appeared in "Strip For Action," "Bells Are Ringing," "Wildcat," "Subways Are For Sleeping," "Anything Goes" (Off-Bdwy), "Something More."

LISA, LUBA. Born in Brooklyn. Attended American Theatre Wing. Made Broadway debut in 1961 in "Carnival," followed by "I Can Get It For You Wholesale," "West Side Story" (City Center), "I Had A Ball."

LODEN, BARBARA. Born in Marion, N.C., July 8. Appeared in summer stock before making Bdwy debut in "Compulsion," followed by "Look After Lulu," "The Long Dream," "After The Fall" for which she received a THEATRE WORLD Award.

LOGGIA, ROBERT. Born in Staten Island, N.Y., Jan. 3, 1930. Attended U. of Mo. and Actors Studio. Has appeared in "The Man With The Golden Arm" (Off-Bdwy), "The Three Sisters."

LONDON, MARC. Born in Boston, Mass., Sept. 30, 1930. Graduate of Harvard. Appeared in stock before making NY bow Off-Bdwy in "The Secret Life of Walter Mitty."

LUCKINBILL, LAURENCE. Born Nov. 21, 1938 in Ft. Smith, Ark. Graduate of U. of Ark. and Catholic U. Appeared Off-Bdwy in "Oedipus Rex," "There Is A Play Tonight," "The Fantasticks" and "Tartuffe." Made Broadway bow in "A Man For All Seasons," followed by "Beekman Place."

LUNT, ALFRED. Born in Milwaukee, Aug. 19, 1893. Attended Carroll College and Harvard. Has appeared in "Clarence," "Outward Bound," "The Guardsman," "Arms and The Man," "Goat Song," "At Mrs. Beam's," "Juarez and Maximillian," "Ned McCobb's Daughter," "The Brothers Karamozov," "The Second Man," "The Doctor's Dilemma," "Marco Millions," "Volpone," "Caprice," "Elizabeth The Queen," "Reunion In Vienna," "Design For Living," "The Taming Of The Shrew," "Idiot's Delight," "Amphitryon '38," "The Sea Gull," "There Shall Be No Night," "The Pirate," "O Mistress Mine," "I Know My Love," "Quadrille," "The Great Sebastians," "The Visit."

MACKENZIE, WILL. Born in Providence, R.I., July 24, 1938. Graduate of Brown U. Trained with Stratford, Conn., Shakespeare Festival Theatre Co. Has appeared Off-Bdwy in "Wonderful Town" (1963 City Center), "Put It In Writing" and "Morning Sun," "Brigadoon" (City Center), "Half A Sixpence."

MADDEN, DONALD. Born in NYC, Nov. 5 1933. Attended CCNY, Theatre Workshop, and University Playhouse. Made Bdwy bow in 1958 in "Look Back In Anger," followed by "First Impressions," "Julius Caesar" in Central Park for which he received a THEATRE WORLD Award, Off-Bdwy in "Lysistrata," "Pictures In A Hallway," "Henry IV, Part I," "She Stoops To Conquer," "Octaroon" and Hamlet," "Step On A Crack," "One By One."

MANN, PAUL. Born in Toronto, Can., Dec. 2, 1913. Studied at Neighborhood Playhouse, and Group Theatre School. Has appeard in "Johnny Johnson," "Flight To The West," "Macbeth" (1948), "The Whole World Over," "Flight Into Egypt," "Too Late The Phalarope," Lincoln Center Repertory.

Bernice Massi

Joan McCall

Earl McDonald

Buzz Miller

Eli Mintz

MANNING, JACK. Born in Cincinnati, June 3. Graduate of U. of Cincinnati. Has appeared in "Junior Miss," "The Great Big Doorstep," "Harriet," "Mermaids Singing," "Alice In Wonderland," "Man and Superman," "Billy Budd," "The Tender Trap," "Say, Darling," "Do I Hear A Waltz?"

MARCH, FREDRIC. Born in Racine, Wisc., Aug. 31, 1897. Attended U. of Wisc. Made NY bow in 1920 in "Deburau." After several years in Hollywood, returned to Bdwy in 1938 in "Yr. Obedient Husband," followed by "The American Way," "Hope For A Harvest," "The Skin Of Our Teeth," "A Bell For Adano," "Years Ago," "Now I Lay Me Down To Sleep," "An Enemy Of The People," "The Autumn Garden," "Long Day's Journey Into Night," "Gideon."

MARIE, JULIENNE. Born in Toledo, Ohio in 1943. Attended Juilliard School of Music. Has appeared in "The King and I," "Whoop-Up!," "Gypsy," "Foxy," and Off-Bdwy revival of "The Boys From Syracuse" for which she received a THEATRE WORLD Award, "Othello" (Off-Bdwy), "Do I Hear A Waltz?"

MARKEY, ENID. Born in Dillon, Colo. Silent film star before making Bdwy debut in 1919 in "Up In Mabel's Room," followed by many productions among which are "Barnum Was Right," "The Women," "Morning's At Seven," "Ah, Wilderness," "Mr. Sycamore," "Beverly Hills," "Snafu," "Happy Birthday," "The Silver Whistle," "Buy Me Blue Ribbons," "Mrs. McThing," "Mrs. Patterson," "The Southwest Corner," "Only In America," "Ballad Of The Sad Cafe."

MARTIN, MARY. Born in Weatherford, Tex., Dec. 1, 1914. Attended Ward-Belmont College. Made Bdwy debut in 1938 in "Leave It To Me," followed by "One Touch of Venus," "Lute Song," "Annie Get Your Gun," "South Pacific," "Kind Sir," "Peter Pan," "The Skin Of Our Teeth" (1955), "A Sound Of Music," "Jennie," "Hello, Dolly!" on tour.

MARTIN, NAN. Born in Decatur, Ill., July 15, 1927. Attended Max Reinhardt School, Actors Lab, and Actors Studio. Made Bdwy debut in 1950 in "A Story For A Sunday Evening," followed by "The Constant Wife," "J.B.," "Hearts Delight," "Under The Yum Yum Tree," and Off-Bdwy in "Mary Stuart," "The Great God Brown," "Lysistrata," "Henry IV," "Camino Real," "The Merchant Of Venice" and "Hamlet."

MASSI, BERNICE. Born in Camden, NJ, Aug. 23. Graduate of Camden Catholic High School. Made professional debut in National Co. of "South Pacific," followed by Bdwy productions of "Wish You Were Here," "Can-Can," "By The Beautiful Sea," "No Strings," "What Makes Sammy Run?"

MATHEWS, GEORGE. Born in NYC, Oct. 10, 1911. Has appeared in "Escape This Night," "Processional," "Life of Reilly," "Cuckoos On The Hearth," "Eve of St. Mark," "Kiss Them For Me," "Antigone," "Temper The Wind," "The Silver Whistle," "A Streetcar Named Desire," "Barefoot In Athens," "The Desperate Hours," "Holiday For Lovers," "The Shadow Of A Gunman," "Triple Play," "Luther," "Catch Me If You Can."

MATTHAU, WALTER. Born Oct. 1, 1923 in NYC. Made Broadway bow in 1948 in "Anne Of A Thousand Days," followed by "The Liar," "Season In The Sun," "Twilight Walk," "Fancy Meeting You Again," "One Bright Day," "In Any Language," "The Grey-Eyed People," "A Certain Joy," "The Ladies Of The Corridor," City Center revivals of "Guys and Dolls" (1953) and "The Wisteria Trees" (1954), "Will Success Spoil Rock Hunter?," "Maiden Voyage," "Once More, With Feeling," "Once There Was A Russian," "A Shot In The Dark," "My Mother, My Father, and Me," "The Odd Couple."

McCALL, JOAN. Born Jan. 31, 1943 in Grahn, Ky. Graduate of Berea College. Appeared in stock before making Broadway debut April 29, 1965 in "A Race Of Hairy Men."

McCARTHY, KEVIN. Born in Seattle, Wash., Feb. 15, 1914. Attended Georgetown U. and U. of Minn. Made NY bow in 1938 in "Abe Lincoln In Illinois," followed by "Flight To The West," "Winged Victory," "Truckline Cafe," "Joan of Lorraine," "Death Of A Salesman," "Anna Christie," "Love's Labour's Lost," "The Deep Blue Sea," "The Sea Gull," "Red Roses For Me," "The Day The Money Stopped," "Two For The Seesaw," "Advise and Consent," "Something About A Soldier," "The Three Sisters."

McDONALD, EARL. Born Nov. 15, 1905 in Chicago. Graduate of U. of Ill. Made Bdwy bow in 1926 in "White Wings," followed by "Merchant Of Venice," "Fredrika," "Three Waltzes," "Two On An Island," "Three's A Family," "Maid In Heaven," "Dream Girl," "Regina," "Brigadoon" (City Center).

McGRATH, PAUL. Born in Chicago. Attended Carnegie Tech. Made NY bow in 1920 in "The First Year," followed by "Ned McCobb's Daughter," "John Ferguson," "The Green Bay Tree," "Ode To Liberty," "Susan And God," "Lady In The Dark," "Tomorrow The World," "Common Ground," "Command Decision," "The Big Knife," "The Small Hours," "Love and Let Love," "Touchstone," "A Girl Can Tell," "A Case Of Libel," "The Child Buyer" (Off-Bdwy).

McKAY, SCOTT. Born in Pleasantville, Iowa, May 28, 1917. Attended U. of Colo. Made Broadway bow in 1938 in "Good Hunting," followed by "The American Way," "Letters To Lucerne," "The Moon Is Down," "The Eve Of St. Mark," "Dark Eyes," "Pillar To Post," "Another Part Of The Forest," "Born Yesterday," "Bell, Book and Candle," "Sabrina Fair," "Teahouse Of The August Moon," "Brigadoon" (City Center), "Nature's Way," "Requiem For A Nun."

McVEY, PATRICK. Born in Ft. Wayne, Ind., March 17, 1913. Graduate of Ind. Law School, and Pasadena Playhouse. Has appeared in "State Of The Union," "Detective Story," "Hold It," "Bus Stop," "Catch Me If You Can."

MEDFORD, KAY. Born in NYC, Sept. 14. Has appeared in "Paint Your Wagon," "Two's Company," "John Murray Anderson's Almanac," "Lullaby" for which she received a THEATRE WORLD Award, "Black-Eyed Susan," "Almost Crazy," "Wake Up, Darling," "Mr. Wonderful," "A Hole In The Head," "Carousel" (City Center), "Handful of Fire," "Bye, Bye, Birdie," "In The Counting House," "The Heroine," "Pal Joey" (City Center), "Funny Girl."

nthony Newley   Mary Ann Niles   Clarence Nordstrom   Frederick O'Neal   Jerry Orbach

MEREDITH, BURGESS. Born in Cleveland, Ohio, Nov. 16, 1908. Attended Amherst, then joined Eva LeGallienne's repertory company. Has appeared in "Little Ol' Boy," "She Loves Me Not," "The Barretts of Wimpole Street," "Flowers Of The Forest," "Winterset," "High Tor," "Liliom," "Candida," "The Playboy Of The Western World," "The Fourposter," "The Remarkable Mr. Pennypacker," "Teahouse Of The August Moon," "Major Barbara," "I Was Dancing."

MILLER, BUZZ. Born in Snowflake, Ariz., Dec. 23, 1928. Attended Ariz. State College. Has appeared in "Magdalena," "Pal Joey," "Two's Company," "Me and Juliet," "Pajama Game," "Bells Are Ringing," "Redhead," "Bravo Giovanni," "Hot Spot," "Funny Girl."

MINTZ, ELI. Born Aug. 1, 1904 in what is now Poland. Had wide experience in European and American Yiddish theatres before making Broadway bow in 1948 in "Me and Molly," followed by "The Fifth Season," "A Worm In The Horseradish," "The 49th Cousin," "I Was Dancing," "Catch Me If You Can."

MORISON, PATRICIA. Born in NYC in 1919. Made Broadway debut in 1938 in "Two Bouquets." Made many films before returning to NY in 1948 in "Kiss Me, Kate," followed by "The King and I," and 1965 City Center revival of "Kiss Me, Kate."

MORROW, KAREN. Born in Chicago, Dec. 15, 1936. Attended Clarke College, Iowa, and Workshop "M" in Milwaukee. Made NY debut Off-Bdwy in 1961 in "Sing, Muse!" for which she received a THEATRE WORLD Award, followed by 1963 Off-Bdwy revival of "The Boys From Syracuse," "I Had A Ball."

MURPHY, ROSEMARY. Born in Munich, Ger., Jan. 13, 1927. Received stage training with Stratford Shakespeare Festival Theatre. Has appeared in "Look Homeward, Angel," "Period Of Adjustment," "Any Wednesday."

NATWICK, MILDRED. Born in Baltimore, June 19, 1908. Made Bdwy debut in 1932 in "Carrie Nation," followed by "The Wind and The Rain," "The Distaff Side," "End of Summer," "Love From A Stranger," "Candida," "The Star Wagon," "Missouri Legend," "Blithe Spirit," "The Playboy of The Western World," "The Grass Harp," "Coriolanus," "The Waltz Of The Toreadors," "The Day The Money Stopped," "The Firstborn," "Critic's Choice," "Barefoot In The Park."

NEWLEY, ANTHONY. Born in Hackney, London, Eng., Sept. 21, 1931. Received training with Dewsbury Repertory Co. Made Broadway bow in 1956 in "Cranks," followed by "Stop The World—I Want To Get Off" and "The Roar Of The Greasepaint—The Smell Of The Crowd" both of which he co-authored.

NEWMAN, PAUL. Born in Cleveland, Ohio, Jan. 26, 1925. Attended Kenyon College and Yale. Made Broadway bow in 1953 in "Picnic" for which he received a THEATRE WORLD Award, followed by "The Desperate Hours," "Sweet Bird Of Youth," "Baby Want A Kiss."

NILES, MARY ANN. Born in NYC, May 2, 1933. Attended Miss Finchley's School, and Ballet Academy. Made Broadway debut in 1945 in "Girl From Nantucket," followed by "Dance Me A Song," "Call Me Mister," "Make Mine Manhattan," "La Plume de Ma Tante," "Carnival," "Flora The Red Menace."

NOLTE, CHARLES. Born in Duluth, Minn., Nov. 3, 1926. Attended U. of Minn. and Yale. Made Bdwy bow in 1947 in "Antony and Cleopatra," followed by "Uniform of Flesh," "Caesar and Cleopatra," "Design For A Stained Glass Window" for which he received a THEATRE WORLD Award, "Mister Roberts," "Billy Budd," "The Caine Mutiny Court Martial," "Medea" (1955), and Off-Bdwy in "Do Not Pass Go" which he wrote.

NORDSTROM, CLARENCE. Born March 13 in Chicago. Graduate of Woodstock College. Made Broadway bow in 1916 in "You're In Love." Among the many productions in which he has appeared are "Ziegfeld Follies," "Greenwich Village Follies," "Queen High," "Knickerbocker Holiday," "The Visit," "Donnybrook," City Center 1964 revival of "Brigadoon."

OLAF, PIERRE. Born in Cauderan, France, July 14, 1928. Attended Lycee. Made Broadway bow in 1958 in "La Plume de Ma Tante," followed by "Carnival," "A Murderer Among Us," "That Hat!" (Off-Bdwy).

OLSON, JAMES. Born in Evanston, Ill., Oct. 8, 1930. Attended Northwestern U. and Actors Studio. Made Bdwy bow in 1955 in "The Young and Beautiful," followed by "The Sin Of Pat Muldoon," "J.B.," "The Chinese Prime Minister," "The Three Sisters" (1964).

O'MALLEY, REX. Born in London, Jan. 2, 1901. Has appeared in "The Marquise," "The Apple Cart," "Wonder Bar," "The Mad Hopes," "Revenge With Music," "You Never Know," "The Simpleton of The Unexpected Isles," "The Taming Of The Shrew," "No More Ladies," "Many Happy Returns," "Lady Windermere's Fan," "Charley's Aunt," "The Sleeping Prince," "The Lady of The Camellias," "Say Nothing" (Off-Bdwy).

O'NEAL, FREDERICK. Born in Brooksville, Miss., Aug. 27, 1905. In 1940 co-founded American Negro Theatre. Appeared in 7 of their productions before making Bdwy bow in 1944 in "Anna Lucasta," followed by "Take A Giant Step," "The Winner," "House Of Flowers," and Off-Bdwy in "The Man With The Golden Arm" and "Ballad Of Bimshire." Is president of Actors Equity.

ORBACH, JERRY. Born in NYC, Oct. 20, 1935. Attended U. of Ill. and Northwestern U. Appeared Off-Bdwy in "The Threepenny Opera," "The Fantasticks" and "The Cradle Will Rock." Made Broadway bow in 1961 in "Carnival," followed by "Guys and Dolls" (1965 City Center).

ORLANDI, FELICE. Born in Italy, Sept. 18, 1925. Graduate of Carnegie Tech. Has appeared in "Romeo and Juliet" (1951), "Idiot's Delight" (1952 City Center), "The Girl On The Via Flaminia," "27 Wagons Full Of Cotton," "Diamond Orchid," "Matty and The Moron and Madonna" (Off-Bdwy).

O'SULLIVAN, MAUREEN. Born in Roscommon, Ire. Attended Sacred Heart Convent, Dublin. After a long career in films, made Bdwy debut in 1962 in "Never Too Late."

Dick Patterson

Gilles Pelletier

Don Porter

Gilbert Price

Lester Rawlin

O'SULLIVAN, MICHAEL. Born in Phoenix, Ariz., March 4, 1934. Attended Regis College, U. of Denver, and Goodman School in Chicago. Appeared Off-Bdwy in "Six Characters In Search of An Author" and "In White America." Made Bdwy bow May 19, 1964 in "The White House," followed by Lincoln Center Repertory Co.'s "Tartuffe" for which he received a THEATRE WORLD Award.

PAGE, GERALDINE. Born in Kirksville, Mo., Nov. 22, 1924. Studied at Goodman Theatre, Chicago. Appeared in many Off-Bdwy plays before making Bdwy debut in 1953 in "Mid-Summer" for which she received a THEATRE WORLD Award, followed by "The Immoralist," "The Rainmaker," "The Innkeepers," "Separate Tables," "Sweet Bird of Youth," "Strange Interlude" (1963), "The Three Sisters" (1964), "P.S. I Love You."

PALMER, PETER. Born in Milwaukee, Wisc., Sept. 20, 1931. Attended U. of Ill. Made Broadway bow in 1956 in "Li'l Abner" for which he received a THEATRE WORLD Award, followed by City Center revivals of "Brigadoon."

PARSONS, ESTELLE. Born in Lynn, Mass., Nov. 20, 1927. Attended Conn. College, and Boston U. Law School. Has appeared in "Whoop-Up!," "Beg, Borrow or Steal," and Off-Bdwy in "The Threepenny Opera," "Automobile Graveyard," "Mrs. Dally Has A lover" for which she received a THEATRE WORLD Award, and "In The Summer House," "Ready When You Are C. B."

PATTERSON, DICK. Born in Clear Lake, Iowa. Graduate of UCLA. Appeared in nightclubs and stock before making Broadway bow in "Vintage '60," followed by "The Billy Barnes People," "Bye Bye Birdie," "Fade-Out, Fade-In."

PELLETIER, GILLES. Born in Quebec, Can., March 22, 1925. Attended College Ste.-Marie, and College Jean-de-Breboeuf. Appeared in many Canadian productions before making Broadway bow Nov. 19, 1964 in "P.S. I Love You."

PERKINS, JOHN. Born in Boston, May 7, 1927. Studied at Irvine Studio. Has appeared in "Romeo and Juliet" (1951), "Wish You Were Here," "The Balcony" Off-Bdwy, "The Physicists."

PETTET, JOANNA. Born in London, Nov. 16, 1944. Studied in Canada and at Neighborhood Playhouse. Made Broadway debut in 1962 in "Take Her, She's Mine," followed by "The Chinese Prime Minister," "Poor Richard."

PLEASENCE, DONALD. Born in Worksop, Nottingham, Eng., Oct. 5, 1920. Attended Sheffield School. Served apprenticeship with Birmingham Repertory Co. Broadway appearances include Olivier's "Antony and Cleopatra" and "Caesar and Cleopatra" "The Caretaker," "Poor Bitos."

PLUMMER, CHRISTOPHER. Born in Toronto, Can. in 1927. Toured with "The Constant Wife" before making Bdwy bow in 1954 in "The Starcross Story," followed by "Home Is The Hero," "The Dark Is Light Enough" for which he received a THEATRE WORLD Award, "Medea," "The Lark," "The Night Of The Auk," "J.B.," "Arturo Ui."

POOLE, ROY. Born in San Bernardino, Calif., March 31, 1924. Graduate of Stanford. Has appeared in "Now I Lay Me Down To Sleep," "St. Joan" (1956), "The Bad Seed," "I Knock At The Door," "Long Day's Journey Into Night," "Face Of A Hero," "Moby Dick," "Poor Bitos."

PORTER, DON. Born in Miami, Okla., Sept. 24. Attended Oregon Inst. of Technology, and Portland Civic Theatre School. Has appeared on Bdwy in "Calculated Risk," "Any Wednesday."

PRESTON, ROBERT. Born in Newton Highland, Mass., June 8, 1918. Studied at Pasadena Playhouse. Made many films before Bdwy bow in 1951 in "Twentieth Century," followed by "The Male Animal," "Men Of Distinction," "His and Hers," "The Magic and The Loss," "The Tender Trap," "Janus," "The Hidden River," "The Music Man," "Too True To Be Good," "Nobody Loves An Albatross," "Ben Franklin In Paris."

PRICE, GILBERT. Born in NYC, Sept. 10, 1942. Graduate of Erasmus High School, Brooklyn. Received training at American Theatre Wing School. Has appeared in "Kicks and Company," "Fly Blackbird," "Jerico-Jim Crow" (Off-Bdwy) for which he received a THEATRE WORLD Award, "The Roar Of The Greasepaint—The Smell Of The Crowd."

PRIMUS, BARRY. Born Feb. 16, 1938 in NYC. Attended City College. Made Broadway bow in 1960 in "The Nervous Set," followed by "Oh, Dad, Poor Dad . . .," and Lincoln Center Repertory productions.

RAWLINS, LESTER. Born in Farrell, Pa., Sept. 24, 1924. Attended Carnegie Tech. Has appeared in City Center revivals of "Othello" and "King Lear," "The Lovers," "A Man For All Seasons," and Off-Bdwy in "Endgame," "The Quare Fellow," "Camino Real," "Hedda Gabler," "The Old Glory" and "The Child Buyer."

REDFORD, ROBERT. Born in Santa Monica, Cal., Aug. 18, 1937. Attended U. of Colo., Pratt Inst., and American Academy of Dramatic Arts. Has appeared in "The Highest Tree," "Little Moon of Alban," "Sunday in New York," "Barefoot In The Park."

REDGRAVE, MICHAEL. Born in Bristol, Eng., March 20, 1908. Attended Clinton and Magdalene Colleges. Appeared in many English films and plays before making Bdwy bow in 1948 in "Macbeth," followed by "Tiger At The Gates," "The Sleeping Prince," "The Complaisant Lover."

REILLY, CHARLES NELSON. Born Jan. 13, 1931 in NYC. Attended U. of Conn. Appeared Off-Bdwy in "Nightcap," "Fallout," "Lend An Ear," "Parade," "The Inspector General," "3 Times 3," and "Apollo of Bellac," before making Broadway bow in "Bye Bye Birdie," followed by "How To Succeed In Business Without Really Trying," "Hello, Dolly!"

RICH, DORIS. Born in Boston, Aug. 14, 1905. Studied at American Academy of Dramatic Art. Made Broadway debut in 1927 in "Getting In The Movies," followed more recently by "The Mad Hopes," "The Taming Of The Shrew," "Sophie," "Flamingo Road," "Strange Bedfellows," "The Madwoman of Chaillot," "Affair of Honor," "Redhead," "The Physicists."

250

rles Nelson Reilly   Charles Rydell   Ulla Sallert   Paul Sand   Lorraine Serabian

RITCHARD, CYRIL. Born in Sydney, Australia, Dec. 1, 1898. Attended St. Aloysius College and Sydney U. Appeared on Australian and London stages before making Bdwy bow in 1947 in "Love For Love," followed by "Make Way For Lucia," "The Relapse," "Peter Pan," "A Visit To A Small Planet," "The Pleasure of His Company," "The Happiest Girl In The World," "Romulus," "Too True To Be Good," "The Irregular Verb To Love," "The Roar of the Greasepaint—The Smell of The Crowd."

RIVERA, CHITA. Born Jan. 23, 1934 in Washington, DC. Made Broadway debut in 1952 in "Call Me Madam," followed by "Guys and Dolls," "Seventh Heaven," "Can-Can," "Shoestring Revue," "Mr. Wonderful," "West Side Story," "Bye Bye Birdie," "Bajour."

ROBARDS, JASON, JR. Born in Chicago, July 26, 1922. Attended American Academy of Dramatic Arts. Made Bdwy bow in 1947 with D'Oyly Carte Opera Co., followed by "Stalag 17," "The Chase," Off-Bdwy in "American Gothic," and "The Iceman Cometh," "Long Day's Journey Into Night" for which he received a THEATRE WORLD Award "The Disenchanted," "Toys In The Attic," "Big Fish, Little Fish," "A Thousand Clowns," "After The Fall," "But For Whom Charlie," "Hughie."

RYDELL, CHARLES. Born Oct. 28, 1931 in Jamestown, N.Y. Has appeared Off-Broadway in "The Threepenny Opera" and "The Secret Life Of Walter Mitty."

SALLERT, ULLA. Born March 27 in Stockholm, Sweden. Studied at Royal Musical Academy, and became one of Sweden's most popular and versatile actresses. Made Broadway debut Oct. 27, 1964 in "Ben Franklin In Paris."

SAND, PAUL. Born in Santa Monica, Calif., Mar. 5, 1935. Attended CCLA. Trained with Marcel Marceau. Made Bdwy bow in 1961 in "From The Second City," followed by "Journey To The Day," and "Wet Paint" (Off-Bdwy).

SANDERS, BYRON. Born in Charlotte, N.C., Sept. 24, 1927. Attended U. of Vienna. Made Broadway bow in 1955 in "The Desk Set," followed by "Friday Night" (Off-Broadway).

SANDS, DIANA. Born in NYC, Aug. 22, 1934. Attended High School of Performing Arts. Has appeared in "A Raisin In The Sun," "Tiger Tiger Burning Bright" for which she received a THEATRE WORLD Award, Off-Bdwy in "The World of Sholom Aleichem," "Major Barbara," "The Man With The Golden Arm," "Land Beyond The River," and "Brecht On Brecht," "Blues For Mister Charlie," "The Owl and The Pussycat."

SCAMMELL, TERENCE. Born March 1, 1937 in London. Attended Royal Academy of Dramatic Art. Toured with National Repertory Co., appeared with American Shakespeare Festival, and Off-Bdwy in "The Mousetrap," and "The Giants' Dance."

SCOTT, MARTHA. Born in Jamesport, Mo., Sept. 22, 1914. Attended U. of Mich. Made NY debut in 1938 in "Our Town," followed by "Foreigners." "The Willow and I," "Soldier's Wife," "The Voice of The Turtle," "It Takes Two," "Design For A Stained Glass Window," "The Remarkable Mr. Pennypacker," "Cloud 7," "A Distant Bell," "The Tumbler," "The 49th Cousin," "Never Too Late."

SERABIAN, LORRAINE. Born June 12, 1945 in NYC. Graduate of Hofstra U. Has appeared Off-Broadway in "Sign of Jonah," "Electra," "Othello," and "The Secret Life of Walter Mitty."

SEYMOUR, ANNE. Born in NYC, Sept. 11, 1909. Attended Cathedral School and American Laboratory Theatre School. Has appeared in "Mr. Moneypenny," "At The Bottom," "The Seagull," "Puppet Show," "School For Scandal," "Sunrise At Campobello."

SHAW, ROBERT. Born in Westhoughton, Eng., Aug. 9, 1927. Studied at Royal Academy of Dramatic Arts. Made Broadway bow in 1961 in "The Caretaker," followed by "The Physicists."

SHEEN, MARTIN. Born in Dayton, Ohio, Aug. 3, 1940. Received training with The Living Theatre. Made Bdwy bow in 1964 in "Never Live Over A Pretzel Factory," followed by "The Subject Was Roses." Off-Bdwy credits: "The Connection," "Many Loves," and "In The Jungle of Cities."

SHERWOOD, MADELEINE. Born in Montreal, Can., Nov. 13, 1926. Attended Yale Dramatic Workshop. Has appeared in "The Chase," "The Crucible," "Cat On A Hot Tin Roof," "Invitation To A March," "Camelot," "Arturo Ui," "Do I Hear A Waltz?"

SHYRE, PAUL. Born in NYC, March 8, 1926. Attended U. of Fla., and American Academy of Dramatic Art. Has appeared Off-Broadway in "Purple Dust," "Pictures In The Hallway," and "I Knock At The Door."

SNOW, HARRY DAVID. Born in Altoona, Pa., Dec. 28, 1928. Attended Franklin and Marshall College, and Curtis Inst. of Music. Has appeared in "Pardon Our French," "Wish You Were Here," "John Murray Anderson's Almanac," "Once Upon A Mattress," "Brigadoon" (1964 City Center).

SPINETTI, VICTOR. Born Sept. 2, 1932 in South Wales, British Isles. Attended Cardiff Drama College. Made NY bow in 1960 in "The Hostage," followed by "Oh, What A Lovely War."

STANLEY, KIM. Born in Tularosa, N. Mex., Feb. 11, 1925. Attended U. of N. Mex. and U. of Tex. Made Bdwy debut in 1949 in "Montserrat," followed by "The House of Bernarda Alba," "The Chase" for which she received a THEATRE WORLD Award, "Picnic," "The Traveling Lady," "Bus Stop," "A Clearing In The Woods," "Cat On A Hot Tin Roof" in London. "A Touch of The Poet," "Cheri," "A Far Country," "Natural Affection," "The Three Sisters" (1964).

STAPLETON, JEAN. Born in NYC, Jan. 19, 1923. Attended Hunter College and American Theatre Wing School. Made Bdwy debut in 1953 in "In The Summer House," followed by "Damn Yankees," "Bells Are Ringing," "Juno," "Rhinoceros," "Funny Girl."

STAPLETON, MAUREEN. Born in Troy, NY, June 21, 1925. Toured in "The Barretts of Wimpole Street" before making Bdwy debut in 1946 in "The Playboy of The Western World," followed by "Antony and Cleopatra," "Detective Story," "The Bird Cage," "The Rose Tattoo" for which she received a THEATRE WORLD Award, "The Emperor's Clothes," "The Crucible," "Richard III," "The Seagull," "27 Wagons Full of Cotton," "Orpheus Descending," "The Cold Wind and The Warm," "Toys In The Attic," "The Glass Menagerie" (1965).

251

Marco St. John

Elaine Swann

Jo Tract

Rudy Tronto

George Voskov

STEELE, TOMMY. Born Dec. 17, 1936 in London, Eng. Became one of England's most popular performers in clubs, films, and on stage before making Broadway bow April 25, 1965 in "Half A Sixpence" which he created in London.

STERLING, JAN. Born in NYC, Apr. 3, 1923. Made Broadway debut in 1938 in "Bachelor Born," followed by "When We Are Married," "Grey Farm," "This Rock," "The Rugged Path," "Dunnigan's Daughter," "This Too Shall Pass," "Present Laughter," "Two Blind Mice," "Small War On Murray Hill," "The Perfect Setup," "Friday Night" (Off-Bdwy).

STERNHAGEN, FRANCIS. Born in Washington, D.C., Jan. 13, 1932. Attended Vassar, and Catholic U. Has appeared Off-Broadway in "The Admirable Bashful," "Thieves' Carnival," "The Country Wife," "Ulysses In Nightown," "The Saintliness of Margery Kempe," "The Room" and "A Slight Ache." Broadway debut in 1962 in "Great Day In The Morning."

STEWART, DAVID J. Born in Omaha, Neb. Attended Neighborhood Playhouse and Actors Studio. Has appeared in "Antigone," "Antony and Cleopatra," "That Lady," "The Rose Tattoo," "Barefoot In Athens," "Camino Real," "The Immoralist," "The Making of Moo" (Off-Bdwy), "A Man For All Seasons," "Marco Millions," "After The Fall," "Incident At Vichy."

STEWART, DON. Born in Staten Island, NY, Nov. 14, 1935. Attended Wichita U. Made Bdwy bow in "Camelot," followed by "The Student Gypsy." Off-Bdwy credits: "The Fantasticks," "Jo," "Babes In The Wood."

STICKNEY, DOROTHY. Born in Dickinson, S.D., June 21, 1900. Attended Northwestern Dramatic School. Made NY debut in 1926 in "The Squall," followed by "Chicago," "March Hares," "The Beaux Stratagem," "The Front Page," "Philip Goes Forth," "Another Language," "On Borrowed Time," "Life With Father," "Life With Mother," "The Small Hours," "To Be Continued," "Kind Sir," "The Honeys," "The Riot Act," "A Lovely Light" (solo show).

ST. JOHN, MARCO. Born in New Orleans, May 7, 1939. Graduate of Fordham U. Appeared Off-Bdwy in "Angels of Anadarko" and "Man of Destiny." Made Broadway bow Nov. 14, 1964 in "Poor Bitos" followed by "And Things That Go Bump In The Night."

STREISAND, BARBRA. Born in Brooklyn, Apr. 24, 1942. Made Bdwy debut in 1962 in "I Can Get It For You Wholesale," followed by "Funny Girl."

STRONG, MICHAEL. Born in NYC Feb. 8, 1918. Attended Brooklyn College, and Neighborhood Playhouse. Has appeared in "The American Way," "Spring Again," "The Russian People," "Counterattack," "The Eve of St. Mark," "Men To The Sea," "It's A Gift," "The Whole World Over," "Detective Story," "An Enemy of The People," "The Emperor's Clothes," "Anastasia," "A Month In The Country," and with Lincoln Center Repertory Co.

SULLIVAN, JOSEPH. Born in NYC, Nov. 29, 1918. Attended Fordham U., and American Theatre Wing. Has appeared in "Sundown Beach," "Command Decision," "The Live Wire," "The Country Girl," "Oh, Men! Oh, Women!," "The Rainmaker," "The Best Man," "Fiddler On The Roof."

SUROVY, NICOLAS. Born in Los Angeles, June 30, 1944. Attended Northwestern U., U. of Cannes, and Neighborhood Playhouse. Appeared in stock before making NY bow Off-Broadway in "Helen" for which he received a THEATRE WORLD Award.

SWANN, ELAINE. Born in Baltimore, Md., May 9. Attended U. of NC. Received training with Maryland Hilltop Theatre. Made Bdwy debut in 1957 in "The Music Man," followed by "Greenwillow," "A Thurber Carnival," "My Mother, My Father and Me," "Jennie."

SWENSON, INGA. Born in Omaha, Neb., Dec. 29, 1932. Attended Northwestern. Made Bdwy debut in "New Faces of 1956," followed by "Twelfth Night," "The First Gentleman" for which she received a THEATRE WORLD Award, American Shakespeare Festival productions, "110 In The Shade," "Baker Street."

TANDY, JESSICA. Born in London, June 7, 1909. Made NY debut in 1930 in "The Matriarch," followed by "The Last Enemy," "Time and The Conways," "The White Steed," "Geneva," "Jupiter Laughs," "Anne of England," "Yesterday's Magic," "A Streetcar Named Desire," "Hilda Crane," "The Fourposter," "The Honeys," "A Day By The Sea," "The Man In The Dog Suit," "Triple Play," "Five Finger Exercise," "Stratford American Shakespeare Festival, and Minneapolis Festival productions, "The Physicists."

TRACT, JO. Born in Urbana, Ohio, Dec. 25, 1939. Attended Ohio State. Made Broadway debut in "Fade Out—Fade In," followed by "Catch Me If You Can."

TRONTO, RUDY. Born in Peekskill, N.Y., July 14, 1928. Attended Colgate U. Made Broadway bow in 1960 in "Irma La Douce," followed by "Carnival." Has appeared Off-Bdwy in "The Boys From Syracuse," and "The Secret Life of Walter Mitty."

VOSKOVEC, GEORGE. Born in Sazava, Czech., June 19, 1905. Attended Dijon College, France, and Charles U. in Prague. Made NY bow in 1945 in "The Tempest," followed by "The Love Of Four Colonels," "His and Hers," "The Sea Gull," "Festival," "Uncle Vanya" (Off-Bdwy), "Do You Know The Milky Way?," Burton's "Hamlet" (1964), "The Physicists."

WALLACH, ELI. Born in Brooklyn. Attended CCNY, U. of Tex., and Neighborhood Playhouse. Has appeared in "Henry VIII," "Androcles and The Lion," "Alice In Wonderland," "Yellow Jack," "What Every Woman Knows," "Skydrift," "Antony and Cleopatra," "Mister Roberts," "The Lady From The Sea," "The Rose Tattoo" for which he received a THEATRE WORLD Award, "Mlle. Colombe," "The Teahouse of The August Moon," "Major Barbara," "The Chairs," "The Cold Wind and The Warm," "Rhinoceros," Off-Bdwy in "The Typists" and "The Tiger," "Luv."

WATSON, DOUGLAS. Born in Jackson Ga., Feb. 24, 1921. Attended U. of NC. Made Bdwy bow in 1947 in "Antony and Cleopatra" for which he received a THEATRE WORLD Award, followed by "The Leading Lady," "Richard III," "The Happiest Years," "That Lady," "The Wisteria Trees," "Romeo and Juliet," "Desire Under The Elms," "Sunday Breakfast," "Cyrano de Bergerac," "The Confidential Clerk," "Portrait of A Lady," "The Miser," "The Young and The Beautiful," "Little Glass Clock," "The Country Wife," "A Man For All Seasons," "The Chinese Prime Minister," Stratford American Shakespeare Festival Productions.

| Collin Wilcox | Eugene R. Wood | Donald Woods | Richard Woods | Irene Worth |

WATSON, SUSAN. Born in Tulsa, Okla., Dec. 17, 1938. Attended Juilliard School of Music. Appeared Off-Bdwy in "The Fantasticks" and "Lend An Ear." Made Broadway debut April 6, 1960 in "Bye Bye Birdie," followed by "Carnival," "Ben Franklin In Paris."

WAYNE, DAVID. Born in Traverse City, Mich., Jan. 31, 1916. Attended Western State U. Made Bdwy bow in 1938 in "Escape This Night," followed by "Dance Night," "The American Way," "Scene of The Crime," "The Merry Widow," "Peepshow," "Park Avenue," "Finian's Rainbow" for which he received a THEATRE WORLD Award, "Mister Roberts," "The Teahouse of The August Moon," "The Ponder Heart," "The Loud Red Patrick," "Say, Darling," "Send Me No Flowers," "Venus At Large," "Too True To Be Good," "Marco Millions" (1964), "But For Whom Charlie," "Incident At Vichy."

WEAVER, FRITZ. Born in Pittsburgh, Jan. 19, 1926. Attended U. of Chicago. Appeared Off-Bdwy in "The Way of The World," "The White Devil" and "The Doctor's Dilemma" before making Bdwy bow in 1955 in "The Chalk Garden" for which he received a THEATRE WORLD Award, followed by "Protective Custody," "Miss Lonelyhearts," Phoenix productions of "The Family Reunion," "The Power and The Glory," "The Great God Brown," "Peer Gynt" and "Henry IV, Parts I & II," "All American," "Lorenzo," "The White House," "Baker Street."

WEDGEWORTH, ANN. Born in Abilene, Tex., Jan. 21. Attended U. of Tex. Has appeared on Bdwy in "Make A Million," "Blues For Mister Charlie." Off-Bdwy credits: "Chaparral," "The Crucible," "The Days and Nights of Beebee Fenstermaker," "The Last Analysis."

WEST, JENNIFER. Born in Ft. Smith, Ark., Sept. 22, 1939. Attended CCLA. Made NY debut March 24, 1964 Off-Bdwy in "Dutchman," followed by "After The Fall," "Diamond Orchid."

WHITE, JANE. Born in NYC, Oct. 30, 1922. Attended Smith College, and New School. Made Bdwy debut in 1945 in "Strange Fruit," followed by "Razzle Dazzle," "The Insect Comedy," "The Climate of Eden," "Take A Giant Step," "Jane Eyre," "The Power And The Glory," "Once Upon A Mattress," Off-Bdwy in "Hop, Signor!" and "The Trojan Women."

WHITE, JESSE. Born in Buffalo, N.Y., Jan. 3, 1918. Made Broadway bow in 1943 in "Sons and Soldiers," followed by "My Dear Public," "Mrs. Kimball Presents," "Helen Goes To Troy," "Harvey," "The Cradle Will Rock," "Red Gloves," "Born Yesterday," "Kelly," "Kiss Me, Kate" (1965 City Center).

WICKWIRE, NANCY. Born in Harrisburg, Pa., Nov. 29, 1925. Attended Carnegie Tech, and Old Vic School, London. Has appeared in "Jane," "Dial 'M' For Murder," "St. Joan," "The Grand Prize," Off-Bdwy in "The Way of The World," "The Cherry Orchard," "Measure For Measure," "The Girl Of The Golden West," "As You Like It," "A Clearing In The Woods," and "Rosmersholm," "Seidman and Son," "The Golden Age," "Abraham Cochrane," "Traveller Without Luggage."

WILCOX, COLLIN. Born in Highlands, N.C., Feb. 4, 1937. Attended U. of Tenn. Has appeared in "The Day The Money Stopped," "Off-Bdwy in "Season of Choice," and "Camino Real," "The Good Soup," "Look: We've Come Through," "Too True To Be Good," "The Family Way."

WILLIAMS, CLARENCE III. Born Aug. 21, 1939 in NYC. Made Broadway bow in 1960 in "The Long Dream," followed by Off-Bdwy performances in "The Egg and I," "Walk In Darkness," "Doubletalk," and "Sarah and The Sax," "Slow Dance On The Killing Ground" for which he received a THEATRE WORLD Award.

WILLIAMS, EMLYN. Born in Mostyn, Flintshire, Wales, Nov. 26, 1905. Attended Christ Church School, Oxford. Made NY bow in 1927 in "And So To Bed," followed by "Criminal At Large," "Night Must Fall," "Montserrat," "Readings From Charles Dickens," "Bleak House," "A Boy Growing Up," "Daughter of Silence," "A Man For All Seasons," "The Deputy."

WISEMAN, JOSEPH. Born in Montreal, Can., May 15, 1919. Has appeared in "Abe Lincoln In Illinois," "Journey To Jerusalem," "Candle In The Wind," "The Three Sisters," "Storm Operation," "Joan of Lorraine," "Antony and Cleopatra" (1947), "Detective Story," "That Lady," "King Lear" (1950), "Golden Boy" (1952), "The Lark," "The Duchess of Malfi," Lincoln Center Repertory productions.

WOLFIT, DONALD. Born in Newark-on-Trent, Eng., April 29, 1902. Made Broadway bow in 1947 in Shakespearean repertoire including "King Lear," "Hamlet," "The Merchant of Venice," and "As You Like It," "Volpone," "All In Good Time."

WOOD, EUGENE R. Born in Bowling Green, Mo., Oct. 27, 1903. Attended Colo. State College, and Cornell. Has appeared in "Porgy and Bess," "The Pajama Game," "Look Homeward, Angel," "Subways Are For Sleeping," "West Side Story," Off-Bdwy in "Borak," "The Crucible," "The Anvil," and "Night of The Auk," "Kiss Me, Kate" (1965 City Center).

WOOD, PEGGY. Born in Brooklyn, Feb. 9, 1894. Made Bdwy debut in 1910 in "Naughty Marietta," followed by "The Lady of The Slipper," "Love O' Mike," "Maytime," "Candida," "Trelawney Of The Wells," "The Merchant of Venice," "Bitter Sweet," "Old Acquaintance," "Blithe Spirit," "The Happiest Years," "Getting Married," "Charley's Aunt" (1954 City Center), "The Transposed Heads" (Phoenix), "Girls In 509," "Opening Night," and "Pictures In The Hallway" (Off-Bdwy).

WOODS, DONALD. Born Dec. 2, in Brandon, Manitoba, Can. Appeared in stock and touring companies before making Broadway bow in 1941 in "Quiet Please." After numerous films, returned to NY in Off-Bdwy productions of "Rosmersholm," "Riverside Drive," and "One By One."

WOODS, RICHARD. Born May 9, 1930 in Buffalo, N. Y. Graduate of Ithaca College. Has appeared on Broadway in "Beg, Borrow Or Steal," "Capt. Brassbound's Conversion," "Sail Away," Off Broadway in "The Crucible," "Summer and Smoke," "American Gothic," "Four-In-One," "My Heart's In The Highlands," "Eastward In Eden," "The Long Gallery," "The Little Hut," American Shakespeare Festival, and with APA since 1962.

WORTH, IRENE. Born in Nebraska, June 23, 1916. Graduate of UCLA. Made Broadway debut in 1943 in "The Two Mrs. Carrolls." Has since divided her time between U.S., English and Canadian productions. Has appeared in NY in "The Cocktail Party," "Toys In The Attic," "King Lear" (1964 Royal Shakespeare Co.), "Mary Stuart" (Phoenix), "Tiny Alice."

OBITUARIES

William Bendix

Elizabeth Brice

Alan Bunce

ADLER, FRANCES, 73, actress, and member of famous theatrical family, died Dec. 13, 1964 of a heart ailment in her New York apartment. She was the eldest daughter of famed Yiddish actors Jacob and Sarah Adler, and was leading lady to her father in a wide repertory, including Shakespeare, Tolstoy, and Gortdin. In recent years she has been teaching, but appeared in 1947 in "The Flies," and in 1959 in "Electra." Surviving are her two daughters, three brothers and three sisters.

ALLEN, GRACIE, 62, beloved comedienne, wife and partner of George Burns, died Aug. 28, 1964 of a heart attack in Cedars of Lebanon Hospital, Hollywood. For 34 years Burns and Allen were the best-loved and most celebrated team in show business. She had toured the vaudeville circuits with her older sisters, and as a "single" before meeting Burns in 1923. They were an instant success in films, radio, and television. She retired in 1958. Surviving are her husband, and their two adopted children Sandra and Ronald. She was buried in Forest Lawn Memorial Park, Glendale.

BARRETT, MINNETTE, 80, retired actress, died June 20, 1964 in the Clearview Nursing Home, Whitestone, Queens, N.Y. She had appeared as a headliner in vaudeville, and in "The Bat" (original and 1937 revival), "The Show Off," "Lovely Lady," "Mrs. McThing," and the 1952 revival of "Desire Under The Elms." She headed the American Theatre Wing's Drive for sales of World War II bonds.

BENDIX, WILLIAM, 58, stage, screen, and television actor, died Dec. 14, 1964 in Good Samaritan Hospital, Hollywood, from lobar pneumonia. He appeared in several Theatre Guild productions but his recognition came with the role of Policeman Krupp in "The Time Of Your Life," and he went to Hollywood where he was in 50 films. He returned to Broadway in 1960 when he succeeded Jackie Gleason in "Take Me Along." His greatest success was as Chester Riley in the radio and TV series "The Life of Riley." He is survived by his wife of 37 years, and two daughters. Burial was in San Fernando Mission Cemetery.

BLUM, DANIEL, 65, founder and editor of THEATRE WORLD, died of a heart attack in New York's Mt. Sinai Hospital on February 24, 1965. He was widely known for his pictorial books on the theatre, movies, television, and opera. He took a keen interest in encouraging young actors with the annual THEATRE WORLD Awards. He also edited 16 volumes of SCREEN WORLD, a film annual, A PICTORIAL HISTORY OF THE AMERICAN THEATRE, and GREAT STARS OF THE AMERICAN STAGE. For several years he was New York drama critic for the "Chicago Journal of Commerce." He was co-producer of several plays, the last of which was the 1957 revival of "The Country Wife." Interment was in the family mausoleum in Chicago's Rosehill Cemetery. Three sisters survive.

BRICE, ELIZABETH, retired musical comedy and vaudeville singer and dancer, died Jan. 25, 1965 in New York. She appeared in "The Chinese Honeymoon," "Ziegfeld Follies," "Nearly A Hero," "The Belle of New York," "Lady Teazle," "Mlle. Mischief," "The Mimic Girl," "The Motor Girl," "The Jolly Bachelors," "The Sun Princess," "The Winsome Widow," "The Overseas Revue," and her last in 1920, "Buzzin' Around." A sister survives.

BROWN, RUSS, 72, singer and actor, died in the Englewood, N.J., Hospital, Oct. 19, 1964. His career on stage, in movies, and television spanned more than 50 years. He is probably best remembered for introducing "Ya Gotta Have Heart" in "Damn Yankees," and "Politics and Poker" and "Little Tin Box" in "Fiorello!" He had appeared in vaudeville with Bert Wheeler, and with his wife Gertrude Whitaker. Other Broadway credits include "The Firefly," "Flying High," "One Good Year," "Howdy Stranger," "Hold On To Your Hats," "Good Night Ladies," "Hollywood Pinafore," "Up In Central Park," "Finian's Rainbow," "The Pajama Game," and "The Biggest Thief In Town."

BUNCE, ALAN, 61, stage, radio, and television actor, died Apr. 27, 1965 in the Columbia-Presbyterian Hospital, NYC, after a brief illness. He appeared in some 35 plays starting in 1921 with "S.S. Tenacity," and including "Tommy," "Pigs," "Unexpected Husband," "Laff That Off," "A Perfect Alibi," "Dream Child," "DeLuxe," "The Golden Journey," "Valley Forge," "Kind Lady," "Copper and Brass," "Sunrise At Campobello," "A Cook For Mr. General," "Mary, Mary," and "The Child Buyer" his last in Jan. 1965. He was probably best known for his Albert on the radio and TV show "Ethel and Albert." He served as president of the American Federation of Television and Radio Artists, and on the council of Actors Equity. He is survived by his widow, actress Ruth Nugent, a daughter and two sons.

CALDER, KING, 65, stage and television actor, died June 28, 1964 of a heart attack in Hollywood's Good Samaritan Hospital. Made his Broadway debut in 1930 and appeared in "Five Star Final," "Black Widow," "Bravo," "The Trial of Mary Dugan," "Cafe," "The Doughgirls," "Born Yesterday," "Season In The Sun," "Seventeen," "My Sister Eileen," "No Time For Sergeants." He spent his later years portraying television lawmen. His wife Ethel survives.

CANTOR, EDDIE, 72, beloved banjo-eyed song and dance man, and comedian of stage, vaudeville, films, radio, and television, died Oct. 10, 1964 of a heart attack in his Beverly Hills home. From vaudeville, he was signed by Ziegfeld for his "Follies" and appeared in several editions. He also starred in "Make It Snappy," "Whoopee," "Banjo Eyes," and "Kid Boots" which took him to his great Hollywood success. He became one of radio's most popular stars, and tried television before going into semi-retirement in 1953. Four of his five daughters survive. His wife Ida, to whom he always referred, died in 1962.

CHANDLER, HELEN, 59, stage and screen actress, died as a result of surgery in a Hollywood hospital on April 30, 1965. Before leaving Broadway, she had appeared in "It's A Bet," "It's You I Want," "Pride and Prejudice," "The Wild Duck," "Springtime For Henry," "Lady Precious Stream," and "Outward Bound." Her husband, Walter Piascik, survives.

CLARKE, GAGE, 64, stage and film actor, died of cancer Oct. 23, 1964 in Hollywood. His film career began in 1957 after many years on Broadway in such productions as "A Ledge," "Jezebel," "Lost Horizons," "Parnell," "Many Mansions," "I Know What I Like," "Outward Bound," "Another Love Story," "The Happy Time," "The Bad Seed."

CLOVELLY, CECIL, 74, former actor and photographer, died Apr. 25, 1965 in NY's St. Clare's Hospital after a long illness. A native of England, he came to The States in 1914 to appear in "Justice." Other plays in which he appeared were "Peter Ibbetson," "The Jest," "Richard III," "Hamlet," "In A Garden," "Love For Love," "The Dybbuk," "Family Affairs," "Life With Father," "Emperor Jones," and "Anne Of The Thousand Days." He appeared in several films before becoming a professional photographer. His widow and a daughter survive.

COMPTON, FRANCIS, 79, an actor for nearly 60 years, died Sept. 18, 1964 in St. Joseph's Hospital, Stamford, Conn., after a long illness. From a noted English theatrical family, he made his New York debut in 1912 in "The Whip." He performed with many great stars, and in such plays as "Cyrano de Bergerac," "Othello," "Idiot's Delight," "Witness For The Prosecution," and "Caesar and Cleopatra," but he was quoted as saying he received his greatest satisfaction from playing the butler in a dozen or so drawing room comedies. He is survived by his wife Mary Wetmore Wells, three sons and a daughter, a brother, and three sisters.

DANE, CLEMENCE, 77, English playwright and novelist, died March 28, 1965 in London. She transformed her third novel "Legend" into the successful play and film "A Bill of Divorcement." Other plays are "Will Shakespeare," "Broome Stages" from her novel, "Come Of Age," and adaptations of Max Beerbohm's "The Happy Hypocrite," and Rostand's "L'Aiglon." She also wrote several film scenarios.

King Calder

Eddie Cantor

Helen Chandler

Francis Compton

Louise Dresser

Margaret Dumont

DRESSER, LOUISE, 86, retired stage and screen actress, died Apr. 24, 1965 in the Motion Picture Country Hospital, Woodland Hills, Calif., after surgery for an intestinal ailment. Her career spanned a half century, beginning as a singer in vaudeville, then scoring several hits in Broadway musicals. She began her film career in 1923, won an Academy Award for her role in "When My Ship Comes In," but had her greatest success in seven films with Will Rogers. She introduced the song "My Gal Sal," and appeared in revues with Weber and Fields. She was DeWolf Hopper's leading lady in "Matinee Idol," and was in "Chaperones," "About Town," "The Girl Behind The Counter," "The Candy Shop," "Broadway To Paris," "Have A Heart," and "Rock-a-bye Baby." She divorced her first husband, Jack Norworth, and for 42 years was married to singer-actor Jack Gardner, who died in 1950. She retired in the 1940's. Only a sister-in-law survives. Interment was in Forest Lawn Memorial Park, Glendale, Calif.

DUMONT, MARGARET, 75, stage, screen, and television actress and singer, died March 6, 1965 of a heart attack at her home in Hollywood. On stage with the Marx Brothers, and then as a leading lady in their seven films, she was the unperturbed grande dame of high society as the mad foursome created low comedy around her. She began her career as a singer on Broadway with George M. Cohan, toured Europe and played in revues there. She appeared frequently on television, and had just completed taping a skit with Groucho Marx.

EFFRAT, JOHN, 57, actor, director, and producer, died May 14, 1965 of a heart attack in NY's Medical Arts Center Hospital. He was stricken at a meeting of the Episcopal Actors Guild of which he was a council member. He appeared in "Autumn Hill," "The American Way," "The Village Green," "Holy Night," "The Odds On Mrs. Oakley," "The Streets Are Guarded," and "I Like It Here." He was an official of Actors Equity, and of The Actors Fund of America. Since 1948 he has produced the annual showcase productions for unknowns. He was a member of The Players and The Lambs. He is survived by his wife Ann, a son, a brother and sister.

ELIOT, T.S., 76, American-born Nobel prize poet and playwright, died Jan. 4, 1965 in his London home of 50 years. In addition to his two most successful plays, "Murder In The Cathedral," and "The Cocktail Party," he wrote "The Confidential Clerk," "Family Reunion," and "The Elder Statesman." He is survived by his second wife. His ashes were interred in the parish church of East Coker, Eng.

EMERY, JOHN, 59, stage and film actor, died of cancer in his New York home on November 16, 1964. Member of a theatrical family, his Broadway career began in 1925 with "Mrs. Partridge Presents." His many stage credits include "The Barretts of Wimpole Street," "Antony and Cleopatra" with his current wife Tallulah Bankhead, "Romeo and Juliet," "St. Joan," "The Constant Wife," "Hamlet," with John Gielgud, "Skylark," "Liliom," "John Brown," "Wuthering Heights," and "Angel Street." Besides Miss Bankhead, he was married and divorced from Tamara Geva and Patricia Calvert. For many years he was on the council of Actors Equity. There were no immediate surviving relatives.

FORBES, MARY ELIZABETH, 84, stage and screen actress, died Sept. 3, 1964 in her apartment in Hollywood. At the turn of the century, she was Harrison Fisher's favorite "cover girl," and appeared in such plays as "Wildfire," "Barbara Frietchie," "Earl of Pawtucket," "Walls of Jericho," "Alias Jimmy Valentine," "Trelawney of The Wells," "Romance," "Peter Pan," "The Boomerang," "Smilin' Through," "Victoria Regina," "To The Ladies," "What Every Woman Knows," "Our Town," "The Virginian," "Tomorrow and Tomorrow." Her ashes will be placed in the family plot in Mt. Hope Cemetery, Rochester.

GOSFIELD, MAURICE, 51, stage, radio, and television actor, died Oct. 19, 1964 in Will Rogers Memorial Hospital, Saranac Lake, N.Y., after a long illness. He had appeared in "Siege," "The Lady Comes Across," "Darkness At Noon," "The Petrified Forest," "Three Men On A Horse," and "Room Serivce." He was best known for his Pvt. Doberman in the "Sgt. Bilko" TV series. His mother, two brothers and a sister survive.

HANSBERRY, LORRAINE, 34, one of America's most promising playwrights, died Jan. 12, 1965 of cancer in University Hospital, N. Y. C. Her first play "A Raisin In The Sun," won the Drama Critics Circle Award for the 1958-59 season, and was made into a movie. Her second play, "The Sign In Sidney Brustein's Window" was presented this season. At the time of her death, she was working on two new plays and a musical. She is survived by her husband, songwriter-producer Robert Nemiroff, her mother, a sister and two brothers. Burial was at Beth El Cemetery, Croton-on-the-Hudson, N.Y.

HANSON, LARS, 78, one of Sweden's most prominent dramatic actors on stage and screen, died April 8, 1965 in Stockholm after a brief illness. He last appeared in New York in 1962 in the Royal Dramatic Theater production of "The Father."

HARDWICKE, CEDRIC, 71, versatile English-born stage and film actor, died Aug. 6, 1964 in New York University Hospital of a chronic lung condition. When knighted in 1934 for his Shavian performances, he was the youngest actor ever to receive that honor. He made his Broadway debut in 1936 in "Promise," and subsequently appeared in over 30 plays including "The Amazing Dr. Clitterhouse," "Shadow and Substance, "Pygmalion" with Gertrude Lawrence, "Candida," "Antigone," "Caesar and Cleopatra," "Don Juan In Hell," "A Majority Of One." He was married and divorced from Helena Pickard and Mary Scott, both actresses, who each bore him a son. After cremation, his ashes were flown to London for burial.

HARE, LUMSDEN, 90, stage and film actor, died Aug. 28, 1964. Began acting in London at age of 18, and came to the United States in 1905 where he supported such stars as John Drew, Billie Burke, and Ethel Barrymore, and appeared in "Elmer Gantry," "What Every Woman Knows," and "The Land of Promise." He went to Hollywood in the 1920's where he appeared in over 30 films. He was married to Selene Johnson, an actress. A daughter survives.

HART, BERNARD, 53, stage manager, producer, and brother of the late Moss Hart, was found dead from a heart attack in his Manhattan apartment on Aug. 18, 1964. He was co-producer of "Dear Ruth," "Anniversary Waltz," "Christopher Blake," "The Survivors," "The Secret Room," "Light Up The Sky," "The Climate of Eden," and stage manager for "My Fair Lady" and "Camelot." There were no immediate survivors.

HYLTON, JACK, 72, English producer and impresario, died Jan. 29, 1965 in a London hospital of a heart ailment. He had presented more than 100 productions, including many American hits, and was a co-producer of several Broadway shows, including "La Plume de Ma Tante," "Women of Twilight," and "Rugantino." His widow, Beverley Prowse, survives, as do a son and daughter by a former marriage.

KILBRIDE, PERCY, 76, character actor, died Dec. 11, 1964 in Chase Sanitarium, Hollywood, from arteriosclerosis and terminal pneumonia after brain surgery necessitated by a head injury he received in an accident. He appeared on Broadway in "Lily Turner," "Post Road," "Three Men On A Horse," "Cuckoos On The Hearth," "Little Brown Jug," and "George Washington Slept Here" which took him to Hollywood. His greatest success was in the "Pa and Ma Kettle" film series, although he played more than 800 roles on stage and in films. He was a bachelor with no immediate surviving relatives.

John Emery

Lars Hanson

Cedric Hardwicke

Lumsden Hare

Winifred Lenihan

Jeanette MacDonald

KOLB, CLARENCE, 90, veteran vaudeville star, film and television character actor, died Nov. 25, 1964 in Orchard Gables Sanitarium, Hollywood, after a lengthy illness from a stroke. He achieved fame first with his vaudeville partner Max Dill. After the team broke up in 1931, he appeared in over 75 films, and numerous television shows including "My Little Margie." His actress wife, Mabel Sarah Larsen, survives. Interment was in Forest Lawn Memorial Park.

LASCOE, HENRY, 50, a veteran Broadway and television character actor, died Sept. 1, 1964 in Hollywood of a heart attack while taping a television show. His many Broadway credits include "Me and Molly," "Call Me Madam," "Silk Stockings," "Fanny," "Romanoff and Juliet," "Fiorello," "Wonderful Town," and "Carnival." His wife and three children survive.

LAWRENCE, LAWRENCE SHUBERT, SR., 70, nephew of the legendary Shubert brothers, died April 15, 1965 in Lankenau Hospital, Philadelphia. He had served as general manager of the Shubert interests since 1914, and was the producer of several plays, including "My Maryland," "Congratulations," and "The Man Who Corrupted Hadleyburg." His son Lawrence, and his widow, the former Frances von Summerfield survive.

LENIHAN, WINIFRED, 66, retired actress, died July 27, 1964 of a heart attack in her Sea Cliff, L.I., home. She made her stage debut in 1918 in "The Betrothal," and in 1923 was the first American actress to play Shaw's "St. Joan." She also appeared in "For The Defense," "The Dover Road," "White Wings," "Major Barbara," and in 1936 "Black Limelight" her last play. In 1925 she became the first director of the Theatre Guild's School of Acting in NY, and for a short while was a radio director. She appeared in one film "Jigsaw." She was the widow of Frank W. Wheeler, a vice president of the A & P. Surviving are a son, and a step-son and step-daughter.

MacDONALD, JEANETTE, 57, red-haired soprano star of stage and film operettas, died Jan. 14, 1965, in Methodist Hospital, Houston, Texas, of a heart ailment. Her career began in 1914 as a chorus girl, but she soon moved up to leading roles in "The Magic Ring," "Tip Toes," "Bubbling Over," "Yes, Yes, Yvette," "Sunny Days," "Boom Boom," and "Angela" which took her to Hollywood where her greatest success was in musicals with Nelson Eddy. In 1942 she left movies to make concert tours. She made her opera debut in Montreal in "Romeo and Juliet," followed by "Faust" with the Chicago Civic Opera. In recent years she limited her appearances to occasional television performances. In 1937, she was married to Gene Raymond, actor, who survives. Interment was in Forest Lawn Memorial Park.

MARBLE, MARY, 91, retired musical comedy star, died Feb. 5, 1965 in the Percy Williams Home in East Islip, L.I. She had appeared in musicals from the 1890's until the early part of this century, including "Off The Earth," "Milk White Flag," "Babes In Toyland," and "Dream City." Her last appearance was in "Green Pastures" in 1930. She had been in vaudeville as part of the team of Chip and Marble. She was the widow of producer John W. Dunne.

MARX, HARPO, 70, comedian, died Sept. 28, 1964 in Mt. Sinai Hospital, Hollywood, after heart surgery. He wore a blond wig and was the silent, harp-playing member of the famous Marx Brothers, who kept audiences laughing for 50 years. Before launching their successful film career, they appeared in vaudeville and on Broadway in "I'll Say She Is," "The Cocoanuts," and "Animal Crackers." Harpo broke his stage silence once, in 1940 when he played in "The Man Who Came To Dinner." Surviving are his wife, film actress Susan Fleming, their four adopted children, and his brothers Groucho, Zeppo and Gummo.

MAYER, JEROME, 55, Broadway and stock producer and director, died March 3, 1965 in Columbus Hospital, N.Y., after being struck by a hit-and-run driver. He produced and directed in New Hope, Carnegie Tech, Corning, San Juan, Honolulu and Broadway. His productions include "Noah," "Russet Mantle," "Young Couple Wanted," "Goodbye In The Night," "Lullaby." He is survived by four brothers and a sister.

MOORE, EULABELLE, 61, actress, died Nov. 30, 1964 in New York She had appeared in numerous Broadway productions, including "Three's A Family," "A Streetcar Named Desire," "The Male Animal," "Brother Rat," "Great Day In The Morning," "The Skin of Our Teeth," "Another Part of The Forest," and "Jason." A sister survives.

MURRAY, MAE, 75, musical comedy dancer, Ziegfeld girl, and blond film vamp, died March 23, 1965 at the Motion Picture Country Home in Woodland Hills, Calif., after a long illness. Before becoming the golden girl of Hollywood, she appeared on Broadway in "About Town," "Ziegfeld Follies" of 1908, 1909, 1915, and "Watch Your Step." She was married and divorced four times. A son survives. Burial was in Valhalla Memorial Park, North Hollywood.

O'CASEY, SEAN, 84, Irish playwright, died Sept. 18, 1964 of a heart attack in a nursing home in Torquay, England. His dramas and prose-poetry were an inspiration to many writers, actors, and producers throughout the world. World acclaim came in 1925 with the production of his play "Juno and The Paycock." His other plays include "The Shadow of A Gunman," "The Plough and The Stars," "Cathleen Listens In," "Nannie's Night Out," "The Silver Tassie," "Within The Gates," "The End of The Beginning," "The Star Turns Red," "Red Roses For Me," "Purple Dust," "Oak Leaves and Lavendar," "Time To Go," "Bedtime Story," "The Bishop's Bonfire," "Drums of Father Ned," "Cock-A-Doodle Dandy," and "Hall of Healing." He was married to Irish actress Eileen Reynolds Carey, by whom he had two sons and a daughter.

O'NEIL, NANCE, 90, retired tragedienne, died Feb. 7, 1965 at the Actors Fund Home in Englewood, N.J. Her most notable successes were in Belasco's "The Lily" and "The Passion Flower." Critics at home and abroad, hailed her as one of America's greatest tragic actresses. Other plays in which she appeared successfully were "Judith of Bethulia," "Magda," "Hedda Gabler," "The Jewess," "Monna Vanna," "The Wanderer," "The House of Women," "Bitter Oleander," "Camille," "Macbeth," "Stronger Than Love." She also appeared in several films, but retired in 1935. She was the widow of Alfred Hickman, British actor. No immediate relatives survive.

OSTRANDER, ALBERT A., 61, theatrical designer, died of a heart attack in NY's St. Vincent's Hospital, on Sept. 29, 1964. He was designer and technical director for Norman Bel Geddes on such shows as "Panama Hattie," "Jumbo," "Madame DuBarry," "The Great Waltz," and "The Eternal Road." He was also designer for Ringling Brothers —Barnum and Bailey Circus. His wife and daughter survive.

PORTER, COLE, 71, one of America's greatest song and musical comedy writers, died Oct. 15, 1964 in St. John's Hospital, Santa Monica, Calif., from complications following surgery for a kidney ailment. He wrote the music and lyrics for scores of songs that became all-time favorites, and for some of Broadway's and Hollywood's great musicals. His stage hits were "Hitchy-Koo of 1919," "Fifty Million Frenchmen," "Jubilee," "Anything Goes," "DuBarry Was A Lady," "Panama Hattie," "Wake Up and Dream," "The New Yorkers," "Leave It To Me," "You Never Know," "Mexican Hayride," "Let's Face It," "Something For The Boys," "The Gay Divorcee," "Red, Hot and Blue," "Kiss Me, Kate," "Can-Can," and his last in 1955 "Silk Stockings." He is survived by two cousins. Burial was in his native Peru, Ind., between his mother, and his wife of 25 years, Linda Lee Thomas.

PREISSER, CHERRY, 46, retired acrobatic dancer, died July 12, 1964 at her home in Sydney, Australia. With her sister June, the team won international fame in vaudeville and revues in the 1920's and 1930's. They appeared in the "Ziegfeld Follies" of 1934 and 1936. She is survived by her sister, Mrs. June Terry of Los Angeles, her husband David J. Hopkins, six daughters, and a son. She retired after her marriage in 1937.

Mae Murray

Sean O'Casey

Nance O'Neil

259

Cole Porter

Grace Valentine

Robert Warwick

ROSSE, HERMAN, 78, set designer for more than 200 stage and screen productions, died Apr. 14, 1965 from a heart attack in the Nyack, N.Y., Hospital. Shows which he designed were "Casanova," "The Swan," several "Ziegfeld Follies," "The Great Magoo," "Ulysses In Nighttown" Off-Broadway in 1958. He designed the medallions for the American Theatre Wing's annual Antoinette Perry Awards. He won an "Oscar" for his film set "King of Jazz" in 1930. His widow, four sons and five daughters survive.

SARGENT, MARGHERITA, 81, actress and widow of actor Augustin Duncan, died Sept. 10, 1964 in Wilton, Conn., at the home of her son, Angus Duncan, executive secretary of Actors Equity. She made her Broadway debut in 1907 in "When Knights Were Bold." Her many credits include "Macbeth" with Lionel Barrymore, "The Great Gatsby," "The First Lady," "Homecoming," "Lute Song," and her last appearance in 1957 in "Inherit The Wind." Surviving, besides her son, are two daughters.

SWANN, CAROLINE BURKE, 51, producer, writer, and former actress, died Dec. 5, 1964 in NY's Memorial Hospital. She appeared on Broadway in "Brooklyn, U.S.A.," and "Heart Of A City," and produced "The Tenth Man," and "The Hostage." Off-Broadway she produced "The Dumbwaiter," "The Collection," "The Room," "A Slight Ache," and "One Way Pendulum." From 1946 to 1956 she was producing, writing, and directing network television for NBC. Surviving are her husband, advertising executive Erwin D. Swann, her mother, and a brother.

THOMAS, CALVIN, 79, character actor for more than 50 years, died Sept. 26, 1964 in Essex General Hospital, Caldwell, N.J. Made his Broadway debut in "Peer Gynt" with Richard Mansfield, and subsequently appeared in approximately 100 productions, including "Rosalie," "Six Cylinder Love," "Rio Grande," "Tiger Rose," "The 13th Chair," "The Night of January 16," "We The People," "Abe Lincoln in Illinois," "The Village Green," "Sweet Charity," "Kiss and Tell," "Carousel," "The Traveling Lady," and his last in 1956 "Pipe Dream." Surviving are his actor brother Thomas, his widow Delia, and two sons.

VALENTINE, GRACE, 73, actress, died Nov. 14, 1964 in Bellevue Hospital in New York. She made her Broadway debut in 1914 in "Yosemite," and among the many plays in which she appeared are "Johnny Get Your Gun," "Lombardi, Ltd.," "The Fabulous Invalid," "The American Way," "George Washington Slept Here," "Happy Birthday," "A Story For Strangers," "Season In The Sun," and the 1952 revival of "Anna Christie." Interment was in Kensico Cemetery, Valhalla, N.Y.

VAN SICKLE, RAYMOND, 79, actor and playwright, was found floating in Tokyo's Kobe Harbor on July 10, 1964. It was believed he slipped and fell into the water and drowned. He had appeared in over 30 plays, including "The Fight," "Journeyman," "Chicken Every Sunday," "Christopher Blake," "Summer and Smoke," his last "Cut of The Axe" in 1960. He wrote "Best Years" and "Sun Kissed" which were produced on Broadway, and radio scripts and scenarios for the films.

WARWICK, ROBERT, 85, stage and film matinee idol, and later character actor, died June 6, 1964 in Saltair Convalescent Hospital, West Los Angeles, after a long illness. Began his career in 1903 in "Glad Of It," followed by "The Education of Mr. Pipp," "Anna Karenina," "The Worth Of A Woman," "The Balkan Princess," "The Kiss Waltz," "Rosedale," "The Secret," "A Celebrated Case," "Captain Brassbound's Conversion," "In The Night Watch," "Drifting," "To Love," "Cheaper To Marry," "A Lady's Virtue," "The Two Orphans," "Sherlock Holmes," "Within The Law," "Nice Women," "A Primer For Lovers," "Ode To Liberty." In the 1920's he began another successful career in films, and until shortly before his death he was active in television. His daughter and two grandchildren survive. Burial was in Holy Cross Cemetery.

INDEX

262

264

269